Redeeming
the Time

Other Books by Leland Ryken

Redeeming the Time

A Christian Approach to Work and Leisure

Leland Ryken

Baker Books

A Division of Baker Book House Co
Grand Rapids, Michigan 49516

To Philip, Lisa, and Josh,
who work and play in the Spirit

© 1995 by Leland Ryken

Published by Baker Books
a division of Baker Book House Company
P. O. Box 6287, Grand Rapids, Michigan 49516-6287

Printed in the United States of America

Library of Congress Cataloging-in-Publication Data

Ryken, Leland.
    Redeeming the time: a Christian approach to work and leisure/ Leland Ryken.
      p.   cm.
    Includes bibliographical references.
    ISBN 0-8010-5169-X (paper)
    1.Work—Religious aspects—Christianity. 2. Leisure—Religious aspects—Christanity. I. Title.
BT738.5.R94   1995
241'.64—dc20   95-18568

Contents

Preface

Work and leisure are God's gifts to the human race. Attitudes toward them in our society are dominated by a secular outlook. Within the Christian church they are topics of neglect. In our thinking moments we know that work and leisure deserve better than this.

This book attempts to fill several gaps that I quickly noted as I got into the subject. Most of the writing on work and leisure is the product of secular thinking. While it delineates the contemporary issues to which the Christian faith speaks, it offers almost no help in thinking Christianly about work and leisure.

Of course secular writers do not hesitate to make negative comments about the role of religion in the history of work and leisure. "The Protestant ethic" has long been the favorite whipping post, in Christian circles as well as secular ones. A small part of my enterprise has been to set the record straight regarding the unjustly maligned Puritans.

I have written from the presupposition that the Bible is the final authority on the issues about which it speaks. Of course it is important to adduce the biblical data that is actually relevant to the subjects of work and leisure. I have read books and articles that bombarded me with biblical verses but left me wondering what the relevance of the data was to work and leisure.

The most distinctive feature of this book is that it combines the subjects of work and leisure. There are lots of books on work and many on leisure. But it is self-defeating to keep these in separate compartments. Work and leisure together make up a whole, and they derive much of their meaning from each other rather than by themselves. They also influence each other, partly because they compete for our time.

The divisions of this book suggest the logic that underlies it. I begin by describing work and leisure as they are in themselves. Then I analyze the contemporary crisis in work and leisure, accompanied by a historical survey of how we got where we are. Having looked at proposed solutions that are failing, I turn at last to Christian solutions to the problems of work and leisure. The underlying principles are thus integration of social data with the Christian faith and a problem-solution format.

This book is a sequel to my earlier book *Work and Leisure in Christian Perspective,* which has been out of print for several years. For this sequel, I doubled the scope of my research, added four new chapters, incorporated over a hundred additional sources, quoted the Puritans at first hand rather than from secondary sources, added an analysis of time, and completely repackaged the material that appeared in the earlier book to accentuate the interconnectedness of work and leisure.

Introduction
Why We Need to Think about Work and Leisure

Work and leisure have forced themselves on the agenda of contemporary concerns. Businesspeople know all about the problem of work, as Chuck Colson and Jack Eckerd's book *Why America Doesn't Work* makes clear.[1] Surprising as it may sound, America doesn't play any better than it works.

Christians have their own version of the contemporary crisis in work and leisure. They feel guilty about their work and they feel guilty about their leisure. They do not understand either of them very well.

Mixed Messages

Our society at large displays contradictory attitudes toward both work and leisure. Workaholics have turned work into their religion. One writer found that they spend nearly half their time—seventy hours per week or more—working at their job.[2] But two of my acquaintances who have sat next to business executives on plane trips tell a different story. Employers generally think that the work ethic is either dead or dying. The head of a business with branches throughout the country said his company tries to hire workers from the Midwest because they tend to have a better work ethic and work habits.

We betray our impoverished work ethic by our slogans. I was passed on a Kansas interstate by a truck with the following jingle painted on

---

1. Chuck Colson and Jack Eckerd, *Why America Doesn't Work* (Dallas: Word, 1991).
2. Richard Phillips, "The New Calvinists," *The Chicago Tribune* 5, November 1986, section 7: 5–8.

the back: "I owe, I owe, so off to work I go." Here, in rather crude form, is a dominant attitude toward work today. It views work in mercenary terms as the thing that makes our acquisitive lifestyle possible. Or consider the sign that I saw on the office door of a colleague: "I'd rather be fishing." Here is another prevalent attitude toward work: work is a necessary nuisance and unpleasant duty. Leisure is what we value. Work is something we put up with as a means to that end.

We signal our uneasiness about our attitudes toward work by our quips.

"Work fascinates me—I can sit and watch it for hours."

"Thank God it's Friday."

"Hard work may not kill me, but why take a chance?"

"I'm not lazy—I just don't like to work."

A mail-order catalog advertises a license plate frame that reads, "Retired—no more worry, no more hurry, no more boss."

Work is a problem for nearly all of us. We do not go around saying, "Thank God it's Monday." When we overwork we feel guilty about the way work robs us of time for other areas of life, including family activities and religious activities. At other times we feel guilty for disliking our work. Who does not resonate with Thoreau's comment that the laboring person "has not leisure for a true integrity day by day. He has no time to be anything but a machine."[3]

Our slogans may seem to indicate that work is our problem and leisure the perceived solution. But the messages we send regarding leisure are as contradictory as our attitudes toward work. If we valued leisure as much as our complaining about work seems to indicate, why do we make so little time for it? If we think that leisure is the antidote to our overwork and dislike of it, why do we feel guilty about the time we devote to leisure rather than work?

The Church's Silence about Work

The church should be proclaiming a clear message on a subject of such universal concern as work. It once did. For the original Protestants and Puritans, work was a favorite sermon topic, as surviving sermons show. New England Puritan Cotton Mather preached about the uses of leisure during the winter months. When was the last time you heard (or preached) a sermon on work?

The church is responsible to relate Christian doctrine to all of life in terms that are understandable and relevant to lay people. There was a

3. Henry David Thoreau, as quoted by Tim Hansel, *When I Relax I Feel Guilty* (Elgin, Ill.: David C. Cook, 1979), 34.

time when it did so in regard to work. But work has become one of the "lost provinces of religion."[4] The time has come to enlarge the province of Christianity so it again influences the public forum on the subject of work.

The result of the retreat of Christian thinking about work is that attitudes toward work among Christians are not much different from those in society at large. We find the normal quota of workaholics in the pews on Sunday morning. And what percentage of Christians view their work with the sense of calling that the Reformers proclaimed with such clarity?

Not surprisingly, the church has passed on secular attitudes toward work to the coming generation. Sociologist James Hunter surveyed attitudes among young people enrolled at Christian colleges and seminaries. One of the conclusions that Hunter drew was this:

> What has been seen thus far merely confirms what is already well known about the place and value of work for Evangelicalism—that work has lost any spiritual and eternal significance and that it is important only insofar as it fosters certain qualities of the personality.[5]

It is time to shore up an eroding work ethic.

The Church and Leisure

The church has never been able to make up its mind about leisure. The Bible says little about leisure directly. Christians through the centuries have also said and thought little about it, preferring to feel guilty about time spent in leisure. As the title of Tim Hansel's book on the subject suggests, when Christians relax they feel guilty.

The church has often opted for easy answers to the question of leisure. In the Catholic Middle Ages, church leaders such as Augustine and Tertullian advised Christians to stay away from cultural amusements such as plays and festivals and stick to the spiritual life. The distrust of "worldly amusements" has also run strong throughout the history of Protestantism, even when the younger generation resists the bias.

4. W. R. Forrester, *Christian Vocation* (New York: Charles Scribner's Sons, 1953), 169. The opening chapter of Elton Trueblood's *Your Other Vocation* (New York: Harper and Brothers, 1952) has a good discussion of various lost provinces of religion related to work.

5. James Davison Hunter, *Evangelicalism: The Coming Generation* (Chicago: University of Chicago Press, 1987), 56.

The other extreme is to ignore the question of leisure. The resulting problem is that whenever the church has refused to think about any area of culture it has usually ended up imitating the practices of a secular society. This has been a common trend in our century. Christians adopt cultural practices just as they are going out of vogue in the secular world. What we casually watch on television today would have shocked Christians just twenty years ago. Robert K. Johnston correctly observes that

> it is surprising that . . . the Christian Church has put so little thought into the person at play. Rather than ground their discussion in biblical reflection and careful observation of play itself, Christians have most often been content to allow Western culture to shape their understanding of the human at play.[6]

The time is ripe for the church to grapple with the question of leisure more seriously than it has.

Summary

Earlier in this century someone claimed that we work at our play and play at our work. Today the confusion has deepened: we worship our work, work at our play, and play at our worship.

Christians need to think about work and leisure for at least three reasons. First, work and leisure are pressing daily problems for us as individuals and as a society. They are problems that show no sign of going away, and our personal and corporate future might well depend on whether we can reach solutions.

Second, Christians have begun to search for solutions among themselves, as the rise of institutes and workshops attests. Almost all of the attention is currently focused on restoring a sense of vocation to work, to the neglect (once again) of leisure. The important point is that Christians increasingly recognize that the time has come to do something about a problem that has been allowed to fester for decades.

Third, the world at large is farther from solving its problems of work and leisure than it has ever been. If the Christian faith has the answers to the problems of work and leisure, then Christians should contribute to the public discussion in the hope that the accuracy of their solutions will be apparent.

---

6. Robert K. Johnston, *The Christian at Play* (Grand Rapids: Eerdmans, 1983), 83.

Understanding Work and Leisure

1

"There Is No Fine Thing But Needs Much Laboring"

The Many Faces of Work

Before we analyze the problems of work and leisure, and before we explore Christian solutions, we need to understand the nature of work and leisure. Sociological studies of both work and leisure have poured from the presses during the past two decades. They tell us much that we need to know.

The Nature of Work

We need to begin by distinguishing between *job* and *work*. Work for which we are paid or by which we earn our livelihood goes by the common name of *job* or *labor*. But this is only part of the work that we do. Discussions that limit work to one's job end up being much less helpful than they seem. We need, of course, to develop a Christian perspective on labor, but to stop there is to leave some of the most problematic areas of our daily lives untouched. We also need to make sense of vacuuming the house, taking out the garbage, and driving children to music lessons. The problem of work is often most acute in these areas because getting paid for labor at once lends a kind of sanction to it that is lacking in other work.

Work, then, includes the job or labor for which we are paid, but it extends well beyond that. It includes all that we are obliged to do to meet our physical and social needs. With this basic definition in place, we can look at some complementary ways by which we can understand the nature or meaning of work. In doing so, we will be exploring the answers that people give when they are asked, "Why do you work?"

Work as a Means of Providing for Life's Needs and Wants

At the most elemental level, work is a means of providing for the needs and desires of life. As such, it is basically utilitarian. Whatever else work may add to life, it supplies the money or materials by which we acquire goods and services, and it makes life around the house possible. To live our lives, we need to cook meals and take the car to the gas station and mow the lawn.

Of course this acquisitive view of work that links it to consumption extends to more than satisfying the necessities of life. It also becomes the means toward supplying the products and activities that make up a total lifestyle. It is apparent, then, how drastically work becomes affected by the consumer society in which we live, given further impetus by the expectation of upward social mobility.

Such a view of work is on a collision course with certain basic Christian values, as we will see later in this book. If not balanced by other attitudes, the view of work as a source of income robs work of intrinsic value and of other ends besides personal advancement and consumption, and it quickly produces the workaholic syndrome. Still, there is no reason to disparage the role of work in supplying what we need and want for living. To be deprived of such work is the most damaging work problem of all.

Work as Toil: The Curse of Work

Regarding work as a necessity because it supplies the basic needs and wants of life does not have to turn it into a curse, but in fact it often does so because it accentuates the obligatory nature of work. We tend to find burdensome anything to which we are driven by necessity. This link is suggested by the biblical account of how work became toil as a result of the curse pronounced after the fall (Genesis 3:17, 19):

> cursed is the ground because of you;
>   in toil you shall eat of it all the days of your life. . . .
> In the sweat of your face
>   you shall eat bread.

Here the curse of work is put into a context of earning our daily sustenance, and by extension it applies to all work that we are required to do in order to obtain something we want.

The element of curse in work is intrinsic to life in a fallen world. The sociological data that I will explore in chapter 4, as well as people's mutterings about work, all point in this direction, even when people do not acknowledge the theological context of the Fall. Modern poet William Butler Yeats summed it up in his poem entitled "Adam's Curse" when he wrote, "It's certain there is no fine thing / Since Adam's fall but needs much laboring." By "much laboring," Yeats meant toilsome work.

The curse of work cannot be ignored, though we can partly redeem work from its curse. Any naive glorification of work is refuted by a long, hard look around us, as well as by some introspection into our own feelings toward what we do in a typical day. Nor does the Christian faith take a naively optimistic attitude toward work. Taking out the garbage and cleaning the bathroom are nothing less than unpleasant in themselves.

Work as a Means of Production

Work must also be viewed from an economic perspective. Viewed thus, it is a means of production, to be measured in terms of its value to the employer or the laborer. Given this economic context, labor becomes something that an employer "buys" and that a worker "sells." Both work and worker become something that are "worth" this or that amount. Labor becomes another commodity on the market.

Of course this dimension of work carries inherent opportunities for perverted attitudes toward work. Work can become as impersonal as the machinery in a factory. It is sold and bought at the market rate, with the result that some workers naturally view their work as less valuable than that of others. Instead of being viewed as a calling with inherent worth, work often becomes mercenary, a means to financial ends. The laborer's worth and identity become linked to the size of his or her paycheck. And the question, "What good does this work accomplish?" is replaced by, "How much does it pay?" Here is one of the problems about work that the Christian faith must address.

Work as Human Achievement

Thus far I have viewed work in terms of its extrinsic motivations and rewards. But a more idealized view is also possible, quite apart from religious considerations. Some types of work carry their own reward because we regard them in terms of personal accomplishment. The sense of achievement can include either the product resulting from the work or the activity of doing the work itself. The attitude of accomplishment, moreover, often extends to work that in itself is unpleasant or even drudgery. Completing such tasks is perceived as an accomplishment in itself.

There is something primordial about work. It answers a deep-seated human urge to be useful, to master something, to do something skillfully, to produce something tangible. Robert Cohen put it this way:

> Labor is the very touchstone for man's self-realization, the medium of creating the world of his desire. . . . Man labors . . . to transform his world, to put his own mark on it, to make it his, and to make himself at home in it.[1]

Of course this view of work as achievement can lead to either a humanistic view of human greatness or a Christian view of stewardship in which ability and opportunity are accepted humbly as a gift from God.

Work as Psychological Satisfaction

Work can also be studied in psychological terms. Freud theorized that love and work are the two central activities by which people give meaning to life.[2] The importance that Freud attached to work seems plausible when we consider the wide range of psychological needs that work satisfies.

One need is self-esteem, or a sense of personal worth. This is most easily seen in the collapse of self-worth that afflicts the unemployed.[3] It also explains why a study that addressed the question, "Do the poor want to work?" found that poor people "identify their self-esteem with work as strongly as do the nonpoor."[4] The sense of uselessness that accompanies the inability to work only confirms this need. During the summer that I broke both of my arms and was unable even to feed myself or shave I came to feel how debilitating to one's well-being it is to be unable to work. I eventually longed to be able to do even such despised work as taking out the garbage and cutting back the trumpet vines (which had occasioned my accident with the ladder).

1. Robert S. Cohen, "On the Marxist Philosophy of Education," *Modern Philosophies and Education,* ed. N. B. Henry (Chicago: The National Society for the Study of Education, 1955), 190.

2. In *Civilization and Its Discontents,* Freud wrote that "the life of human beings in common . . . had a twofold foundation, i.e., the compulsion to work, created by external necessity, and the power of love" (*Great Books of the Western World,* ed. Robert M. Hutchins [Chicago: Encyclopedia Britannica, 1952], 54:782).

3. See John C. Raines and Donna C. Day-Lower, *Modern Work and Human Meaning* (Philadelphia: Westminster, 1986).

4. L. Goodwin, *Do the Poor Want to Work?* (Washington, D.C.: Brookings Institution, 1972), 112.

Work is also a major determinant in a person's identity. "What do you do for a living?" is a typical question we ask someone we have just met. "Do you have a job outside the home?" we ask women with children. The answers to these questions quickly establish people's identity and status, both in their own eyes and those of others.

Work also serves a social function in our lives. Except for tasks done in solitude, work brings us into contact with other people. These social contacts carry either reward or frustration, but in either case they determine a great deal of what we think and feel in a given day. Retired people, moreover, often complain of the loss of social satisfaction that accompanied their work situations.

Yet another psychological need that work satisfies is the need for activity, which some psychologists regard as a basic human need. Work, whether it consists of one's job or tasks around the house, keeps us occupied. It also lends structure to the day. During the summer of my enforced inactivity, I found myself unable to watch the morning news as I ate breakfast, even though this had been my usual practice, because I sensed that the world of weather forecasts belonged only to the world of active people, and I was not a part of it.

Work as Service

Thus far we have viewed work in terms of self-interest, or what we get out of it. There is, however, a final ingredient in work that pushes it in the direction of altruism. Work is a service to others.

Here the focus shifts outward to the effect one's work has on other individuals and on society as a whole. This, too, is one of the rewards of work: it benefits others as well as oneself. We acknowledge this aspect whenever we pay tribute to a person for what he or she has done for humanity. Of course this ideal is more easily discerned in service-oriented jobs or volunteer work that serves the public. Correspondingly, one of the problems with assembly line or warehouse work, where one does not see the results of one's labor, is that the sense of service tends to evaporate.

Summary

Understanding work requires that we think about it in at least six dimensions. Work provides for life's needs and wants and is a means of economic production. It carries with it a constant possibility of being a curse or drudgery, but it has the potential to supply a sense of human achievement, psychological satisfaction, and service to humanity. These are points at which work intersects with the Christian faith, as we will see in Part 5.

The Ethics of Work

Another general framework within which work must be understood is its ethical dimensions. Here too I will eventually relate the principles to a specifically Christian framework, but for the moment I am interested in the more general ethical terms that apply to work.

The Idea of a "Work Ethic"

The very phrase *work ethic* suggests one such ethical category. It is no doubt true that there are many specific work ethics, but when we use the term in the singular we acknowledge a moral viewpoint that values work and regards it as something good.

A work ethic implies several related things. It assumes that the *active life* and not simply the contemplative life is worthy. It implies that *industriousness* and a degree of *self-reliance* are private and public virtues. In addition, a work ethic usually implies a *social concern* for the health of society, and this is often tinged with a feeling of *patriotism.*

There is no standard term for the ethical viewpoint that opposes the work ethic, but there clearly are individuals and societies that lack a work ethic. They are characterized by a high degree of idleness, low economic achievement, lack of pride in their work, low regard for the quality of work, tolerance of laziness, and a parasitic reliance on others to sustain their life.

Utilitarianism and Service

Another ethical outlook that fosters work is *utilitarianism.* After all, work achieves practical results that are useful to individuals, families, and societies. Conversely, people and societies that have little feeling for what is useful produce an anemic work ethic.

A related ethical stance is that of *servanthood* or *service to the common good.* While work can thrive within an atmosphere governed solely by self-interest, it rarely does so. Not only does a devotion to the welfare of the state or community often buttress motives of self-interest, it can even sustain people in work they do not find personally beneficial.

Work and the Self

Work can flourish within ethical systems that espouse opposite attitudes toward the self, namely, self-fulfillment and self-sacrifice. In systems that value *self-fulfillment,* one works to satisfy certain innate personal needs. An ethical outlook that belittles the individual's self-realization usually ends up with an impoverished work ethic. In fact, this is a major problem in a technological society, where many jobs exist only at the price of disregarding the worker's self-fulfillment.

The opposing ethical viewpoint that might still find value in work is an ethic of *self-sacrifice* or *self-denial*. Given the element of drudgery in work, work still remains an option if one believes that self-denial is inherently virtuous. While this can be given a specifically Christian application, other ethical outlooks have also honored work within a context of self-sacrifice. Needless to say this is not a common stance today.

Summary

Work derives its sanction from a range of ethical premises, including the beliefs that work is inherently virtuous, useful, a service to humanity, self-fulfilling, or self-denying. All of these can be placed in a context of Christian ethics, and when we do this, other ethical considerations such as stewardship and calling also come into play, as we will see later in this book.

Further Reading

Sebastian de Grazia, *Of Time, Work, and Leisure* (1962).
Daniel Yankelovich, "The Meaning of Work," in *The Worker and the Job: Coping with Change*, ed. Jerome M. Rosow (1974), 19–47.
Stanley Parker, *Leisure and Work* (1983).

2

It's Not as Simple as You Think
Toward an Understanding of Leisure

Defining the nature of work is relatively easy. By contrast, the concept of leisure has proved much more elusive. Leisure encompasses such varied pursuits as quiet contemplation on one end of the continuum and active sports and recreation on the other. People's preferences, too, make leisure harder to codify. What some people find leisurely others find exhausting and unpleasant.

Defining Leisure

Definitions of leisure fall into three groupings. These definitions place leisure in relation to time, to activity, and to a state of soul or mind. None of these definitions is complete by itself. Together they establish the issues that are relevant to understanding leisure.

Leisure as Free Time

Time provides a good starting point for understanding leisure. One ingredient of leisure is that it is *nonwork*. Work is done out of a sense of duty or obligation. This is not to prejudge the question of whether some work might have the quality of leisure. But to define leisure in the first place requires that we begin by contrasting it to work and other necessities. One authority notes,

Contemporary leisure is defined by contrast not just to one's job, but to all of the ordinary necessities and obligations of existence, and it must be remembered that they who have and use leisure regard it as part of the dialectic of daily living.[1]

Even the etymology of the word suggests that leisure means free time. The word and concept have been traced back to two roots. One is the old French word *leisir,* from the Latin *licere,* meaning "to be allowed or to be lawful." Our word *license* comes from the same root. The key concept is freedom to do something. If we ask what we are free *from* in leisure it is obvious that we are free from the constraints of necessity or obligation. Leisure in this sense is freedom to do what we want to do in a relatively unforced manner.

The other root word to which leisure has been traced is the Greek word *skole* or the Latin *schola,* from which we derive our word *school.* The context for this conception is the classical ideal of an aristocracy in which people, freed from the need to work (which was done by slaves), could fulfill the responsibilities of free time by educating themselves to be the leaders of society. At its origin, the word carried the idea "to halt or cease"; applied to leisure, it implied having time free from work to spend as one pleased, including freedom to develop oneself as a person.[2]

The idea of leisure as time in which we are free to choose our own activities underlies some often quoted definitions of leisure by modern authorities, including the following:

Leisure is activity chosen in relative freedom for its qualities of satisfaction.[3]

Leisure is activity apart from the obligations of work, family, and society to which the individual turns at will, for either relaxation, diversion, or broadening his knowledge.[4]

Leisure is time beyond that which is required for existence . . . and subsistence. . . . It is discretionary time, the time to be used according to our own judgment or choice.[5]

1. Joffre Dumazedier, *Toward a Society of Leisure,* trans. Stewart E. McClure (New York: Free Press, 1967), 18–19.
2. Sebastian de Grazia, *Of Time, Work, and Leisure* (New York: Twentieth Century Fund, 1962), 12.
3. John R. Kelly, *Leisure* (Englewood Cliffs, N.J.: Prentice Hall, 1982), 7.
4. Dumazedier, *Toward a Society of Leisure,* 16–17.
5. Charles Brightbill, *The Challenge of Leisure* (Englewood Cliffs, N.J.: Prentice Hall, 1960), 4.

Leisure is time free from work and other obligations and it also encompasses activities which are characterized by a feeling of (comparative) freedom.[6]

All of these definitions agree that leisure is a contrast to work and other obligations, and that it is freely chosen instead of being done under obligation. Of course an activity must *feel* like leisure and must be *perceived* as freely chosen to count as leisure. Planting flowers or attending a party could be either work or leisure, depending on how a person perceives them in terms of obligation or choice.

An important part of leisure—and part of its function in human experience—lies in its status as an escape. By itself, leisure has little meaning and quickly palls. Contrary to what we often think, a life of endless leisure would be boring. Only when leisure is placed as a complement to work does it assume meaning. Robert Johnston has called leisure "a parenthesis in life."[7] Leisure is all the more pleasurable when we experience it as a conscious break from work—we love to see people going about their ordinary work while we are "on vacation" (or "on holiday," as the British quaintly put it).

Although leisure is not synonymous with play, these two have much in common. Johan Huizinga's famous description of play will help fill out the notion of leisure as enlightened escape.[8] Play, claims Huizinga, is a voluntary activity. It is superfluous, beyond the ordinary necessity of life. It is disinterested, standing "outside the immediate satisfaction of wants and appetites." It "adorns" and "amplifies" life. Being different from ordinary life, play is limited in its time and space, and is governed by its own rules. In sum, play is

a free activity standing quite consciously outside "ordinary" life. . . . It is an activity connected with no material interest, and no profit can be gained by it. It proceeds within its own proper boundaries of time and space according to fixed rules and in an orderly manner. It promotes the formation of social groupings.

All of this is true of leisure in general as well as play.

Leisure as Activity

To define leisure as nonworking time in which people are free to choose their activities is a necessary but insufficient definition. Having

6. Stanley Parker, *The Sociology of Leisure* (New York: International Publications Service, 1976), 12.
7. Johnston, *Christian at Play*, 35.
8. Johan Huizinga, *Homo Ludens: A Study of the Play-Element in Culture* (1950; reprinted, Boston: Beacon Press, 1955), 1–27.

cleared a space for leisure, as it were, we need to put some positive ingredients into that space. For this reason it has seemed natural to think
of leisure as the pursuit of certain activities.

Cultural pursuits, for example, have traditionally been classified as
leisure. Reading a book, attending a concert or play, visiting an art gallery or museum, and listening to music are leisure activities.

Recreation is a second main category of leisure activities. Such recreation runs the gamut from sports to vacationing, from playing a table
game to skiing.

The broad category of *entertainment* ranks as a third major leisure activity in the modern world, with mass media topping the list. Watching
television, going to see a movie, listening to the radio or cassette player,
and reading magazines have absorbed an increasing share of the leisure
scene in the later twentieth century. The latest published survey found
that Americans average 15 hours of television viewing per week, while
media expert Quentin Schultze's research led him to conclude in 1994
that "the typical family has the tube on for over seven hours daily."[9]

Hobbies and crafts also belong to the list of activities the world calls
leisure. These could include collecting things (stamps, antiques), restoring things (furniture, cars), and making things (model train sets,
picture frames). Photography, gardening, and many types of puttering
around the house can likewise rise to the level of leisure.

Finally, many *social activities* fall into the sphere of leisure. Visiting
with friends or relatives, informal conversations in the hallway, going
on a family picnic, or attending a church potluck dinner are obvious examples. So are some domestic routines, such as sitting down to breakfast or the evening meal, chatting with a spouse or child while doing
the dishes, and even sex with one's spouse.

Taking time to categorize leisure activities highlights an important
fact: our leisure activities exceed the leisure time we usually feel we
have at our disposal. When asked in the abstract how much leisure
they have, busy people think in terms of leisure *time* and conclude
that they have little leisure in their lives. The range of activities that
make up leisure helps to modify that assessment at least a little. It is
also important to note that defining leisure as time spent in specific activities is incomplete by itself. To rate as leisure, an activity must include the elements of freedom and choice noted earlier. The attitude
accompanying a given activity sometimes determines whether it is
work or leisure.

For some people, jogging or riding the exercise bike is leisure. For others, it is work, an activity governed by the utilitarian end of physical fit-

9. John P. Robinson, "I Love My TV," *American Demographics*, September 1990, 27;
Quentin J. Schultze, *Winning Your Kids Back from the Media* (Downers Grove: InterVarsity, 1994), 42.

ness and therefore drudgery. Golf is leisure for people doing it in their free time but work for those who do it to cultivate a business relationship. Having someone over for dinner can be either a social duty or a leisure activity. Work done as "moonlighting" can be just another job designed to produce extra income or it can meet all the criteria of leisure.

Defining leisure in terms of activity also shows it to be the opposite, not only of necessary work (as noted in the definition of leisure as free time), but also of idleness. Leisure is not synonymous with free time, though free time is usually a prerequisite for it. Leisure is time devoted to freely chosen activities that are inherently pleasurable and satisfying. Many of these activities require effort and are even physically or mentally strenuous, but they are experienced as leisure because they are freely chosen and carry the rewards of leisure.

Leisure as a Quality of Life

Leisure reaches its fullest dignity when we move from considering it in terms of time and activity to defining it in terms of a quality that it bestows on life. One of the standard sources on the subject, Sebastian de Grazia's book *Of Time, Work, and Leisure*, asserts that

> leisure and free time live in two different worlds. We have got in the habit of thinking them the same. Anybody can have free time. Not everybody can have leisure. . . . Leisure refers to a state of being, a condition of man, which few desire and fewer achieve.[10]

What things, then, make up the attitude that merits the designation *leisure?* As a beginning, we can agree that "leisure is a matter of the individual's perception rather than of rigid time-based or activity-based definitions. It is rooted in enjoyment and reflects degrees of pleasure and satisfaction."[11] In other words, leisure is a state of feeling satisfied—a feeling of luxurious well-being.

The most vigorous attempt to define leisure as a positive quality of life has been made from a Catholic perspective by Josef Pieper.[12] Leisure, writes Pieper, "is a mental and spiritual attitude—it is not simply the result of external factors, it is not the inevitable result of spare time, a holiday, a week-end or a vacation. It is, in the first place, an attitude of mind, a condition of the soul." According to Pieper, several ingredients help to produce this condition of soul. One is "an attitude of non-activity, of inward calm, of . . . letting things happen." It is "a receptive

10. de Grazia, *Of Time, Work, and Leisure*, 7–8.
11. J. Allan Patmore, *Recreation and Resources: Leisure Patterns and Leisure Places* (Oxford: Basil Blackwell, 1983), 6.
12. Josef Pieper, *Leisure the Basis of Culture*, trans. Alexander Dru (New York: Pantheon Books, 1964).

attitude of mind," one that eludes "those who grab and grab hold." This is similar in tenor to the experience of "wise passiveness" championed by the English Romantic poet William Wordsworth.[13]

Pieper also believes that leisure in its highest reaches includes a sense of celebration conceived as joy in the acceptance of one's place in the world. In leisure, moreover, "the truly human values are saved and preserved." Who can doubt it? In leisure we renew our contact with nature, family, and friends, and we take time to ponder or experience the things that matter most to us.

Pieper expresses an obviously high ideal for leisure, asserting that leisure is more than doing; it is also being. While I do not wish to exclude free time activities that fall short of this ideal, a main goal of this book is to encourage readers to upgrade the quality of their leisure pursuits. We have a lamentable tendency to drift by default into mediocrity in our leisure lives instead of actively choosing the excellent. When we define leisure in terms of human enrichment, it again emerges as the opposite, not only of work, but also of idleness.

Summary

Definitions of leisure include three complementary aspects. Leisure begins as time free from constraints of obligation or necessity. Beyond that, it consists of certain activities that are conventionally classified as leisure. In their highest forms these activities add important qualities to human life, including satisfaction, enrichment, receptivity to experiences of beauty and to insights that would otherwise go unnoticed, recovery of human values, and celebration.

The Rewards and Functions of Leisure

Defining leisure is one way to understand it. Identifying the rewards and goals that people attach to leisure is equally helpful, since these, too, help us understand what it is and what it is designed to accomplish. For example, leisure serves the purpose of balancing or compensating for the strain of work and obligation. While it would belittle leisure to see it only in its relationship to work, it is necessary to see it partly in the context of what Dumazedier calls "the search for repose."[14]

There are, of course, other rewards to leisure. Dumazedier identifies

13. William Wordsworth, "Expostulation and Reply." Wordsworth had in mind the effects that come when we open ourselves to the influences of nature, but his phrase "wise passiveness" extends to many moments in which we surrender ourselves to something in a receptive mood.
14. Dumazedier, *Toward a Society of Leisure*, 82.

three primary functions of leisure: relaxation, entertainment, and personal development.[15] Relaxation "provides recovery from fatigue" and "repairs the physical and nervous damage wrought by the tensions of daily pressures." This is "the recuperative function of leisure." Entertainment, in turn, "spells deliverance from boredom." As for personal development, leisure "permits a broader, readier social participation on the one hand and on the other, a willing cultivation of the physical and mental self over and above the utilitarian considerations of job or practical advancement."

Geoffrey Godbey has approached the subject by identifying the ideals that leisure at its best can meet. The list includes pleasure, learning, playfulness, celebration, and self-actualization.[16] Writing from a Christian perspective, Robert Lee paints a similar picture:

> Leisure is the growing time of the human spirit. Leisure provides the occasion for learning and freedom, for growth and expression, for rest and restoration, for rediscovering life in its entirety.[17]

In the previous chapter I noted that one of the psychological and social functions of work is that it helps to establish a person's identity. The same is potentially true for leisure, though our overvaluing of work and undervaluing of leisure tend to obscure this potential. There is no logical reason why my friend at church should be more identified as an investment banker than an expert harpsichord player. In fact, his education was in music, and he chose work that would allow him to cultivate his avocation in music. John Kelly has rightly said that leisure is "the crucial life space for the expression and development of selfhood, for the working out of identities that are important to the individual."[18]

Most people would take more responsibility for the quality of their leisure and choose it more carefully if they saw how important it can be in establishing a meaningful identity. It is partly in leisure that we discover who we are and what we can become. We might note in this regard that everyone has a leisure history made up of past experiences, opportunities seized or lost, satisfactions, and frustrations. Together these make up a significant part of our identity.

One authority on leisure believes that leisure is part of an innate human pursuit of what a person regards as a desirable identity.[19] To the

15. Ibid., 14–16.
16. Geoffrey Godbey, *Leisure in Your Life: An Exploration* (Philadelphia: Saunders College, 1980), 289–91.
17. Robert Lee, *Religion and Leisure in America* (Nashville: Abingdon, 1964), 35.
18. John R. Kelly, *Leisure Identities and Interactions* (London: Allen and Unwin, 1983), 23.
19. Ralph Glasser, "Leisure Policy, Identity and Work," in *Work and Leisure*, ed. J. T. Haworth and M. A. Smith (Princeton: Princeton Book Co., 1976), 36–52.

extent that people are free to make choices, they build their lives around an ideal they hold for themselves. People thus reveal "by their choices, in clothes, furniture, speech, manners, leisure activities, friends, and as far as possible work, their individual interpretation of the ideal identity they are pursuing. The goals of leisure and of life are inseparable."

Leisure is also important in establishing social relations. For one thing, many leisure activities are done with other people, so leisure pursuits place us into interest groups with those who enjoy the same leisure activity. Our leisure activities either enlarge or narrow the circle of people with whom we have contacts. We also choose leisure pursuits partly by how they affect the expectations of other people in our nonworking time.

The social function of leisure has specific application to the types of unity the church or other Christian groups have always sought to establish. Although the following statement was not made with the church in mind, it is strikingly similar to the ideal of a Christian community or group as a closely knit body:

> The social nature of much leisure would indicate that leisure has the special function of building community in society. In the chosen activities and relationships of leisure, the bonding of intimate groups such as the family and larger groups of the community takes place.[20]

To speak of the leisure function of the church may seem like trivializing the church but in fact a large part of the spiritual and social activities of a dynamic and unified church fall within the sphere of leisure. We need to upgrade the dignity that leisure holds in the Christian world.

The role of leisure in family living is especially important. Leisure is one of the largest things that families share—or at least ought to share. Kelly notes that "the family provides the first context of leisure learning, the primary socialization about leisure values, the companions for most leisure through the life cycle, and (in the residence) the location of most leisure. . . . It is the family which usually takes the vacation trip, eats as a group, and goes to church together."[21] One study found a positive correlation between couples' satisfaction with their marriage and the proportion of time spent in shared leisure activities.[22]

Concerning the social context of leisure it is important to note that leisure is always a learned behavior. At every stage of life, we do in our

20. Kelly, *Leisure*, 12.
21. Ibid., 174. See also his helpful chapter on leisure and the family in his book *Leisure Identities and Interactions* (cited above).
22. Dennis Orthner, "Leisure Activity Patterns and Marital Satisfaction over the Marital Career," *Journal of Marriage and the Family* 37 (1975):91–102.

leisure time what we have learned to do. Of course this process of learning can be greatly aided by educational opportunities (broadly defined). To minimize the role of education for leisure is to settle for a rather low level of achievement through a process of inertia. Philosopher Bertrand Russell correctly said that "the wise use of leisure . . . is a product of civilization and education," adding that a person who has known only work will be bored if he or she suddenly comes into possession of free time.[23]

A final function of leisure is that it provides the arena within which we express personally held values. Our very choice of leisure pursuits is based on our personal values. Leisure also tests people's values or lack of them. As Robert Lee puts it,

> The problem of leisure is . . . the problem of life. . . . Leisure is a part of man's ultimate concern. It is a crucial part of the very search for meaning in life. . . . Increasingly it is in our leisure time that either the meaningfulness or the pointlessness of life will be revealed.[24]

Leisure not only expresses and tests our values but can also enrich them. As Charles Obermeyer notes,

> Leisure is not something added to life, a . . . diversion or . . . sigh that is often indistinguishable from boredom. It is the process that builds meaning and purpose into life.[25]

Leisure is not peripheral to life but essential to it. One study found that people's satisfaction with life as a whole was more strongly related to satisfaction with leisure than satisfaction with their job.[26]

Summary

At its best, leisure serves many functions. It provides rest, relaxation, enjoyment, and physical and psychic health. It allows people to recover the distinctly human values, to build relationships, to strengthen family bonds, and to put themselves in touch with the world and nature.

Leisure can lead to wholeness, gratitude, self-expression, self-fulfillment, creativity, personal growth, and a sense of achievement. It expands our horizons beyond the confines of the workaday world and lib-

23. Bertrand Russell, *In Praise of Idleness and Other Essays* (London: Allen and Unwin, 1935), 19.

24. Lee, *Religion and Leisure*, 25–26.

25. Charles Obermeyer, "Challenges and Contradictions," in *Technology, Human Values and Leisure*, ed. Max Kaplan and Phillip Bosserman (Nashville: Abingdon, 1971), 222.

26. Godbey, *Leisure in Your Life*, 40.

erates our spirits from the bondage of the everyday routine. Anything that has these potential rewards deserves more thought and understanding than it typically receives in Christian circles.

The Ethics of Leisure

Like work, leisure can be placed into a context of traditional ethical viewpoints. This framework, too, will help us to understand leisure itself before we relate it to specifically Christian morality.

Ethical Viewpoints Hostile to Leisure

We can begin by noting the outlooks to which leisure stands opposed. One of these is *idleness*. Leisure in its ideal sense is not the absence of activity or effort; it is joyous effort in activities that carry their own reward. Leisure is the enemy of a do-nothing outlook on life. In fact, the people most deprived of leisure include the unemployed and the depressed.

Belief in the worth of leisure is also the enemy of a *utilitarian ethic* that values only activities that are directly useful to meeting one's physical needs. By its very nature, leisure is something that is nonutilitarian, if we define utilitarian in the ordinary sense of mastering one's environment. There is something joyously gratuitous about the fact that in leisure we go beyond the requirements of life. It is true that a utilitarian ethic sometimes finds room for leisure, but not as something inherently worthwhile in itself. People with a strong work ethic have often acknowledged the necessity and goodness of leisure, but only as something that makes a person able to work better. This is not genuine leisure because it makes leisure utilitarian instead of viewing it as having value in itself.

Leisure also opposes an ethic of *self-abasement*. Leisure is intrinsically pleasurable. It produces delight and satisfaction. It is no wonder, therefore, that leisure fares poorly in ethical systems that denigrate pleasure. If pleasure is wrong, leisure and play are virtually the first things to go.

Hedonism and Humanism

Turning, then, to the positive side, the pursuit of leisure presupposes a *hedonistic ethic*, by which I mean an outlook that accepts the desirability of pleasure and enjoyment. There are, of course, Christian and non-Christian versions of what constitutes legitimate pleasure, but what I call hedonism or pleasure-seeking is the seedbed within which leisure grows, and it is compatible with Christianity, as John Piper has shown.[27]

Leisure also presupposes *humanism*. This term, too, has been sullied in the minds of some Christians because of its twentieth-century secular definitions. But humanism through the centuries has meant the striving to perfect all human possibilities in this world. It is devoted to human development and fulfillment. Such humanism can be either God-centered or human-centered. God-centered humanism values human fulfillment only in subordination to God's purposes and in relationship to him. The other type views people as self-reliant in their pursuit of human fulfillment.[28] Leisure depends on the affirmation of human fulfillment.

Summary

Leisure is not ethically neutral. It flourishes only when people believe in the goodness of pleasure and human fulfillment. It withers when people are lazy, preoccupied with what is useful, or given to self-denial. Perhaps we can see here the seeds of some of the negative attitudes toward leisure that have prevailed throughout the history of Christianity.

Further Reading

Sebastian de Grazia, *Of Time, Work, and Leisure* (1962).
Joffre Dumazedier, *Toward a Society of Leisure* (1967).
Harold D. Lehman, *In Praise of Leisure* (1974).
Geoffrey Godbey, *Leisure in Your Life: An Exploration* (1980).
John R. Kelly, *Leisure* (1982).
Stanley Parker, *Leisure and Work* (1983).
Leonard Doohan, *Leisure: A Spiritual Need* (1990).
Paul Heintzman, Glen Van Andel, Thomas Visker, eds., *Christianity and Leisure: Issues in a Pluralistic Society* (1994).

27. John Piper, *Desiring God: Meditations of a Christian Hedonist* (Portland, Ore.: Multnomah, 1986).

28. For discussions of Christian humanism, see Ronald B. Allen, *The Majesty of Man: The Dignity of Being Human* (Portland, Ore.: Multnomah, 1984); and J. I. Packer and Thomas Howard, *Christianity: The True Humanism* (Waco: Word, 1985).

PART 2

The Trouble with Work and Leisure Is . . .

3

Time's Wingéd Chariot
The Time Famine

T here is a time for every matter under heaven," claimed the ancient wiseman. While it is still true, a new twist has developed: there is no longer *enough* time for everything—perhaps not enough time for *anything* that we truly value. It is no wonder that recent years have produced the concept of "the time famine."

The result of this famine is that most people feel rushed and frantic in their weekly routine, as well as guilty about what they have not accomplished. A 1977 study asked respondents how often they felt rushed to complete their day's activities. One-fourth said they "always feel rushed," 53 percent said they "sometimes feel rushed," and only 22 percent said they "almost never feel rushed."[1] In other words, four out of five people felt continuously or regularly rushed. By 1990, the percentage of people who said that they "always feel rushed" had risen to a third of the population.[2]

Running Out of Time

In 1989 *Time* magazine ran a cover story on the time famine that has engulfed American society, and its analysis of the problem remains a

1. John P. Robinson, *How Americans Use Their Time: A Social Psychological Analysis of Everyday Behavior* (New York: Praeger, 1977), 48.
2. John P. Robinson, "The Time Squeeze," *American Demographics*, February 1990: 30.

37

good starting point for understanding the context of our current crisis in work and leisure.[3] The thesis of the article was that America has run out of time, and the article predicted that "time could end up being to the '90s what money was to the '80s." The symptoms and causes of the time famine are everywhere around us.

The Technological Revolution

We can begin with what lies behind much of the current over stimulated lifestyle—the technological revolution. Technology has accelerated the pace of life. In the office, computers have multiplied the amount of information to which we have access and the speed with which we can access it. Fax machines and computer mail have enabled us to shrink the time required to forward information from days to seconds. Laptop computers allow us to type on the airplane, and portable telephones enable us to make business calls while driving. A Hollywood publicist quoted in the *Time* article claimed that people call him on the telephone to tell him that his fax line is busy!

One result of this technological acceleration is that people feel more rushed at work. With voice mail able to pile up messages, more messages need to be answered each day. If mail can be sent in seconds, we tend to feel that it needs to be answered within minutes. Having grown accustomed to the speed of computers, we now get frustrated waiting for the machine to access a document or perform our commands. Employees at fast-food restaurants who typically serve drive-thru customers in twelve seconds report that the horns start honking if the food hasn't arrived in fifteen.[4]

The technology frenzy has also invaded the home. Telephones appear in more and more rooms of the typical home. Microwaves speed up the preparation of food, and takeout food is always an option if the microwave does not appeal. More than 530 microwaveable food products have been introduced since the early 1990s.[5] New television sets allow the family to see two channels at once or record a program simultaneously while viewing another one. One architect reports a growing request for media centers in homes, and he himself believes that "technology is a diversion from life."[6]

One of the unexplained results of the technological revolution is that "time-saving" devices have consumed our time instead of freeing it up. Around the house, for example, the number of hours that women

3. Nancy Gibbs, "How America Has Run Out of Time," *Time*, 24 April 1989, 58–67.
4. Juliet B. Schor, *The Overworked American: The Unexpected Decline of Leisure* (New York: Basic Books, 1991), 17.
5. Blair Kamin, "Consumers' Cries for Convenience Beckon Business in a Big Way," *Chicago Tribune*, 29 April 1991, section 1, 10.
6. James Trunzo, quoted in *Time* article, 61.

spend on housework (around 53 per week) has remained constant—and one study concluded that "technical sophistication may *increase* the amount of time given over to household work" (with the microwave oven being the only major appliance that has saved significant amounts of time).[7] Jeremy Rifkin, author of the book *Time Wars*, notes the irony "that in a culture so committed to saving time we feel increasingly deprived of the very thing we value."[8]

The Accelerated Pace of Life

It is nearly impossible to exaggerate the impact of technological speed on our individual and family lives. For one thing, technology has increased the number of options that we have at our disposal. It has given us more products (such as VCRs and endless gadgets) and with them more potential activities (such as watching movies or grinding our own coffee beans). If we own a camcorder, we have to find the time to take pictures and view them. The problem is that the amount of time we have to do things is fixed. As long ago as 1965, economist Gary Becker argued that as our affluence allows us to buy more and more goods, we have less and less time to spend on each of them.[9] The result is that we try to cram more and more activities into a fixed span of time.

The increased opportunities to do things has affected many areas of life. Sometimes it is fueled by the success syndrome. Parents, for example, want to make sure that their children have every possible opportunity to succeed—in school, in sports, in music, in social life. Parents themselves want to share—or at least give appearances of sharing—the current version of the American dream; they want to keep up a social life, see the movies or attend the concerts that people of their station do, and go on the types of outings their friends do. In short, no one wants to miss out on what everyone else seems to be enjoying. John Robinson, head of the American's Use of Time project at the University of Maryland, has observed that "people's schedules are more ambitious," adding that "there just isn't enough time to fit in all the things one feels have to be done."[10]

A salient feature of all this acceleration is the information overload that our society has developed. With access to more and more data, we are naturally expected to do something with it. As a result we are drowning in information. Television news and commercials come

---

7. Schor, *Overworked American*, 86–88.

8. Jeremy Rifkin, *Time Wars: The Primary Conflict in Human History* (New York: Simon and Schuster, 1987), 19.

9. Gary Becker, "A Theory of the Allocation of Time," *Economic Journal* 75 (1965):493–517.

10. John Robinson, quoted in *Time* article, 59.

packaged in smaller and smaller bytes—which means, of course, that there are *more* individual items that bombard us.

All of this would be more manageable if it didn't cost so much. Relatively few families can sustain the accelerated lifestyle to which we aspire on a single income. Most families depend on either both parents' working (as was the case with 57 percent of American families in 1989) or on the primary wage earner's working an excessive number of hours. The more we gain of the good life (conceived in technological terms) the more we have to work to pay for it. Sociologist Paula Rayman, who speaks of "falling behind while getting ahead," claims that "the American Dream is very much intact. It's just more expensive."[11]

We have become a shortcut society. According to the *Time* article, in 1922 Emily Post declared that the proper time of mourning for a widow was three years. Fifty years later Amy Vanderbilt asserted that the bereaved could return to a normal routine after a week! Not surprisingly, the shortcut society is also a throwaway society. Everything from cameras to spouses has become disposable.

The accelerated life has generated expectations that make frustration inevitable. One eyeglass franchise promises glasses "in about an hour." In such a world, it is small wonder that when we come upon a car traveling 50 miles per hour in a 55 mile per hour zone we become irritated at having to slow down before we pass it.

The Human Toll

The personal toll that the pace of life has exacted from us is something that nearly everyone has observed and felt. For one thing, our lives have become overly scheduled as they are dominated by the calendar and the clock. Appointment books have become increasingly elaborate and sophisticated, and more people carry them than ever before. We are a booked-up culture. Workshops and books on time management have proliferated, and some of the experts are hailed as celebrities.

We schedule our leisure times and then peer at our watches anxiously to make sure that our leisure does not exceed its allotted time. This may seem innocuous, but in the previous chapter I noted that leisure must be *felt* to be leisurely for it truly to count as such.

Professional people, armed with time-saving devices, end up working harder to meet the inexhaustible needs and deadlines of their superiors and clients (a trend expected to expand as the economy moves from an industrial to a service economy). Who ever ends up doing *less* work after purchasing a fax machine or voice mail?

Family life has also been transformed. Increasingly family activities must be arranged by appointment. It is a full-time job to keep the fam-

11. Paula Rayman, quoted in *Time* article, 60.

ily's schedule coordinated and updated. The kitchen table used to be a daily meeting point for the family. Today Hallmark, which launched a 125-card "To Kids with Love" series in 1989, prints cards that parents can put on the breakfast table urging children to "Have a super day at school." Families do fewer and fewer things as a complete unit.

No statistics can record the physical, psychic, and emotional strain that the time famine places on us. For the most part, all of us know from personal experience the syndrome of always feeling harried and tired. Even if a few hours miraculously appear some evening, most people resort to television because they lack the energy to do anything else. Arlie Hochschild, author of the book *The Second Shift* that studied working couples, found that people "talked about sleep the way a hungry person talks about food."[12] Sleep researchers, who have coined the phrase "sleep deficit," claim that a majority of Americans are getting between sixty and ninety minutes less sleep per night than they should.[13]

Summary

Any significant analysis of work and leisure must begin with a consideration of time. Time is the medium within which we work and play. The English Renaissance poet Andrew Marvell wrote a poem in which he begins with the hypothesis, "Had we but world enough, and time." But the hypothesis is faulty, for the simple reason that "at my back I always hear / Time's wingéd chariot hurrying near."[14] While the problem is perennial, it is even more acute in our own day. To solve our problems of work and leisure will require us to solve the problem of time as well.

The Time Continuum

Work and leisure together make up our daily lives, and what they share is time—twenty-four hours a day. Not surprisingly, therefore, theorists on work and leisure have long talked about "the time continuum."

Obligatory and Discretionary Activities

The simplest dichotomy into which we can divide the twenty-four hours that make up the day is between activities that are obligatory and those that are discretionary—between activities we have to do and

12. Arlie Hochschild, *The Second Shift* (New York: Viking Penguin, 1989), 9.
13. Schor, *Overworked American*, 11.
14. Andrew Marvell, "To His Coy Mistress."

those we choose to do. These should be viewed as two poles on a continuum, not as two separate columns of activities.

On the obligatory end of the spectrum we find those daily activities that are required to sustain life. They include personal care (sleeping, eating, dressing), housework (preparing meals, cleaning the house, cutting the lawn), the job that produces one's income, task-related studying, and social obligations (helping a spouse or roommate, overseeing a child's homework, helping a friend move). While work does not comprise all that exists on the obligatory end of the scale, it belongs with other activities that cluster together in the realm of obligations. In saying this, I do not mean to prejudge whether we find these obligations enjoyable or burdensome.

At the discretionary end of the spectrum we find those activities that are usually placed in the category of leisure—entertainment, sports, recreation, hobbies, and other free-time activities. These are things that we do because we want to, and for their own sake. If we choose not to do such activities things do not fall apart as they do when we fail to meet our obligations.

Semileisure Activities

As we ponder the continuum it becomes evident that some activities fall into a middle category. They are either a mixture of obligation and freedom, or they fall into one category or the other depending on the person or occasion. Examples include gardening, decorating a room, or serving on a committee. Traveling to work or some other required activity is work for some people and recreation for others. So are physical exercise, building bookshelves, or refinishing a piece of furniture.

Then, too, we all have obligations that do not fall into the category of work, though their obligatory nature at the same time removes them from the realm of leisure. Attending Little League practices, reading a book in order to stay informed, caring for pets, and optional shopping are examples.

It is small wonder, therefore, that authorities on the subject have coined the term *semileisure* to cover activities that do not fall clearly into the category of either work or leisure. One of them explains, "Here is an activity part practical, part nonpractical, so to speak, in varying proportions."[15] Activities that fall into this category often stem from relationships. It is also common for these activities to begin as freely chosen and gradually assume the quality of a duty. One thinks, for example, of doing extra work for pay and of various types of volunteer work.

15. Dumazedier, *Toward a Society of Leisure*, 18–19.

In sum, we can picture our daily activities as falling somewhere on the following scale:

Obligation	Semileisure	Freedom
(work)		(leisure)

The Practical Implications of the Time Continuum

The time scale will be important throughout this book. It shows at a glance how interrelated work and leisure are. They are not separate elements of our lives but rather complementary aspects of a single whole. To talk about leisure without considering the constraints of the obligatory activities in our daily routine is unrealistic. We can increase one segment of the continuum only by subtracting something else, which in turn relates to the focus of this chapter: time.

It is also apparent that necessary work takes precedence over leisure in our daily routine. Leisure is something we can engage in only after our basic physical necessities are satisfied. To define leisure as nonwork is not an adequate definition, but the scale shows at a glance that freedom from obligation or necessity is at least a prerequisite for leisure.

It is equally important to recognize the category of semileisure activities. For many activities in life, it is up to us whether they will be experienced as work or leisure. To move work toward the right side of the scale and to enlarge the sphere in which we feel the spirit of freedom and choice is a laudable goal. Christianity does not endorse masochism or gloom. Even leisure in work becomes possible if we approach work in the right spirit. A main theme of this book is the desirability of enlarging the freedom side of the ledger.

Finally, the scale I have discussed has a special relevance to Christian activities. Many spiritual and moral acts that Christians perform have a combined sense of duty and pleasure. Christians pray, attend Bible studies and worship services, serve on committees of Christian organizations, and volunteer their time to help people in need, partly because they regard these as obligations of the Christian life and partly because they want to do them. The whole area of "Christian ministry" occupies a huge part of the middle of the scale for many Christians, though secular writers do not mention religious activities in their analysis of time usage.

How the Time Famine Has Affected Work and Leisure

Because work and leisure compete for the limited amount of time that we have, it is no wonder that the shortage of time in our weekly lives has drastically affected both our work and leisure. Time studies and statistics tell the story, and as we look at these, we will see how important it is to discuss work and leisure together (something most books on the subject neglect).

Too Much Work

Regarding the relation of work to time we can say unequivocally that the problem is that work takes too much of most people's time. We must remember that work extends far beyond a person's primary job and beyond work done for pay, though the problem for many people begins with the time spent on the job.

The trends are even more important than the specific statistics. Juliet Schor's book *The Overworked American*, from which I have drawn the following data, conveniently summarizes the latest findings. Beginning in the late 1960s, the United States entered an era of rising worktime—on the job and off. In the last twenty years, the average amount of time that Americans have spent on the job has risen by about nine hours (i.e., slightly more than one additional day of work) per year. Over the span of two decades, therefore, the average employed person works an additional 163 hours per year—the equivalent of an extra month a year.

Another source notes a study showing that in 1948 thirteen percent of Americans with full-time jobs worked more than 49 hours a week; in 1979, 18 percent; in 1989, 24 percent.[16] Nearly half of those who work more than 49 hours a week actually work 60 hours or more.[17]

The phenomenon of double-jobbing or moonlighting is an important part of the picture. Moonlighting is more prevalent today than at any time during the three decades for which we have records, with over six percent of employed people holding two or more jobs.[18] In one survey, a third of American workers expressed a willingness to work more hours than they currently did for pay.[19] A 1969 study revealed that two out of five moonlighters in the United States believed they needed to work for extra income in order to pay for regular household expenses, while 60 percent did it for reasons other than economic necessity.[20] An often cited case is the rubber workers in Akron, Ohio, who worked a six-hour work day. Over half the workers took either another full-time job or an additional part-time job.[21]

16. Witold Rybczynski, *Waiting for the Weekend* (New York: Viking, 1991), 216.
17. Schor, *Overworked American*, 30.
18. Schor, *Overworked American*, 31; Rybczynski, *Waiting for the Weekend*, 217.
19. Godbey, *Leisure in Your Life*, 106.
20. Parker, *Sociology of Leisure*, 67.
21. Johnston, *Christian at Play*, 11.

But working for pay is only part of the time we allot to work. We must add to it the work involved in other necessities of life. The household routine is a major element. The more goods and property we possess, the more time they take. Keeping in mind the time scale noted earlier, it is obvious that nonleisure obligations take up by far the biggest chunk of a person's time, even though some of the items may not ordinarily be considered work (for example, driving to various activities or telephoning people).

Various studies come up with different figures on how many hours per week men and women actually spend in their total work on the job and at home. One study showed that married mothers average 85 hours of work on job, homemaking, and childcare, while married fathers average 66 hours.[22] Another study had the figures at 87 hours and 76 hours.[23] A third study found that married couples averaged 76–89 hours of work for each spouse.[24] What all these studies show is the high number of weekly hours we spend working.

Not Enough Leisure

The time squeeze has also affected leisure. As time spent in work has increased, time available for leisure has dwindled. Again it is the trends that tell us the most.

John Robinson's time survey in the 1970s found that, of the 168 hours available to people each week, 80 percent were devoted to job, housework, personal needs, and related travel, not counting some types of obligatory activities.[25] This was similar to the finding of someone a decade earlier that people had between twenty and thirty hours left after work and household chores for additional obligatory activities and leisure.[26] But in 1987 a Harris poll showed that Americans claimed to have 16.6 hours of leisure time each week.[27] This was 9.6 fewer hours than in 1973, a loss of nearly one and half hours a day.[28] Placed into a time sequence, the number of leisure hours per week declined by these steps: 1973—26.2; 1975—24.3; 1980—19.2; 1984—18.1; 1987—16.6.[29] In other words, Americans' leisure time shrank by 37 percent in less than two decades.

22. Study summarized in Hochschild, *Second Shift*, 278.
23. Ibid.
24. Schor, *Overworked American*, 21.
25. Robinson, *How Americans Use Their Time*, 89.
26. Dumazedier, *Toward a Society of Leisure*, 81.
27. Schor, *Overworked American*, 175.
28. Blair Kamin and Flynn McRoberts, "Leisure Slips on Time Treadmill," *Chicago Tribune*, 29 April 1991, section 1:10.
29. *New York Times*, 3 June 1990, section E, 4.

One of the fallacies that is commonly accepted as truth is that the growth of technology increases our free time. But an international study of time usage found that the United States, representing the most technologically developed culture in the world, showed *less* leisure time than cities in other countries.[30] Such statistics are buttressed by the personal observation of E. F. Schumacher:

> The amount of genuine leisure available in a society is generally in inverse proportion to the amount of labor-saving machinery it employs. If you would travel, as I have done, from England to the United States and on to a country like Burma, you would not fail to see the truth of this assertion.[31]

Summary

The time famine of the technological age is more than a set of statistics and trends. It is a daily reality for all of us. We do not need to conduct a poll to know that we have run out of time. All we need is a long, hard look at our daily and weekly lives, and a bit of introspection to uncover how we feel about our daily and weekly routine. A century and a half ago Henry David Thoreau told an audience in a factory town, "Work, work, work. It would be glorious to see mankind at leisure for once."[32]

Further Reading

Robert Banks, *The Tyranny of Time: When 24 Hours Is Not Enough* (1983).

Jeremy Rifkin, *Time Wars: The Primary Conflict in Human History* (1987).

Nancy Gibbs, "How America Has Run Out of Time," *Time*, 24 April 1989, 58–67.

Juliet B. Schor, *The Overworked American: The Unexpected Decline of Leisure* (1991).

30. Alexander Szalai, ed., *The Use of Time: Daily Activities of Urban and Suburban Populations in Twelve Countries* (The Hague: Mouton, 1972), 464.

31. E. F. Schumacher, *Good Work* (New York: Harper and Row, 1979), 25.

32. Henry David Thoreau, "Getting a Living"; quoted in Daniel T. Rodgers, *The Work Ethic in Industrial America, 1850–1920* (Chicago: University of Chicago Press, 1979), 1.

4

The Experiment That Failed

Trying to Get Too Much out of Work, and Getting Too Little

A job should be a job, not a death sentence."

"Jobs are demeaning. You walk out with no sense of satisfaction."

"One minute to five is the moment of triumph. You physically turn off the machine that has dictated to you all day long."

These are the statements of three of the 133 workers interviewed by Studs Terkel for his book *Working: People Talk about What They Do All Day and How They Feel about What They Do.*[1] Terkel's 589-page book, now a classic on contemporary attitudes toward work, does much to confirm that our society is suffering from a work crisis. The opening paragraph of Terkel's introduction suggests the extent of the crisis:

> This book, being about work, is by its very nature, about violence—to the spirit as well as to the body. It is about ulcers as well as accidents, . . . about nervous breakdowns as well as kicking the dog around. It is, above all (or beneath all), about daily humiliations. To survive the day is triumph enough for the walking wounded among the great many of us.

Books built around interviews of workers, as well as those written by

1. Studs Terkel, *Working: People Talk about What They Do All Day and How They Feel about What They Do* (New York: Pantheon Books, 1972).

writers who went to work in a factory, suggest that this grim assessment is backed by the experiences of people in the workplace.[2]

The Grand Experiment

The background against which we must understand the contemporary crisis in work is the mid-twentieth century's acceptance of what I will call the "success ethic." Several strands made up this attitude toward work that became the dominant work ethic of our century.

Money and Career Status as the Goals of Work

Most important of all was the economic goal of work. Work was no longer a calling in the sense of being a service to God and society. Instead its motivation was to make money as a means toward attaining the good life. The good life, in turn, was conceived in material terms, with emphasis on an attractive home replete with conveniences, plenty of clothes, nice cars, expensive entertainment and vacations, and maximum opportunities for one's family. The goal, in short, was what we call a "high" standard of living.

A second ingredient that made up the success ethic was a preoccupation with career status. People valued themselves and others in terms of a successful career. Rising the corporate or professional ladder was the most visible measure of success in a career. The urge for success measured in terms of career advancement produced the phenomenon of "the organization man" of which William Whyte wrote in the 1950s.[3] Of course the ascent up the ladder was expected to be accompanied by an increase in salary, thereby reinforcing the economic motivation of work.

This preoccupation with one's career produced the phenomenon of careerism. Douglas LaBier claims that "careerism has become the main work ethic of our times," and he describes the phenomenon thus:

> At root, careerism is an attitude, a life orientation in which a person views career as the primary and most important aim of life. . . . Successful career development means feeling motivated by the prospect of up-

2. Specimen books include Barbara Garson's *All the Livelong Day: The Meaning and Demeaning of Routine Work* (Garden City, N.Y.: Doubleday, 1975) , a collection of interviews of factory workers; and Goran Palm's *The Flight from Work*, trans. Patrick Smith (New Haven: Cambridge University Press, 1977), an exposé written by a poet-author who worked as an hourly factory worker as a means of researching the topic of attitudes toward work.

3. William H. Whyte, Jr., *The Organization Man* (New York: Simon and Schuster, 1956), 150.

ward movement with a large organization to positions of increasing responsibility or managerial authority. . . . The implication is that our career should be equivalent with our identity. . . . Some even describe phases and developmental tasks of adult life in terms of career development.[4]

The Search for Social Status and Self-Fulfillment

In the work ethic that became dominant in the mid-twentieth century, success was measured not only by the size of one's income and one's position on a professional ladder but by one's social status as well. Social mobility and respectability based on one's economic and professional rise became an axiom of the workplace. Lee Braude made a sociological analysis of the transformations of work in this century, observing that "the acquisition of money, rather than work, as a bridge to enhanced status became a dominant goal orientation of Americans."[5]

Of course this life-absorbing quest to rise economically, professionally, and socially required immense dedication to one's work. People who accepted the premises of the success ethic were willing to pay the price. They sacrificed leisure, personal fulfillment, and family time to make the dream possible. (Note the paradox of neglecting one's familiy for the sake of one's family, that is, to make possible their standard of living.)

With success thus elevated to the highest value, we could predict the list of virtues that became dominant. Self-denial was one of them, as workers performed epic feats of denying themselves the pleasures of life while pursuing economic and professional success. An insatiable capacity for work, accompanied by the physical and mental energy required for it, were equally evident. Ambition likewise became a prime virtue in the success ethic, as did a competitive spirit.

Sociologists such as Robert Bellah and Daniel Yankelovich have documented that, beginning in the 1970s, a new preoccupation with self-fulfillment ushered in changed attitudes toward work.[6] These analysts erred, however, in calling the quest for self-fulfillment a replacement of the older success ethic. All that changed was ideas about what constitutes self-fulfillment. Like their predecessors, workers in search of self-fulfillment view work as a means toward the fulfillment of personal goals. Their concern with individual fulfillment is merely an extension of the

---

4. Douglas LaBier, *Modern Madness: The Emotional Fallout of Success* (Reading, Mass: Addison-Wesley, 1986), 25–26.

5. Lee Braude, *Work and Workers: A Sociological Analysis* (New York: Praeger, 1975), 188.

6. Robert N. Bellah *et al.*, *Habits of the Heart: Individualism and Commitment in American Life* (Berkeley: University of California Press, 1985); Daniel Yankelovich, *New Rules: Searching for Self-Fulfillment in a World Turned Upside Down* (New York: Random House, 1981).

success ethic that has been around for half a century. We should also note that, whereas the earlier version of the success ethic was particularly slanted toward the male wage-earner of a family, the feminist movement has extended the domain of the success ethic and the quest for self-fulfillment to also include a large female segment of the population.

The Loss of the Sense of Vocation

Most of all, old and new versions of the success ethic represent a secularized substitute for older religious conceptions of work as a calling. The loss of the sense of vocation—a concept developed in later sections of this book—is the dominant element in twentieth-century attitudes toward work. Instead of working primarily to please God and serve humanity, adherents of the success ethic work to satisfy themselves. As one analyst of the phenomenon describes it, "With work shorn of its transcendent moral imperative, the person required others to legitimate his progress, which was itself measured differently."[7]

Summary

Here, then, is the grand experiment that has dominated American life in the second half of the twentieth century. Work is a means to achieving personal goals, including money, professional stature, social standing, and self-fulfillment. I have spoken of the success ethic in the past tense, but this does not mean it does not continue to be the dominant work ethic of our time. Even Christians who repudiate its value system tend to live by a modified success ethic. It is simply part of our ingrained way of life. LaBier says, "We all subscribe to it, adapt to it, and are influenced by it to some degree."[8]

How has the great experiment fared? By Christian standards, the values underlying the success ethic are at best secondary motivations for work. Pursued as most of American society has pursued it, the success ethic has produced a form of idolatry, accompanied by moral impoverishment. Quite apart from any religious critique, the success ethic has produced a contemporary crisis in work, to which we now turn.

How the Experiment Failed

An analysis of the contemporary crisis in work reveals three major problem areas. Together they tell us how the experiment has failed.

7. Braude, *Work and Workers*, 188.
8. LaBier, *Modern Madness*, 25.

The Workaholic Syndrome

The most obvious effect of the experiment is the workaholic syndrome.[9] Workaholics are people whose desire to work is compulsive. People of both sexes and every occupation can be workaholics. Workaholics think about work even when they are not on the job. They are intense, energetic, competitive, and driven. Workaholics prefer work to leisure, and they fear failure, boredom, and laziness. They are incapable of setting limits to their work or of saying "no." They do not delegate well, and they demand a lot from themselves and others. Finally, although workaholism is often discussed as though it were a disease, most workaholics are satisfied and content with their lives, though their lifestyle does produce problems for people who have to live with them.

Douglas LaBier made a social-psychoanalytic study of 230 successful careerists and wrote about his findings in *Modern Madness: The Emotional Fallout of Success*.[10] His survey of "today's new breed of success-oriented career professionals" is a litany of ways in which these people "can become troubled, conflicted, or emotionally damaged by their work and career climb" (p. v). What LaBier discovered was "feelings of guilt over self-betrayal or of trading off too much," feelings that "underlie the rage, depression, anxiety, and escapism found among many otherwise successful careerists" (p. 4). Psychological symptoms include anger, paralysis, alcoholism, psychosomatic ailments, and loneliness (pp. 33–35).

Added to the emotional depletion of people who overwork are the physical symptoms, with fatigue heading the list. One sociologist of work has stressed "the importance of fatigue in today's urban and industrial civilizations."[11] A study that asked industrial workers what they would do with an extra hour per day found that most people said "sleep."[12] Fatigue has become a way of life in contemporary society.

Wayne Oates, in his book *Confessions of a Workaholic*, looks at the workaholic syndrome in a religious light.[13] According to Oates, workaholics with a religious orientation practice a religion of solitude, works, and productivity. Not surprisingly, they are preoccupied with thoughts

9. My summary of the workaholic syndrome in this paragraph is based especially on Marilyn Machlowitz, *Workaholics: Living with Them, Working with Them* (Reading, Mass: Addison-Wesley, 1980).

10. See n. 4 above.

11. Dumazedier, *Toward a Society of Leisure*, 81.

12. Robert S. Weiss and David Riesman, "Some Issues in the Future of Leisure," in *Work and Leisure: A Contemporary Social Problem*, ed. Erwin O. Smigel (New Haven: College and University Press, 1963), 172.

13. Wayne Oates, *Confessions of a Workaholic: The Facts about Work Addiction* (New York: World, 1971).

of work even during church services, and they follow the extremes of either not having time for church activities or turning those activities into yet another form of compulsive work.

In recent years we have added not only *workaholic* to our vocabulary but also the dreaded word *burnout.* This, too, has become the object of sophisticated psychological study and is further evidence of the problem of overwork in our society.[14] A study of employees in eighteen public and private organizations found that just under half suffered from psychological burnout.[15]

What has produced this excessive compulsion to work in our society? The workaholic syndrome is fed by the twin streams of an acquisitive culture that wants more and more things and a success-oriented culture that wants success at any cost. At the root of it all is a system of misplaced values.

The mid-eighties coined the term *yuppies* to designate young, upwardly mobile, ambitious people preoccupied with wealth and success. Many of them spend nearly half of their week—close to seventy hours—at their job.[16] These are people for whom work has become an idol. We should note, too, that this devotion to success has become institutionalized in the form of jobs and professions that require people to be workaholics in order to hold a job.

"Downsizing" and Its Discontents

Whereas we tend to associate overwork with successful people who get carried away with their careers, a whole new category of overworked people has emerged from the recent trend toward "downsizing" in American business. Although the impact of this trend has entered the statistics mainly in the form of people who have lost their jobs, counselors have become aware of another side of the problem. As staffs have shrunk, businesses and bosses have continued to expect the same quantity of work from those who remain. These workers complain about receiving agendas for work that they cannot possibly achieve in the time allotted. To keep their jobs some of these people are forced to work far beyond the hours for which they are paid. The time they have for leisure and family responsibilities has been reduced in ways that have hurt both workers and their families.

14. See Whiton Steward Paine, ed., *Job Stress and Burnout: Research, Theory, and Intervention Perspectives* (Beverly Hills: Sage Publications, 1982); and Christina Maslach, *Burnout: The Cost of Caring* (Englewood Cliffs, N.J.: Prentice-Hall, 1982).

15. Muriel Dobbin, "Is the Daily Grind Wearing You Down?" *U. S. News and World Report,* 24 March 1986, 76.

16. Richard Phillips, "The New Calvinists," *Chicago Tribune,* 5 November 1986, section 7, pp. 5–8.

Dissatisfaction in Work

A second problem with work today is a decline in the satisfaction that people feel in their work. The available research focuses on the dissatisfaction of employees with their jobs, which is similar to the feelings we all have about much of the routine work that we do *off* the job.

The picture is not equally negative with every occupation. For example, four out of ten professionals and managers reported that they were "very satisfied" with their work, while little more than one out of ten unskilled workers responded that positively.[17] The same study showed that whereas professionals would generally choose similar work again, fewer than half of the workers at lower levels would do so.

Other surveys reveal more discontent in the workplace. Less than half of a group of blue collar workers claimed to be satisfied with their jobs most of the time.[18] When asked, "What type of work would you try to get into if you could start all over again?" less than half of a cross section of white collar workers and less than one-fourth of a cross section of blue collar workers indicated they would choose the same type of work.[19]

One of the problems of work is simply that much of it is inherently unsatisfying. In a survey of how Americans use their time, work was mentioned more frequently as the least enjoyable daily activity than as the most enjoyable one.[20] On occasions when I teach the poem in Ecclesiastes about the meaningless cycle of life under the sun (Ecclesiastes 1:4–11), I find that housewives resonate deeply with the weariness over life expressed by the ancient teacher. I resonate with it as I perform such weekly tasks as mowing the lawn and vacuuming the house.

Much of the dissatisfaction with work can be linked to technology and industrialism. The machine and assembly line have introduced a high degree of tedium and stress into modern industry. Many jobs have become depersonalized, repetitive, and uncreative. These problems go by the name *alienation in work*, referring to the fact that machine-related work does not engage the personality of the worker. Workers thus become alienated from the task they do for a living. Robert Blauner diagnoses the problem as having four dimensions:

---

17. Robert L. Kahn, "The Meaning of Work," in *The Human Meaning of Social Change*, ed. Angus C. Campbell and Philip E. Converse (New York: Russell Sage Foundation, 1972), 182.

18. *Work in America: Report of a Special Task Force to the Secretary of Health, Education, and Welfare* (Cambridge, Mass.: Massachusetts Institute of Technology Press, 1973), 15.

19. Ibid.

20. Noted by John Neulinger, *The Psychology of Leisure*, 2d ed. (Springfield, Ill.: Charles C. Thomas, 1981), 89.

powerlessness (inability to control the work process), *meaninglessness* (inability to develop a sense of purpose connecting the job to the overall productive process), *isolation* (inability to belong to integrated industrial communities), and *self-estrangement* (failure to become involved in the activity of work as a mode of self-expression).[21]

The congressional study *Work in America* concluded that "significant numbers of American workers are dissatisfied with the quality of their working lives. Dull, repetitive, seemingly meaningless tasks, offering little challenge or autonomy, are causing discontent among workers at all occupational levels."[22] A main theme in Daniel Yankelovich's book *New Rules* is that the level of discontent has risen as the search for self-fulfillment has collided with the willingness of previous generations to tolerate unfulfilling work to provide for their family.

Dissatisfaction with one's work takes its final toll in a declining work ethic, a major problem in the workplace today. A healthy work ethic is one in which the workers in a society believe in the inherent value of doing good work. But the work ethic in the United States and elsewhere has deteriorated in recent years.[23] Only 25 percent of American workers say they are performing to their full capacity. A majority of jobholders, business leaders, and labor-union leaders believe people are not working as hard as they did ten years ago. When one group of workers kept diaries between 1965 and 1975, the results showed that the time actually spent working on the job fell by ten percent. Someone who clocked the time people actually worked over a two-year period found that only half of the time on the job was spent working; the other half was spent on coffee breaks, late starts, early quits, waiting, and otherwise idle time.[24]

Harris's study in 1981 produced similar results.[25] Three-fourths of all working Americans felt that "people take less pride in their work than they did 10 years ago," while nearly the same number believed that workmanship is worse than it was. And 63 percent felt that "most people do not work as hard today as they did 10 years ago."

21. Robert Blauner, as summarized by Stanley Parker, *Leisure and Work* (London: Allen and Unwin, 1983), 31. Blauner's book is entitled *Alienation and Freedom: The Factory Worker and His Industry* (Chicago: University of Chicago Press, 1964).

22. *Work in America*, xv.

23. See especially Chuck Colson and Jack Eckerd, *Why America Doesn't Work* (Dallas: Word, 1991).

24. Daniel Yankelovich and John Immerwahr, "Putting the Work Ethic to Work," *Society*, Jan.-Feb. 1984, 58–76.

25. Daniel Yankelovich, "The Work Ethic Is Underemployed," *Psychology Today*, May 1982, 6.

A declining work ethic naturally produces poorer work. From time to time the decline in the quality of services receives feature-article coverage in our major news magazines. One study showed that a fourth of American workers are ashamed of the quality of goods they produce, while well over three-fourths of business and government executives believe that the leading factor in diminishing U. S. competitiveness in business is a low commitment to quality products.[26] The trend is the same in the service industry; think of how hard it is to find friendly and helpful assistance from store clerks.

We often associate dissatisfaction in work with people whose work is inherently unsatisfying, but Douglas LaBier's book challenges that premise. He documented the "vague dissatisfaction" of successful career people and their admission "of feeling empty and detached, of a lack of meaning, despite career success."[27]

In sum, there is abundant reason to accept John Kelly's opinion that "there is little more evidence of an active and operative 'work ethic' among American wage earners today than there was in the days of child labor, the sweat shop, and the seventy to eighty hour week."[28] The grand experiment of overvaluing work as the avenue to success failed partly because it could not satisfy the inner longings of its workers—not even the longing to find one's work pleasurable and fulfilling.

The Disenfranchised

If too much work is the main problem associated with the success ethic, too little work is also a problem today. The success ethic is slanted from beginning to end toward those who are fortunate enough to have careers that offer the possibility of vocational success and the upward mobility that it can buy. Most people are barred from even entering the playing field.

Unemployment is an economic and social problem that lies beyond the scope of this book, but its reality must be noted. The problems of unemployment are as much psychological as economic. If too much work damages people, so does too little. In the success ethic, people's sense of personal worth and their purpose in life depend on their ability not simply to work productively but to perform work that gains money and status—possibilities denied to the unemployed.[29]

26. Yankelovich and Immerwahr, "Putting the Work Ethic to Work," 72.
27. LaBier, *Modern Madness*, 3.
28. Kelly, *Leisure*, 117.
29. For more on the problems of the unemployed, see Raines and Day-Lower, *Modern Work*.

While statistics on unemployment are ever before us, those on underemployment are not. Yet the underemployed—those who cannot find permanent, full-time work or work that matches their mental or physical abilities—are one of the most numerous groups in the work force today. A 1994 report by a fact-finding commission found that the U. S. economy is creating a split-level labor market—"an upper tier of high-wage skilled workers and an increasing 'underclass' of low-paid labor."[30] Employers increasingly circumvent the need to pay health insurance and fringe benefits by hiring part-time workers. The success ethic has nothing to say to workers who are stuck with inadequate jobs. One study found that "the most dissatisfied workers are those who are too highly educated for their jobs."[31]

The success ethic also disenfranchises work done without pay. The largest group of such workers is homemakers; they are the biggest losers in the wake of the feminist movement and its premise that careers and paid work are the only worthy type of work. Various types of volunteer workers have also taken a hit. And then there is the work done around the house, such as cooking, cleaning, doing laundry, and caring for children. By valuing only work done for pay and work that leads to career advancement, the success ethic has nothing to offer people when they work without the rewards of that system.

A final group whose work is beyond the reach of the success ethic is the retired. If one's identity and worth depend on one's career, what remains for those who have completed their career? The success ethic has no answer to this question.

Summary

There can be no doubt that work is in trouble in contemporary society. The problems include overwork, dissatisfaction in work, insufficient or inadequate work, and work that does not qualify for the reward system of the job-oriented success ethic. These are problems without a solution as long as they are confined within the success syndrome and as long as they are exempted from such religious considerations as vocation and service to God and humanity.

Why the Experiment Failed

When put against a background of Christian attitudes toward work, the deficiencies of the success ethic will stand out. As an interim report,

---

30. Bernard Baumohl, "Unions Arise—With New Tricks," *Time,* 13 June 1994, 57.
31. Godbey, *Leisure in Your Life,* 107.

however, we can identify five reasons why work based on the premises of the success ethic has failed.

First, *the success ethic is guilty of misvaluing work.* It either overvalues work or values it for the wrong reasons. It makes success in work the basis of a person's identity, and it values work as the means of acquiring possessions. But as Jesus' aphorism put it, "A person's life does not consist in the abundance of his possessions" (Luke 12:15).

Second, *the success ethic provides an inadequate motivation for work.* This is not to say that it is wrong to value such rewards of work as material provision and a good reputation. It is only to say that financial and social self-interest are insufficient to sustain one's devotion to work over the long haul, and they leave some types of unpaid work without any motivation at all. Daniel Yankelovich's book *New Rules* documents the degree to which workers no longer find the old motivations for work satisfactory.

Third, *the success ethic misunderstands human longings.* As a result, it promises more than it can deliver, and its system of rewards is faulty. The success ethic promises satisfaction based on financial well-being, but as the book of Ecclesiastes incisively puts it, "He who loves money will not be satisfied with money" (5:10).

The success ethic is also guilty of moral failure. By elevating work to a centrality that it should not hold, the success ethic leads the worker to neglect the relationships of life, including family, friendships, and church life. Morever, by making financial gain the goal of work, it leads to such moral ills as unrestrained competitiveness and the tendency to stress quantity over quality. The slogan "business is business" tries to cover a multitude of economic sins.

Finally, the success ethic leads to the impoverishment of other important values in life. Foremost among these is leisure. Another frequent casualty is one's devotional life and the life of worship. By stressing doing over being, the success ethic usually eliminates the contemplative and aesthetic dimension of life.

Summary

The Book of Ecclesiastes is one of the most helpful biblical sources on the topics of work and leisure. Among the deadends the writer chased were futile attempts to find meaning and satisfaction in work (2:18–23) and the acquisition of goods (2:4–7). An excerpt that captures the futility of the experiment is 2:22–23:

> What has a man from all the toil and strain with which he toils beneath the sun? For all his days are full of pain, and his work is a vexation; even in the night his mind does not rest. This also is vanity.

Derek Kidner comments that what spoiled work for the ancient teacher was the attempt to get more out of work than it can give.[32]

This is the case against the success ethic. The problem is not that its ideals are utterly unworthy of the human spirit. Subordinated to higher goals, they are part of any solid work ethic. The great experiment failed because it put on work a burden that it was never equipped to carry.

Further Reading

Studs Terkel, *Working: People Talk about What They Do All Day and How They Feel about What They Do* (1972).

Goran Palm, *The Flight from Work*, trans. Patrick Smith (1977).

Marilyn Machlowitz, *Workaholics: Living with Them, Working with Them* (1980).

Douglas LaBier, *Modern Madness: The Emotional Fallout of Success* (1986).

32. Derek Kidner, *A Time to Mourn, and a Time to Dance* (Downers Grove, Ill.: InterVarsity, 1976), 35.

5

The Unfulfilled Promise
How Leisure Has Failed Us

The mid-twentieth century gave us the phrase "the leisure problem." The phrase is still accurate but the writers who popularized the phrase drew exactly the wrong conclusion. They assumed that we were moving toward shorter and shorter work weeks. The result, predicted the experts, would be that people would not know what to do with themselves when they entered the boundless expanses of leisure. It turns out that the predictions were naively optimistic about the quantity of leisure in the modern world, as noted in chapter 3. In addition to the sheer scarcity of leisure in our lives, five factors conspire to create today's leisure problem.

The Harried Leisure Class

The time squeeze on leisure has been accompanied by the phenomenon of the harried leisure class. This phrase was popularized by Staffan Linder's book *The Harried Leisure Class*.[1] Linder's thesis was that the amount of time we have at our disposal is fixed. An acquisitive and affluent lifestyle such as we currently pursue tends to take more and

1. Staffan Linder, *The Harried Leisure Class* (New York: Columbia University Press, 1970).

59

more of our time; as the volume of goods and services consumed increases, so does the time that these things require of us. The net result is a loss of free time. Since the minimum prerequisite for leisure is free time, what we increasingly face is a leisure famine.

To illustrate this point, consider what happens when a family buys a motorboat. Time together on the lake is the leisure goal, but look at the accompanying activities that gobble up leisure time. The boat must be cleaned and maintained. It requires gasoline. It has to be cleaned in the spring and stored in the winter. Traveling to and from the lake takes time; in fact, as the number of people with boats increases, the slower the traffic around the lake becomes. To afford the boat in the first place may have required a wage earner whose work far exceeds a forty-hour-per-week job. Other things being equal, the family without a boat will actually have more leisure time than the family with the boat!

What we see here on a small scale is happening in our society on a grand scale. The time commitment that our consumption requires snatches away the very leisure we thought we were gaining. The more things we have, the larger the house we need, the more time we spend maintaining the things, and the less time we have to enjoy leisure. The crowning irony is that most people in our society acquire more articles than they have time to use. Technology enlarges the possibilities of leisure, but in most people's lives it actually decreases the amount of leisure.

Geoffrey Godbey has extended the theory of a harried leisure class. If we agree that leisure by definition includes an attitude of freedom from coercion, then much of what we think to be leisure is actually anti-leisure. Godbey explains,

> By anti-leisure I refer to activity which is undertaken compulsively, as a means to an end, for a perception of necessity, with a high degree of externally composed constraints, with considerable anxiety, with a high degree of time consciousness, with a minimum of personal autonomy.[2]

A prime example is the obsessive drive of middle- and upper-class families to cater to their children's activities during their growing up years. Life becomes a blur as parents see to it that their children participate in sports, music, school activities, and church and social events. As parents make sure that they provide every opportunity to their children, leisure drops out of their lives.

2. Geoffrey Godbey, "Anti-leisure and Public Recreation Policy," in S. R. Parker *et al.*, *Sport and Leisure in Contemporary Society* (London: Polytechnic of Central London, 1975), 47.

Poor Quality of Leisure

Not only do many Americans lack sufficient *time* for leisure; they also have less *quality* leisure time. In making this indictment I am of course revealing my own sense of values, but, then, our leisure always reflects our values.

It is not surprising, therefore, that the decline of moral and intellectual values in our culture should be reflected in how people spend their leisure time. The moral and intellectual content of most people's leisure pursuits is alarmingly low. The cultural malaise that Paul Elmen has analyzed in his book *The Restoration of Meaning to Contemporary Life* is fully evident in how most people spend their leisure time. Its salient features include boredom, the search for distraction, the fear of spending time by oneself, sensuality, escape into comedy, violence, and the appeal of horror ("the fun of being frightened").[3]

Leisure is more than nonwork. It is an actively chosen, positive use of time for personal enrichment. Judged by such a standard, much of what passes for leisure is less than leisure. One authority cites studies of young people that show "how drab, monotonous, dull and boring" spare time is for them.[4] Someone else has written about a "leisure lack," meaning a lack of leisure "understood as a state of mind."[5] In one study only seventeen percent of an urban sample included leisure as one of the three most important aspects of their life making for satisfaction or dissatisfaction, while the author of another survey "was struck by the slight importance of leisure activity" in the lives of workers.[6]

The technological revolution has contributed to the declining quality of leisure. For one thing, as Linder argues in *The Harried Leisure Class,* in a consumer society people want more and more things. Given the scarcity of time, the time allotted to leisure activity declines. People do not simply listen to music, for example; music is background for some other activity. For the amateur photographer, the need to get good pictures competes with the leisure function of visiting a site. In short, as more and more leisure pursuits compete for our time we enjoy them less and less. The leisure aspect of the lunch or dinner table, the delights of conversation, and the capacity to enjoy beauty are prime examples of this decline.

3. See Paul Elman, *The Restoration of Meaning to Contemporary Life* (Garden City, N.Y.: Doubleday, 1958).

4. Kenneth Roberts, *Contemporary Society and the Growth of Leisure* (London: Longman, 1978), 24.

5. John Neulinger, *The Psychology of Leisure,* 2d ed. (Springfield, Ill.: Charles C. Thomas, 1981), 213.

6. Parker, *Sociology of Leisure,* 147.

Cultural pursuits have also been hard hit by the competition for time. Reading has declined drastically from even three decades ago. A Gallup poll found that 58 percent of Americans have never finished reading a book, while a survey commissioned by a book industry study group similarly revealed that nearly half of Americans never read a book of any type.[7] Alvin Kernan, a Princeton University professor, wrote in 1990 that "something like 60 percent of adult Americans apparently never read a book, and most of the rest read only one book a year on the average."[8]

All of which brings us to the subject of television. A 1983 study concluded that television accounts for nearly half of Americans' leisure time and forty percent of the time not devoted to sleep, employment, and family and personal care.[9] John Robinson's 1990 study on time usage concluded that television consumes 50 percent of Americans' free time.[10]

Aside from the fact that television has replaced more worthwhile leisure activities, it deserves criticism for the passivity it breeds.[11] If we define leisure in terms of activity and oppose it to idleness or mere time killing, much television viewing cannot count as leisure. Psychologists have documented viewers' trance-like fixation that impairs the ability to engage in conscious thought. Studies of brainwave activity demonstrate the inactivity of the brain when focused on television.[12]

Witold Rybczynski believes that the case against television is not that it is passive but that it "offers so little opportunity for reflection and contemplation." It "tells a story in a way that requires no imagination," so that "television watching should more properly be called television staring."[13]

The most significant critique of television is Neil Postman's book *Amusing Ourselves to Death*.[14] Postman shows that in contrast to

---

7. Arthur Schlesinger, Jr., "Implications of Leisure for Government," in *Technology, Human Values, and Leisure*, ed. Max Kaplan and Phillip Bosserman (Nashville: Abingdon, 1971), 77; Herbert Mitgan, "Study Finds Nearly Half of U. S. Do Not Read Books," *New York Times*, 14 November 1978, 13.

8. Alvin Kernan, *The Death of Literature* (New Haven: Yale University Press, 1990), 142.

9. Godbey, *Leisure in Your Life*, 85; John R. Kelly, *Leisure Identities and Interactions* (London: Allen and Unwin, 1983), 131.

10. John P. Robinson, "I Love My TV," *American Demographics* (September 1990): 24–27.

11. Robert Kubey and Mihaly Csikszentmihalyi, *Television and the Quality of Life: How Viewing Shapes Everyday Experience* (Hillsdale, N.J.: Lawrence Erlbaum Associates, 1990).

12. See, for example, Jerry Mander, *Four Arguments for the Elimination of Television* (New York: William Morrow and Company, 1964).

13. Rybczynski, *Waiting for the Weekend*, 192–193.

14. Neil Postman, *Amusing Ourselves to Death: Public Discourse in the Age of Show Business* (New York: Viking, 1985).

written and oral discourse, television encourages passivity, incoherence (inability to perform sustained thinking on a subject), lack of deliberation, and triviality. Television floods us with information without expecting us to do anything with it, and therefore it produces a sense of impotency. As a medium, television has produced a world of broken time and short attention.

Television did not produce mindless and empty leisure all by itself. Television would never have proven so popular a pastime if it were not for the prevailing physical and mental fatigue that characterizes a society given to overwork. Most people lack the physical energy to do anything other than plop down in front of the television. Furthermore, the American preference for recreation over culture (broadly defined) has undermined the intellectual and cultural content of leisure as much as television has.

Still, the electronic media, including television, VCRs, and music systems, influence people's values and leisure tastes as much as they are the product of them. Popular culture deserves to be understood and critiqued, both positively and negatively, from a Christian perspective, as several books have done.[15] The point is not that the media are all bad but that they have lured people into settling for less enriching leisure than they might be enjoying.

Leisure as Work

A third difficulty with leisure today is that it is often valued only in relation to work. This is the syndrome of a utilitarian play ethic that always ends up robbing play or leisure of any intrinsic value. In this view, leisure is of value only as it contributes to work. In our society, which generally overvalues work and success, this has been the fate of leisure. As Robert Johnston puts it, "Leisure is not viewed as an independent occurrence, or even a complementary activity. Rather, it is placed under the tyranny of a work mentality."[16]

Work can thus be an obstacle to leisure even when it does not actually prevent us from engaging in leisure pursuits. Leisure pursued under the constant pressure of knowing that one is taking time from the obligations of work is barely leisure at all. Workaholics blur the distinction between work and leisure, turning work into their hobby and losing the quality of leisure that stems from its contrast to work.[17] In the

---

15. Good critiques of popular culture include Kenneth A. Myers, *All God's Children and Blue Suede Shoes: Christians and Popular Culture* (Westchester, Ill.: Crossway, 1989); and Quentin J. Schultze *et al.*, *Dancing in the Dark: Youth, Popular Culture, and the Electronic Media* (Grand Rapids: Eerdmans, 1991).

16. Johnston, *Christian at Play*, 11.

17. Machlowitz, *Workaholics*, 87–101.

words of William Whyte, "They are never less at leisure than when they are at leisure.[18] At the opposite extreme are workaholics who find leisure time so unstructured that they become lethargic and passive in their free time.[19]

The final result of valuing leisure only as an aid to work is to make leisure like work. People carry over into leisure the same drive for productivity that they require of work. Many sporting activities have more in common with rigorous work than with leisure. In fact, any leisure activity will become just another form of work if pursued with the compulsion of work. This probably explains why many achievers cannot genuinely enjoy leisure. Movie star Burt Reynolds is quoted as saying, "I've worked hard, and I've played hard. But I've never learned how to relax."[20]

One dimension of subordinating leisure to work is the regimentation that has come to characterize much leisure time. We schedule our leisure as rigidly as we schedule our work. Braude says,

> Nonwork time has acquired a character often attributed to work itself. It has become routinized and scheduled so that the cultivation of the good life, usually defined in terms of consumption, is felt to be a task to be pursued. . . . [Leisure] came to be pursued with an intensity that demanded an uninterruptable schedule, a routine within it, and a kind of production quota. . . . Leisure, too, is to be consumed, to be worked at.[21]

In short, one of the problems of leisure today is that it has lost much of the quality of leisure.

Many people introduce elements of competitiveness or the drive to excel at a skill into their leisure pursuits. In his excellent book *Waiting for the Weekend*, Witold Rybczynski notes:

> The list of dutiful recreations includes strenuous disciplines intended for self-improvement (fitness exercises, jogging, bicycling), competitive sports (tennis, golf), and skill-testing pastimes (sailing, skiing). . . . The very frequency of weekend recreations allows continual participation and continual improvement, which encourage the development of proficiency and skill. . . . The modern weekend is characterized by not only the sense of obligation to do something but the obligation to do it well.[22]

18. Whyte, *Organization Man*, 150.
19. Machlowitz, *Workaholics*, 87.
20. Kevin Kerr, "Working Hard at Play," *Adweek's Marketing Week*, 20 January 1992, 12.
21. Braude, *Work and Workers*, 202–3.
22. Pages 222–23.

In an affluent society, leisure becomes professionalized, again making it seem more like work than leisure. Having the right equipment and engaging in recreation at the right places become an obsession. Again Rybczynski has good commentary:

> I'm always charmed by old photographs of skiers that show groups of people in what appear to be street clothes, with uncomplicated pieces of bent wood strapped to sturdy walking boots. These men and women have a playful and unaffected air. Today every novice is caparisoned in skintight spandex like an Olympic racer, and even cross-country skiing, a simple enough pastime, has been infected by a preoccupation with correct dress, authentic terminology, and up-to-date equipment. This reflects a concern for status and consumption, but it also suggests an attitude to play that is different from what it was in the past.[23]

"The lack of carelessness in our recreation," Rybczynski adds, "the sense of obligation to get things right, and the emphasis on protocol and decorum do represent an enslavement of a kind. People used to 'play' tennis; now they 'work' on their backhand."[24]

Leisure also becomes like work when we allow it to exhaust us physically, much as work does. People are often worn out by their leisure activities, partly because the advent of the car raised the scope of what people could undertake in their leisure. Instead of returning to work refreshed by our leisure, we return exhausted.

Finally, social pressure to meet leisure standards can easily make leisure take on a sense of obligation that undermines the very definition of leisure. G. K. Chesterton noted this when he wrote,

> If a man is practically compelled, by a sort of social pressure, to ride in the park in the morning or play golf in the afternoon or go out to grand dinners . . . we describe all those hours of his day as hours of leisure. But they are not hours of leisure at all, in the other sense; as, for instance, on the fanciful supposition that he would like a little time to himself, that he would like to pursue a quite solitary and even unsociable hobby, that he would like really to idle, or, on a more remote hypothesis, that he would like really to think.[25]

Chesterton here describes someone who has free time but not freedom, and his analysis underscores the point of my discussion—that we are often unaware of the ways in which we allow our leisure to assume the qualities of work.

23. Ibid., 17–18.
24. Ibid., 18.
25. G. K. Chesterton, "On Leisure," in *Generally Speaking* (London: Methuen, 1928), 107–8.

Feeling Guilty about Leisure

When a person has a utilitarian attitude toward leisure, it is difficult to enjoy leisure free from guilt. There are many reasons for this bondage.

First, the workaholic syndrome prevents workers from experiencing leisure *as* leisure. Even on vacations they want to "stay on top of the job," and so they never leave the job behind. They pursue leisure activities with the same compulsive drive that they bring to their work.

Second, many people in our society feel guilty about doing something other than work. Among people who overvalue work or have never developed an adequate view of leisure, leisure is viewed as unproductive, of little value to society, and evidence of being privileged. The fact that we live in a permissive and hedonistic society sometimes conceals this problem. Psychologists speak of *anhedonia*—the inability to feel pleasure—and regard it as an abnormality in personality. Applied to leisure, we are talking about people who feel guilty when they relax.[26] The irony is that some of the very people who feel guilty when they take time for leisure also feel guilty because they work too much.

It is not surprising that Walter Kerr wrote a book entitled *The Decline of Pleasure*.[27] The thesis obviously does not fit everyone, but it fits a significant percentage of the population. Kerr said that our society overvalues what is useful, with the result that "we go to our pleasures, when we dare go to them at all, demanding that they surrender to us a kind of knowledge that is not in them. And so we kill them." Unable to invest the pleasure of things and activities with an inherent value, many people in our society miss the pleasure these can give. Bertrand Russell observed that the modern person "thinks that everything ought to be done for the sake of something else, and never for its own sake."[28]

As an example of how the utilitarian impulse can destroy the pleasure of leisure, Kerr cites an experience recounted by the British writer Christopher Fry. Fry once went to see a play, not as a member of the audience, but because he had to write a review of the performance. Recalls Fry, "I could scarcely hear a word of the play for the noise of my own mind wondering how I should write about it."[29] A lot of our leisure today is similarly tainted.

26. See Hansel, *When I Relax I Feel Guilty*.
27. Walter Kerr, *The Decline of Pleasure* (New York: Simon and Schuster, 1962).
28. Russell, *In Praise of Idleness*, 24.
29. Kerr, *Decline of Pleasure*, 234.

Leisure as Idolatry

The final leisure problem stands in contrast to what I have said thus far. Not enough time for leisure, inability actively to choose high-quality leisure pursuits, leisure as an appendage to work, guilt about enjoying the pleasures of leisure—these are the results of undervaluing leisure. But for a sizable minority in our society, the opposite abuse is the problem. They are the ones who overvalue leisure and often turn it into an idol—the central life interest pursued with religious fervor. Along with workaholics there are golfaholics, fitness addicts, television junkies, and rock music addicts.

Overvaluing leisure takes several forms. One is the self-indulgence that leads people to spend virtually all of their nonworking time and resources on having fun or pursuing a hobby. There is no time left for helping others or for worshiping God. Leisure pursuits can tyrannize not only one's time but one's money as well. Another manifestation of the obsession with leisure is the phenomenon known as the "endless weekend"—not only living for the weekend but also talking about it all week long. Or, if not the weekend, then after-work leisure activities.

An additional facet of the problem is the way in which urban living and the orientation of family living around the children have made young people today's leisure class. Farm life once provided an early transition from play to work for adolescents and early teenagers. Today young people begin working later because they must secure outside employment instead of helping with the family's farm work. As a result, their desire to be entertained has become insatiable.

If an excessive devotion to work robs leisure of its joy and meaning, the reverse is also true: excessive devotion to leisure detracts from the value of work. For many Americans, work has ceased to have intrinsic value and has been reduced to that which makes the weekend possible.

The Heart of the Matter: Confusing the Boundaries

The problems discussed in this chapter are variations on a single theme—the confusions that people make when they do not define leisure accurately and protect its boundaries from the things that would devour it. G. K. Chesterton had this to say about our tendency to confuse types of activities that get lumped under the rubric "leisure," as though they were the same:

> I think the name of leisure has come to cover three totally different things. The first is being allowed to do something. The second is being

allowed to do anything. And the third (and perhaps most rare and precious) is being allowed to do nothing.[30]

All three go by the name "leisure," but in fact they are very different, and under some conditions they might not be leisure at all. Chesterton's particular concern was the ease with which the freedom to do something becomes an obligation to do something.

The biggest boundary that gets violated today is the one that should protect leisure from work. The Western value system is dominated by work, and as a society we are much enamored with efficiency. When placed into such a context, leisure fares poorly. People find too little time for leisure. They gravitate to mediocrity in leisure pursuits and are unable to enjoy the pleasures of leisure without feeling guilty. Drawing a boundary around leisure also means that we do not mistake it for the totality of life. To make leisure the central life force is to mistake its nature as a complement to work, to turn it into a god, and to invest it with the qualities of a rival religion.

Further Reading

G. K. Chesterton, "On Leisure," in *Generally Speaking* (1928).
Staffan Linder, *The Harried Leisure Class* (1970).
Robert K. Johnston, *The Christian at Play* (1983).
Robert Kubey and Mihaly Csikszentmihalyi, *Television and the Quality of Life: How Viewing Shapes Everyday Experience* (1990).
Witold Rybczynski, *Waiting for the Weekend* (1991).

30. Chesterton, "On Leisure," 111.

PART 3

Lessons from History:
How We Got Where We Are

6

The Swinging Pendulum
A History of Attitudes toward Work

There are several reasons why it is worth taking a brief excursion through the history of attitudes toward work. We cannot afford the naiveté of beginning anew with each generation. There are lessons to be learned from the past that will help us in the present. Furthermore, the history of attitudes toward work provides an agenda of issues that helps us understand the contemporary scene so that we may focus our presentation of the gospel to this generation.

My overview of how the human race has regarded work (and, in the next chapter, leisure) focuses on the attitudes that have been passed on in written form. To gauge the extent to which ordinary people practiced what the thinkers of their day said is beyond the scope of this survey.

Western culture rests on two foundations—the classical (Greco-Roman) and biblical (Judeo-Christian). The biblical teaching on work and leisure will be saved for the discussion in Part 5.

The Classical View of Work: The Unworthiness of Labor

The status of work got off to an inauspicious start in ancient Greece and Rome.[1] To the Greeks work was a curse, something beneath the

---

1. In order to keep footnotes more manageable, I simply note here the sources from which I took my data regarding classical attitudes toward work: Adriano Tilgher, *Work:*

dignity of a free person. Their word for work was taken from the same root that produced the word *sorrow*. Physical work, especially, was regarded as degrading to human dignity.

Aristotle is a main spokesman for the Greek attitude. For him, leisure was the goal of life. Since physical labor is an obstacle to such leisure, it is unworthy of a free person. The life of a craftsman or trader was a life "devoid of nobility and hostile to perfection of character." According to Xenophon, Socrates held a similar view of work:

> The mechanical arts carry a social stigma and are rightly dishonored in our cities. For these arts can damage the bodies of those who work at them. . . . This physical degeneration results also in deterioration of the soul. Furthermore, the workers at these trades simply have not got the time to perform the offices of friendship or citizenship. Consequently they are looked upon as bad friends and bad patriots.

Underlying such a verdict we can see the Greek urge for freedom. To labor was to be enslaved by necessity. It is not the work alone that is bad, but also the idea of giving up one's independence to work for someone else—or out of physical necessity. According to such a view, the only way to redeem the curse of work was to avoid work. The whole Greek social structure helped to support such an outlook, for it rested on the premise that slaves and artisans did the work, enabling the elite to devote themselves to the exercise of the mind in art, philosophy, and politics.

The poet Hesiod expressed the Greek attitude in mythological form. Work, he said, originated with Eris, goddess of strife, while labor, along with other evils, came from Pandora's box and was a punishment from Zeus. In contrast to the biblical picture of God as worker, the gods in classical mythology lived life serenely above the rigors of work.

Work fared only slightly better in Roman antiquity. Whereas in our own work-oriented society we define leisure as nonwork, the Romans reversed the matter. Their word for work was *negotium,* meaning "nonleisure." In such a climate of opinion, it is not surprising that Cicero wrote,

> The toil of a hired worker, who is paid only for his toil and not for artistic skill, is unworthy of a free man and is sordid in character. . . . Trade on a small retail scale is also sordid.

What It Has Meant to Men through the Ages, trans. Dorothy C. Fisher (New York: Arno Press, 1930), 3–9; Melvin Kranzberg and Joseph Gies, *By the Sweat of Thy Brow: Work in the Western World* (New York: G. P. Putnam's Sons, 1975), 27–31; Robert L. Heilbroner, *The Making of Economic Society* (Englewood Cliffs, N.J.: Prentice-Hall, 1962), 18–29; Hannah Arendt, *The Human Condition* (Chicago: University of Chicago Press, 1958), 80–94; P. D. Anthony, *The Ideology of Work* (London: Tavistock, 1977), 15–22.

Before we leave the classical disparagement of work, we should note that it was based not only on a social structure of slavery but was also rooted in the philosophy of the age. In general, classical philosophy held a low view of the physical world. If, as Seneca put it, the body is necessary rather than important, and if "to despise our bodies is pure freedom," it is obvious that physical work undertaken to supply the needs of the body would be disparaged. This negative view of work produced its own morality in which the virtues were conceived as ones that people could practice only in the absence of work. Such virtues as the pursuit of truth and beauty, living the contemplative life, fulfilling the duties of citizenship, and the exercise of leadership were unavailable to slaves, who were busy working with their hands.

The Middle Ages and the Sacred-Secular Dichotomy

The main contribution of the Middle Ages to the history of attitudes toward work was to divide work into two great categories—the sacred and the secular. The roots of such an attitude were already present in the classical social distinction between free people and slaves. The Middle Ages simply gave this hierarchy a spiritual cast.

Post-biblical Hebraism exalted the contemplative religious life at the expense of physical labor. The school of Rabbi Simeon condemned physical work because it took time from the spiritual life. If people would only do the will of God, ran the argument, their work would be done by others.[2] A similar distinction can be found in a prayer from Talmud in which the rabbi prayed,

> I thank thee, O Lord, my God that thou hast given me my lot with those who sit in the house of learning, and not with those who sit at the street-corners; for I am early to work and they are early to work; I am early to work on the words of the Torah, and they are early to work on things of no moment. I weary myself, and they weary themselves; I weary myself and profit thereby, and they weary themselves to no profit. I run, and they run; I run towards the life of the age to come, and they run towards the pit of destruction.[3]

This division of life into sacred and secular reduced ordinary workers to second-class spiritual citizens.

2. Tilgher, Work, 15.
3. Quoted in Joachim Jeremias, Rediscovering the Parables (New York: Scribner, 1966), 113.

Medieval Roman Catholicism similarly divided work into categories of sacred and secular. This attitude was reflected by Eusebius in the fourth century:

> Two ways of life were given by the law of Christ to His Church. The one is above nature, and beyond common human living. . . . Wholly and permanently separate from the common customary life of mankind, it devotes itself to the service of God alone. . . . Such then is the perfect form of the Christian life. And the other, more humble, more human, permits men to . . . have minds for farming, for trade, and the other more secular interests as well as for religion. . . . And a kind of secondary grade of piety is attributed to them.[4]

The difference between the two types of work was not a difference of degree but of kind. As one authority describes the situation, "Within the monastery or convent, the 'religious' who . . . aimed at perfection devoted themselves largely (though not exclusively) to contemplation, while outside in the family, in the market place, in the field and on the seas, the others kept the wheels of the work of the world running, at the cost of condemning their souls to a second-best spiritual life."[5]

This division of work into sacred and secular was the chief legacy the Middle Ages bequeathed to the world on the subject of work. It has led a vigorous life ever since and persists today, not only in Catholic circles but in conservative Protestant ones as well, where the phrase "full-time Christian service" is used to denote the superior quality of clerical or missionary work.

There were, of course, other developments during the Middle Ages. In some quarters work became an extension of an ascetic outlook. In this tradition, people (including monks and nuns) worked, not because work had inherent dignity in the sight of God, but for the opposite reason—it was painful and humiliating and therefore meritorious as an act of atonement or penance.[6] Physical work was also prescribed for those living in monasteries, but we should not construe this as something that dignified work in general, nor should we see in it a kinship with the Protestant Reformation's attitude toward work. It is true that the bells summoned monks and nuns not only to prayer but also to work, but the bulk of the daily schedule was devoted to the contemplative life, not to active work. Furthermore, to value work as a personal discipline against sin is far from valuing it as a service to God and humanity.[7] Finally, monastic work was done within the confines of the mon-

---

4. Eusebius, *Demonstratio Evangelica*; quoted by Forrester, *Christian Vocation*, 42.
5. Forrester, *Christian Vocation*, 45.
6. Tilgher, *Work*, 35, 38.
7. In the monastic orders, work was enjoined primarily as a means to avoid idleness. The Rule of St. Benedict was particularly influential: "Idleness is the enemy of the soul;

astery and did not extend to work done in the world. As the best-known modern history of attitudes toward work notes, monastic work "is never exalted as anything of value in itself, but only as an instrument of purification, of charity, of expiation. . . . The work done by outsiders in the great world is regarded with indulgent charity but is in no way honored."[8]

This negative picture of work was slightly mitigated as the Catholic church made concessions toward the reality of what was happening in society. Thomas Aquinas, for example, affirmed work as a natural right and duty. He drew up a hierarchy of professions and trades, thereby lending a sanction to what was happening in the social order in which he lived. But Aquinas perpetuated the preference for the contemplative life over active work.[9]

The Renaissance and Reformation: The Dignity of Work

Historians are so preoccupied with what the Reformation did to revolutionize work that they act as though the Renaissance did not even occur. This is surely an oversight. The flowering of humanism that we call the Renaissance asserted the dignity of labor and especially valued the work of one's hands.

This attitude permeates the masterpiece of English Renaissance humanism, Thomas More's *Utopia* (1516). Written by a Catholic, the work expresses a Renaissance attitude toward work. In More's "Nowhere" (which is what "utopia" means), all adults—men and women alike—work equally. In fact, jobs are rotated to insure equality. In this ideal commonwealth, "no loafing is tolerated," and More goes out of

---

therefore at definite times of the day the brethren should be engaged on manual work and at other times on the reading of sacred texts"—(St. Benedict, *S. Benedicti Regula Monasteriorum;* quoted in R. W. Southern, *Western Society and the Church in the Middle Ages* [Grand Rapids: Eerdmans, 1970], 346). Equally instructive is Groote's viewpoint: "I have often told you that labour is wonderfully necessary to mankind in restoring the mind to purity. . . . Don't think however that I wish men or women to be occupied in secular business or human entanglements—let them simply work on those things which bring a daily subsistence from hand to mouth without superfluity. . . . Labour is holy, but business is dangerous" (*Gerardi Magni Epistolae;* quoted in Southern, *Western Society,* 347–348). Jacques Le Goff (*Time, Work, and Culture in the Middle Ages* [Chicago: University of Chicago Press, 1980]) similarly notes that "the meaning of this monastic labor was above all penitential," allowing monks "to set an example of mortification by their labor" (80), and that the medieval theology of work, by regarding work as "a penitential instrument," had "only negative value" (110–111). Claude Mossé (*The Ancient World at Work,* trans. Janet Lloyd [New York: W. W. Norton, 1969]) asserts that "the Fathers of the Church did not think differently from the contemporaries of Plato and Aristotle, and for them too work was still a curse" (113).

8. Tilgher, *Work,* 35–36.
9. Ibid., 39–41.

his way to pay his disrespects to the "multitude of priests and so-called religious men, as numerous as they are idle," that afflicted European society at the time.

Historian de Grazia writes this about the influence of the Renaissance on attitudes toward work:

> Their idea of work expresses their confidence and exuberance. Unwittingly, it sings the praises of the kind of work at which they excelled—the individual, craftsmanlike, artistic. . . . . Their work required that hands touch materials. It was this non-agricultural manual labor they rescued from the contempt in which the ancient world had left it. They gave work the dignity the word craftsmanship carries still.[10]

Even more decisive, however, was the influence of Luther, Calvin, and the Puritans. The "Protestant work ethic" has been so distorted that I will devote a separate chapter to it. For purposes of this historical sketch, I will be content to summarize what the sixteenth and seventeenth centuries contributed to thought of work.

The Reformers began by rejecting the medieval division of work into sacred and secular. To this rejection they added the doctrine of vocation or calling, by which they meant that God called people to tasks in the world. Thus all work done for God's glory was sacred. The dignity of common work never stood higher than at this moment in history. This holy worldliness also found a place for industriousness as a lifestyle and profit as a motive for work, although the Reformers did preach a sense of moderation in work. This affirmation of work and earthly endeavor presupposed a spiritual context in which the godly life was valued supremely and in which no work was divorced from the idea of service to God and others.

If the classical disparagement of work was an extension of the classical worldview, so was the Protestant attitude. The cornerstone of Protestant thought was the sovereignty of God over all of life, and from this flowed an awareness of God's creation of the world and his providential concern for it. Given this affirmation of the world in which God has placed his creatures as stewards, it was inevitable that the Reformation tradition would attach dignity to work in the world.

The Enlightenment: Secularizing the Protestant Work Ethic

The next chapter in the history of attitudes toward work is the saddest of all. It consisted of gradually removing the Protestant work ethic from

10. de Grazia, *Of Time, Work, and Leisure*, 30.

its Christian context. Without the restraining influence of Protestant belief in the primacy of the spiritual, the tenets of the original Protestant
ethic became perverted into a creed of personal success. This secularized
perversion is what most people today mean when they speak glibly of
"the Protestant ethic." The truth is that the people of the Reformation
era would be horrified by what today goes by this label.

The eighteenth-century development is expressed best by Benjamin
Franklin, whose *Poor Richard* proverbs show us what a secularized
Protestant ethic looks like.[11] We might first note what is *not* present.
We do not find a conviction that the purpose of life and work is to glorify God and enjoy him forever. Also gone are the ideas of work as stewardship of what God has given to his creatures and the moral duty to
help those in need. In place of these we find an ethic of self-interest and
expediency. Sloth, for example, is shunned because it brings diseases
and shortens life. Or consider the following Franklin aphorisms:

> Industry pays debts.

> Early to bed, and early to rise,
>   makes a man healthy, wealthy, and wise.

> He that hath a calling hath an office
>   of profit and honor.

> God helps them that help themselves.

Here, indeed, is the exaltation of a humanistic ethic, ordering human
affairs apart from God's grace. Franklin's quip that God gives all things
to industry epitomizes a God-on-a-string mentality.

What comes through most strongly is a preoccupation with money
and getting ahead. Work is only a means to that end, and life itself is
ceaseless work, with no time for leisure or worship. "Be ashamed to
catch yourself idle," says Poor Richard. Again, "Leisure is time for doing something useful." This hoarding of time spent in work is matched
by a hoarding of one's money: "If you would be wealthy, think of saving
as well as of getting."

When William Whyte talks about "the decline of the Protestant
ethic," then, he is actually talking about the humanistic ethic of the
eighteenth century.[12] This is evident from the traits he ascribes to it:
survival of the fittest, thrift, social climbing based on economic success, self-denying work, and self-reliance.

11. All *Poor Richard* quotations are from *Major Writers of America*, ed. Perry Miller
(New York: Harcourt, Brace and World, 1962), 1:120–123.
12. Whyte, *Organization Man*, 14–22.

The names of Adam Smith and John Locke might be added to the list of spokesmen for the new work ethic based on economic self-interest. In *The Wealth of Nations*, Smith begins from the premise that

> it is not from the benevolence of the butcher, the brewer, or the baker that we expect our dinner, but from their regard to their own interest. We address ourselves, not to their humanity but to their self-love.[13]

This is the foundation upon which Smith builds his theory, still with us, of a market system based on the law of supply and demand. Clearly we have left the Puritan world of Christian stewardship and compassion and entered an economic world governed by the mechanism of economic expediency.

John Locke's views of property as the foundation of society fit into this same framework.[14] Labor itself, when joined with nature, produces the property to which people are entitled by natural right. According to Locke, the thing that makes an acre of land valuable or worthless is the amount of human labor that has been expended to make it profitable. Work, in this view, is valued because it is useful, profitable, and the means for acquiring property. In Locke's view, this process of acquisition is what produced the institution of money.

In North America, immigration became an additional ingredient in the growing secularization of the Protestant ethic. The immigrant ethic is based on the principle that hard work and sacrifice will improve the lot of the next generation. This, too, is an ethic of self-interest, but at the family level. One writer correctly notes that "for millions of Americans, . . . the immigrant work ethic came at last to merge with the Protestant work ethic."[15]

Modern historians call the eighteenth century "the Enlightenment," but when viewed from the perspective of a Christian work ethic, it was a dark shadow. It replaced a spiritually controlled work ethic with a humanly governed economic system that regarded work as a means to financial ends. Already during the two centuries of the Reformation and Puritan influence there had been a movement in this direction, but with the eighteenth century the floodgates were opened.[16]

13. Adam Smith, *The Wealth of Nations*, in *Great Books of the Western World*, ed. Robert M. Hutchins (Chicago: Encyclopedia Britannica, 1952), 39:7.

14. John Locke, *The Second Treatise of Civil Government*, 169. Chapter 5.

15. Lance Morrow, "What Is the Point of Working?" *Time*, 11 May 1981, 93.

16. For more on the subject, see Robert S. Michaelsen, "Changes in the Puritan Concept of Calling or Vocation," *The New England Quarterly* 26 (1953):315–36; and Paul Marshall, "John Locke: Between God and Mammon," *Canadian Journal of Political Science* 12 (1979):73–96.

The Nineteenth Century:
Responses to the Industrial Revolution

The view of Locke and Smith that work is the beginning of wealth produced its inevitable results in the nineteenth century, the era of the industrial revolution. Attitudes toward work can best be viewed as responses to the crisis engendered by that revolution.

The crisis is easy to identify. The triumph of the machine greatly accelerated the division of labor into specialized tasks. The growth of factories also heightened the division between owners and laborers, both of whom were driven by the profit motive. In fact, a key question became: Who owns labor—society, industry, or the individual?

For the laborer, specialization produced the phenomenon of the alienated worker. Its features included narrowness and monotony of tasks, bypassing of trained skill (lack of skill required for tasks), inability to see an overall purpose in one's isolated task, denial of the satisfaction that comes from complexity in work, the depersonalized and anonymous nature of work, the sense of never completing a job, lack of a sense of participation, loss of interest in one's task, and loss of pride in one's work.[17]

The Marxist Response

The nineteenth century produced two chief answers to these problems, and so far as I can tell, Christian thinkers did not contribute significantly to the dialogue. The dominant answer was Marxism or socialism. The Marxist diagnosis of the problem was accurate, no matter how much we may disagree with its proposed solutions.

Alienation in work was the problem, and it arose from an inadequate view of work. When work is viewed as an economic commodity that is bought and sold, exploitation is a natural result unless other factors are strong enough to counter it. Exploitation emerges from the division between owner or manager and laborer. If profit is the motive, the owner will naturally try to make as much profit as possible. The worker becomes like a machine, condemned to a life of forced labor. In Marx's own words, the worker becomes converted "into a never-failing instrument," forced "to work with the regularity of the parts of a machine."[18] This is the curse from which Marx sought to free the laborer.

---

17. For an overview of the problems of work in a technological society, see Georges Friedmann, *The Anatomy of Work: Labor, Leisure, and the Implications of Automation*, trans. Wyatt Rawson (Glencoe: Free Press, 1961).
18. Quoted in Anthony, *Ideology of Work*, 124–125.

We should notice that Marxism in theory has a high view of work. Work is the means by which people find their meaning in life. With an idealized view of what work should be, Marxism protested what the industrial society was producing. Engels protested against the demoralization of English textile workers:

> Nothing is more terrible than being constrained to do some one thing every day from morning until night against one's will. . . . Why does he work? For love of work? From a natural impulse? Not at all! He works for money, for a thing which has nothing whatsoever to do with the work itself.[19]

Similarly, Marx's discussion of the estrangement of the worker under capitalism was fired by a high view of what work can and should be.[20] For Marx, labor is "a process in which both man and Nature participate," in which a person "changes his own nature" and "develops his slumbering powers," with the result that work "stamps itself as exclusively human" and enables a person to "realize a purpose of his own."[21]

In its diagnosis of the problems of work in the industrial society, Marxism deserves to be taken seriously. Christian thinking about work cannot afford to ignore the problems Marxism uncovers. When Marx indicts the world for having made money "the god of this world," he asserts a Christian principle.[22]

The Marxist solution, on the other hand, bases itself too thoroughly on the reform of human institutions to win the confidence of Christians, and its credibility has been undermined by the history of societies where Marxism has been attempted. Marxism places its hope in a working class that will redeem society. In the words of Marx,

> A class must be formed which . . . is the dissolution of all classes, a sphere of society which has a universal character because its sufferings are universal. . . . This dissolution of society . . . is the *proletariat*.[23]

This is the collectivist answer to the problem of work in an industrial society. We should not allow its lack of success in Communist coun-

19. Friedrich Engels, *The Condition of the Working Class in England in 1844*, quoted in Roger Mannell and Seppo Iso-Ahola, "Work Constraints on Leisure: A Social Psychological Analysis," in *Constraints on Leisure*, ed. Michael G. Wade (Springfield, Ill.: Charles C. Thomas, 1985), 157.

20. See *The Marx-Engels Reader*, Robert C. Tucker, ed. (New York: W. W. Norton, 1978); Lee Hardy, *The Fabric of This World* (Grand Rapids: Eerdmans, 1990), 29–37; Miroslav Volf, *Work in the Spirit: Toward a Theology of Work* (New York: Oxford University Press, 1991), 55–65.

21. Karl Marx, *Capital*, in *Great Books of the Western World*, ed. Robert M. Hutchins (Chicago: Encyclopedia Britannica, 1952), 50:85.

22. *Marx-Engels Reader*, 50.

23. Ibid., 64.

tries to obscure its insights into the problems of work that are important to an understanding of work in the modern world.

The Romantic Idealization of Work

A second response to the industrial revolution of the nineteenth century was the "Romantic" idealization of work. Looking back, we can see this attitude as part of Victorian optimism and nostalgia for the past. Sensing that industrial work was dehumanizing, these Romanticists urged a return to something more natural. They valued craftsmanship and working with one's hands. In some ways they were forerunners of the "simple lifers" of our own century.

The foremost spokesmen for this tradition were John Ruskin and Thomas Carlyle. They exalted the work of one's hands as the Puritans had done, but without the surrounding theological framework. Ruskin wanted to revive the values of earlier centuries when individual craftsmen could express their ability through their work. His follower William Morris called it "work pleasure." Protesting that the phenomenon of the division of labor was wrongly named ("it is not, truly speaking, the labor that is divided; but the men"), Ruskin longed for a society in which "the dishonor of manual labor" would be "done away with altogether."[24]

Ruskin's fellow Victorian Thomas Carlyle could hardly restrain his enthusiasm for work:

> There is a perennial nobleness, and even sacredness, in Work. . . . The latest Gospel in this world is, Know thy work and do it. . . . Even in the meanest sorts of Labour, the whole soul of a man is composed into a kind of real harmony. . . . All true Work is Religion. . . . All true Work is sacred; in all true Work were it but true hand labour, there is something of divineness.[25]

If we had asked *why* work is this great, the answer apparently would have been, "It just is."

This is the Victorian exaltation of work. It goes by the name of "Puritanism," but this is a misnomer. Writers such as Ruskin and Carlyle valued work in itself, not work as service to God and society. They idealized the work of the craftsman but did not have much to say to the worker who continued to slave away in the factory or the homemaker who cooked the meals and had to wash the dishes.

24. John Ruskin, excerpts from *The Stones of Venice*, in *The Norton Anthology of English Literature*, ed. M. H. Abrams (New York: W. W. Norton, 1962), 2:1125–29.

25. Thomas Carlyle, excerpts from *Past and Present*, in *English Prose of the Victorian Era*, Charles F. Harrold and William D. Templeman, eds. (New York: Oxford University Press, 1938), 229–233.

The Twentieth Century: The Secular Wasteland

No single attitude toward work dominates the present century, but various viewpoints tend to share a secular bias. Work is no longer discussed in a religious context. Whereas theologians were once the people to theorize about work, in our century the discussion is largely conducted by economists and sociologists. Within a prevailingly secular context, the population is divided into a range of attitudes.

The eight-to-five laborer and the homemaker generally resign themselves to work as a necessary evil. Whatever satisfactions life offers, they are more likely to come from family and other home amenities than from work itself. One study, for example, found that only one out of four workers regarded their jobs as a central life interest.[26] For all their dislike of ordinary work, however, no revolution lurks around the corner. These workers have become acclimated to unfulfilling work as the thing that makes the weekend and family life possible.

Among professional classes work is often an idol. The "organization worker," the careerist, and the self-employed professional tend to devote an inordinate amount of their weekly schedule to work.[27] These workers tend to be motivated by self-interest and the ideal of upward social mobility based on wealth. Work is carried out within a framework of the success ethic.

Of course the "simple lifer's'" rejection of the rat race continues to appeal to a small minority within society. These people are belated "Romanticists," heirs of the nature lovers of the nineteenth century who sought to escape from the mechanization of industrial and urban life.

Finally, we should not overlook the continuing appeal of Marxism. Although Communism has fallen into disrepute, many nations in the world live by at least a modified socialist version of Marxism. Its appeal remains strong among intellectuals and those who write on work and leisure. Its continuing vigor as a theory, if not as a practice, stems from the way in which it addresses the problems of work under capitalism, something that any viable work ethic today must take into account.

Although attitudes toward work are in disarray in our century, we should not conclude that the work ethic is dead. When it expresses itself, however, it stems from a secular context. This is epitomized by Richard Nixon's often-quoted Labor Day Message of September 6, 1971:

---

26. Robert Dubin, "Industrial Workers' World: A Study of the 'Central Life Interests' of Industrial Workers," in *Work and Leisure: A Contemporary Social Problem*, ed. Erwin O. Smigel (New Haven: College and University Press, 1963), 60.

27. Harold L. Wilensky found that "those who have freedom to set their own work schedules tend to choose long hours" ("The Uneven Distribution of Leisure: The Impact of Economic Growth on 'Free Time'," in *Work and Leisure*, 131).

Let the detractors of America, the doubters of the American spirit, take note. America's competitive spirit, the work ethic of this people, is alive and well on Labor Day, 1971. The dignity of work, the value of achievement, the morality of self-reliance—none of these is going out of style.[28]

What the Historical Survey Tells Us

Several lessons emerge from the history of attitudes toward work. The ease with which the human race has fallen into inadequate views of work shows that it is a subject that requires careful thought; reaching the right position on work does not occur naturally and spontaneously. Indeed the amount of heartache that has come from bad doctrines of work ought to compel us to think carefully on the issue.

The history of attitudes toward work is also a roadmap to the dead ends that face us in our own cultural setting. We, too, can undervalue or disdain earthly work. We, too, can wrongly decide that "full-time Christian service" is spiritually more distinguished than washing the dishes or working the eight-to-five shift. We can likewise slip into the errors of divorcing work from its context of Christian service to God and others, or making an idol of it, or performing it as a necessary evil.

We should notice, too, that every age has tended to make its view of work conform to prevailing social practices. In a society based on slavery, Greek thinkers decided that work was beneath the dignity of free people. In an era when the clergy dominated society, people were content with a two-track view of work that made ordinary work second best. As Western civilization drifted from its Christian roots, its work ethic became decidedly secular and devoid of a religious base. It should be clear, therefore, that a genuinely Christian view of work must be based on something (the Bible) more authoritative and transcendent than mere human thinking, no matter how helpful that thinking is.

To appeal to biblical authority will of course seem like an anomaly in the larger world of modern thought. This leads me to a final observation. For the last three centuries, work has been discussed in a nonreligious context, chiefly economic and sociological. A topic that was once regarded as a religious issue has fallen victim to the syndrome of the retreating province of the Christian faith in the modern world. The only hope for work in our day is to return it to the religious arena in which it once took its place.

28. Quoted in Gordon Dahl, *Work, Play, and Worship in a Leisure-Oriented Society* (Minneapolis: Augsburg, 1972), 50.

Further Reading

Adriano Tilgher, *Work: What It Has Meant to Men through the Ages* (1930).

Arthur T. Geoghegan, *The Attitude towards Labor in Early Christianity and Ancient Culture* (1945).

W. R. Forrester, *Christian Vocation* (1953).

P. D. Anthony, *The Ideology of Work* (1977).

Lee Hardy, *The Fabric of This World* (1990).

7

Ill at Ease
Leisure through the Ages

The history of attitudes toward leisure is told more quickly than that toward work. Compared to the ongoing discussion of work, leisure has not received its fair share of attention through the centuries.

The Greek Ideal of Leisure

If the history of work got off to an inauspicious start in classical Greece, the reverse is true for leisure. The Greeks had an exalted view of leisure that in important ways remains a standard for today.[1]

Aristotle is the leading spokesman for the Greek ideal, and in his statements we can see both the appeal and the limitations of that ideal. Aristotle believed that the goal of life is happiness, and leisure is necessary to attain it. In his words, "Happiness is thought to depend on leisure; for we are busy [i.e., we work] that we may have leisure, [just as] we make war that we may live in peace."[2] The notion that we work in order to have leisure exactly reverses the Puritan viewpoint, as we shall

1. For my data on classical attitudes toward leisure, I have drawn on these sources: de Grazia, *Of Time, Work, and Leisure*, 11–25; Kelly, *Leisure*, 43–56; and Parker, *Sociology of Leisure*, 22–23.

2. Aristotle, *Nicomachean Ethics*, in *Great Books of the Western World*, ed. Robert M. Hutchins (Chicago: Encyclopedia Britannica, 1952), 9:432.

see. The liability of both formulations is that it slights one-half of the work-leisure equation.

For Aristotle, leisure is more than free time, though it requires freedom from labor as a prerequisite. Freed *from* the need to work, one was freed *to* engage in the life of contemplation and culture. While work is only a means to an end, not an end in itself, the reverse is true for leisure, which is a state of being in which an activity is performed for its own sake.

Philosophers like Plato and Aristotle believed that leisure was especially required for the rulers of society, giving them time to acquire those qualities that made them fit to rule. But while the leisured class was thus liberated from the need to work, they were not free simply to lounge around. Indeed, a great deal of responsibility came with their free time. The Greek work for leisure was *skole,* from which we get our word *school,* implying that leisure was for education, broadly defined.

This ideal of leisure was intimately bound up with Greek humanism. Believing in the value of the individual's self-development, the Greeks sought to fulfill the whole person. Leisure was a means to this wholeness. It "was a quality of life that enabled man to develop and express all sides of his intellectual, physical and spiritual natures."[3]

Greek leisure was almost synonymous with liberal education, and again we can see the logic underlying the word *skole* to designate it. Leisure fostered contemplation, learning, music, literature, and sports. People were educated for these activities in academies, and facilities from theaters to gymnasiums were built for the exercise of these activities. We can see, then, why Aristotle contrasted leisure not only to work, but also to children's play and to recreation that simply restores the worker.

Of course this high ideal of cultured leisure carried with it a price tag. It was reserved for a small minority of the population, mainly males of the ruling class. It was, moreover, based on the premise of slave labor. And like so much contemporary leisure theory, Aristotle was unable to produce a viable leisure ethic without disparaging work in the process.

This brings us to the theme that runs through any history of leisure. In every era, leisure in its highest reaches has been reserved for the intellectual and cultural elite. They are the ones who have had the education and level of cultural sophistication to enjoy leisure. It is a privileged state to be able to enjoy enlightened leisure.

This may make leisure suspect in the eyes of some, but I would suggest a more favorable interpretation. In our own day, when education is

3. Roberts, *Contemporary Society,* 3.

nearly universal and where it costs less to read a book than to drive a car or go to a movie, we can legitimately speak of the democratization of leisure; it is within the reach of anyone who values it. Viewed thus, the Greek ideal of leisure as the fully developed person remains a standard of excellence in leisure.

Rome and Mass Leisure

The Romans followed the pattern of the Greeks in planning and building for leisure. For them, too, it remained a goal of civilization to provide meaningful leisure for its citizens. In its earlier history, the Roman ideal of leisure went by the name of *otium*, a contented rest from work and war. Whereas the Greeks had made contemplation and the life of the mind the goal of leisure, the Romans preferred active pursuits, including physical fitness and spectator sports. Still, among a wealthy few who were able to afford comfortable villas with gardens and pools, leisure took on the quality of what John Milton later called "retired leisure."

Two developments made Roman leisure different from Greek leisure and similar to modern leisure. One was the practice of public leisure for the masses. At one point, the city of Rome had 800 public baths. For this warrior nation, moreover, government and military festivals became an established practice. The Circus Maximus, the largest arena for chariot racing, accommodated 385,000 spectators. The monuments to the Roman tradition of public leisure also included theaters, parks, stadiums, and gymnasiums.

The other development was the politicizing of leisure. As the ruling class became separated from the masses (many of whom were unemployed), leisure became a means of entertaining and distracting the potentially revolutionary masses. Leisure thus became "bread and circuses" for the masses—a manipulation by the ruling class to curtail any discontent that might erupt among the plebeians. The Greek ideal of the educated and cultured person had degenerated to mere consumption—consumption of public entertainment by the lower classes and of a luxurious lifestyle by the rulers.

Here is an early example of a perversion of leisure that is with us today: mass consumption of morally degrading or trivial activities by the masses with modest means, and luxurious self-indulgence by the wealthy minority. This may, in fact, be the dominant feature on the leisure scene today.

Medieval Asceticism

The Middle Ages produced little theorizing about leisure, but one development is important to my attempt later to integrate leisure with Christianity. I noted in an earlier chapter that leisure presupposes the legitimacy of pleasure. Aristotle, in fact, discussed leisure as part of the human quest for happiness, which he regarded as the goal of life. The asceticism (denial of pleasure) and otherworldliness of the Catholic Middle Ages carried with it a relatively low regard for leisure. If the main business of life is to avoid earthly pleasure, then naturally leisure will not hold much appeal.

Tertullian's treatise against Roman festivals is one index to this negative attitude.[4] Beginning with the premise, "What greater pleasure is there than distaste of pleasure itself, than contempt of all the world can give?" Tertullian systematically denied the activities of a Roman festival as fit for Christian participation, asking, "Will the man, seated where there is nothing of God, at that moment think of God?" As for sports, "Never can you approve the foolish racing and throwing feats and the more foolish jumping contests; . . . you will hate men bred to amuse the idleness of Greece." All of the arts are condemned on the ground that the demons from the beginning designed them "to turn man from the Lord and bind him to their glorification," giving "inspiration to men of genius in these particular arts."

Augustine came to regard his classical education in similar terms. He believed that "we were forced to go astray in the footsteps of these poetic fictions."[5] He commended Plato for having "absolutely excluded poets from his ideal state."[6] In retrospect, Augustine believed that he had "sinned" when, as a schoolboy, he disliked the sound of "one and one, two; two and two, four" but loved to hear "the burning of Troy" and "the wooden horse lined with armed men."[7] We see here a distrust of culture and pleasure, which are viewed as enemies of the Christian life. For Augustine, even eating was sinful if one did it for pleasure rather than necessity.[8]

A final example of the negative medieval attitude toward leisure is from a famous letter that the churchman Alcuin wrote in 797. Aware of the monks' fondness for fictional stories about heroes such as Beowulf and Ingeld, Alcuin laid down the rule in a letter to a bishop

4. I have taken all my quotations of Tertullian from *Tertullian: Disciplinary, Moral and Ascetical Works,* trans. Rudolph Arbesmann, in *The Fathers of the Church* (New York: Fathers of the Church, 1959), 40:47–107.

5. Augustine, *Confessions,* I, 17.

6. Augustine, *The City of God,* II, 14.

7. Augustine, *Confessions,* I, 13.

8. Ibid., X, 31.

named Higbald, "Let the words of God be read aloud at table in your re-
fectory. The reader should be heard there, not the flute player; the Fathers of the Church, not the songs of the heathen." To clinch his point,
Alcuin asked rhetorically, "What has Ingeld to do with Christ?"[9]

The Catholic Middle Ages did not discredit all leisure. There were
many holy days in which common people participated. But we must remember that life in the world had two strikes against it from the beginning. The truly spiritual life was what went on in the monasteries,
whose residents were ascetic and otherworldly, a climate that effec-
tively precluded the practice of leisure as a pleasurable and self-rewarding activity. That is why I am less convinced than some that the Middle
Ages constitutes a rich tradition on which to draw for a contemporary
Christian theory of leisure. The question revolves around the medieval
tradition of religious contemplation, a tradition whose importance and
value I do not wish to minimize, but which for several reasons touches
only tangentially on any inquiry into leisure.

To begin with, the medieval tradition of religious contemplation belonged to the life of worship, not to what we mean by leisure. We know
this partly from negative statements that the very people who commended contemplation made about entertainment and leisure activities as we customarily understand them. To attempt to build a case for
leisure on the endorsement of the contemplative life is no more con-
vincing than trying to adduce Puritan views of Sabbath observance or a
statement about the importance of attending worship services as evidence of a positive attitude toward leisure. By contemplation Augustine meant "the contemplation of God."[10] This has a great deal to do
with what one might do on Sunday morning or during one's devotional
time but hardly anything to do with attending a ball game or reading a
novel. In fact, its tendency is to discredit such leisure activities.

Furthermore, medieval contemplation was a religious duty prescribed to those who aspired to the higher reaches of spirituality. It thus
had more in common with work (which is defined partly in terms of its
obligatory nature) than with leisure (which is defined partly in terms of
its nonobligatory nature).

Finally, we should remember that the medieval tradition of religious
contemplation was largely the domain of monks, nuns, and clerics. Augustine's commendation of the pursuit of truth as the best use of leisure
(City of God, XIX, 19) is sometimes offered as a Christian basis for leisure, but it is mainly warmed-over Aristotelianism, urging the contemplative life as a way of avoiding what Augustine calls the "burden" of
active work.

9. Alcuin, letter to Higbald, as quoted by Eleanor S. Duckett, Alcuin, Friend of Char-
lemagne (New York: Macmillan, 1951), 209.

10. Augustine, City of God, XIX, 19.

The Middle Ages did commend more than active work, and as such it affirmed an important aspect of leisure, namely its function of calling to a halt the acquisitive urge. But to claim that it therefore provides a rich basis for a Christian view of leisure is to distort the picture. The very people who commended the contemplative life were virtually unanimous in condemning recreation and cultural pursuits.

Leisure Confronts Humanism and Piety: The Renaissance and Reformation

The sixteenth and seventeenth centuries present a mixed picture. The rebirth of classical, humanistic values resulted in the greatest flowering of artistic creativity in Western civilization. As in ancient Greece, there was general participation in the arts. We can sense the spirit of the age in Thomas More's *Utopia*, a monument to Renaissance humanism. In More's never-never land, people work only six hours a day, not because they despise work, but in order to "give all citizens as much time as public needs permit for freeing and developing their minds." Accordingly, the citizens of this ideal society enjoy such varied leisure pursuits as attending public lectures before daybreak, reading, listening to music during their communal meals, and puttering in their gardens.

Renaissance education is perhaps the best index to the humanistic endorsement of leisure. Education was mainly limited to the males of privileged families (not only aristocratic families, but also prosperous middle class ones). Its ideal was a sound mind in a sound body. It therefore educated students to enjoy such varied leisure activities as reading, music, and physical exercise. Learnéd conversation was highly prized, as were communal meals. We might profitably note the link between education and the enlighted use of leisure time—a principle still relevant today.

We should not set the Renaissance humanists up as antagonists of the Reformers and Puritans. As C. S. Lewis correctly notes, "There was no necessary enmity between Puritans and humanists. They were often the same people, and nearly always the same sort of people."[11] Yet the Reformation's view of leisure cannot be called healthy, although the picture is not as negative as is usually claimed, as I will show in chapter 9. The Protestant ethic was too utilitarian, too work-oriented, and too preoccupied with the possible appearance of evil to allow for a wholehearted endorsement of leisure. Puritans such as Richard Baxter were quick to equate pastimes with timewasting. And even when they af-

11. C. S. Lewis, *Studies in Medieval and Renaissance Literature* (Cambridge: Cambridge University Press, 1966), 122.

firmed legitimate recreation, the Puritans made it part of their work ethic by defending its usefulness in preparing people to work.

Farewell to Leisure: The Triumph of Utilitarianism

The most notable development in attitudes toward leisure between the Reformation and the twentieth century was the growth of utilitarianism.[12] Its chief spokesmen were Jeremy Bentham and John Stuart Mill, but these specific theorists are less important than the general spirit of pragmatism that came to dominate Western society. Bentham equated happiness with utility, pleasure with profit. "What is the use of it?" was his standard test.

As Mill noted, by the time this equation of happiness and utility became popularized, the word *utilitarian* came to mean "the rejection, or the neglect . . . of beauty, of ornament, or of amusement." A later spokesman for the position claimed that if a game "be undertaken solely for the sake of the enjoyment attaching to it, we need scarcely take it under our notice," adding that "value depends entirely upon utility."

Of course this utilitarian spirit expressed itself in the industrial society and its accompanying urbanization. Factories and cities followed the course of what was efficient and useful, not what was beautiful and enjoyable and humanly enriching. Such an outlook was on a collision course with leisure, since leisure lies beyond the bounds of what is strictly useful. "In leisure," writes Josef Pieper, a person "oversteps the frontiers of the everyday, workaday world."[13] Nineteenth-century utilitarianism did what it could to insure that urban workers did not overstep that frontier.

Industrialism also changed the social context in which leisure occurred. It made people less the owner of their own time. It speeded up the pace of life, making leisure more necessary but reducing the amount of time available for it. And it created a more distinct cleavage between work and leisure, since work was increasingly undertaken at specific locations and times separate from the rest of life.

The legacy of utilitarianism has continued to the present day. Individual and communal decisions today tend to be made on the basis of usefulness. Moreover, the test of usefulness is applied with particular rigor by evangelical Christians. The result is a thriving work ethic and an anemic play ethic, along with a virtual neglect of the arts.

12. For this sketch of the growth of the utilitarian spirit I have relied on the informal history provided by Kerr, *The Decline of Pleasure*, 48ff.
13. Pieper, *Leisure the Basis of Culture*, 53.

The Twentieth Century: The Age of Leisure

Our own century is surely the age of leisure. Who can doubt it when in 1989 Americans spent 602 billion dollars on leisure, a billion and a half more than they spent on food and a staggering increase over the 262 billion they spent on leisure just a decade earlier?[14] This is not to deny the point made earlier that in our fast-paced society people have less leisure than they want or need, and that they buy more leisure goods than they have time to use.

What is new in our century, however, is a widespread acceptance of the legitimacy of leisure and recreation. People do not feel that they have to defend watching television or visiting a park. Leisure has become an expectation of life, a natural right.

The study of leisure has also come into its own in our century. Schools offer courses on leisure. Books and articles on the subject multiply each year. In fact, recent decades have produced many more books and articles on leisure than on work, even though (or perhaps because?) leisure is less understood. Recreation and leisure are also closely tied to public policy today.

Leisure today is decidedly pluralistic. Technology has greatly enlarged the range of leisure activities available to people. It has also made the concept of leisure virtually synonymous with mass leisure, with its tendency toward relatively low intellectual and cultural standards.

Finally, modern leisure exists in a largely secular context. Discussions rarely attempt to place it into a religious frame of reference. Most people in our culture pursue their leisure activities without a thought about the morality of what they are doing or whether it is a good use of time. To put it another way, the constraints on most people's leisure are constraints of time and money, not of religious or moral conscience.

What the History of Attitudes toward Leisure Tells Us

Leisure has fared even worse than work in the history of the human race. In the history of work, we can at least look back to two centuries of the Protestant work ethic for a beacon of Christian understanding. But the Christian understanding of leisure is scarcely a flicker, with the result that we will get relatively little help from the past in reaching a Christian perspective on leisure.

The main bright spot we can find is the Christian humanism of the Renaissance. It is admirably epitomized in Puritan John Milton's trea-

14. Kevin Kerr, "Working Hard at Play," *Adweek's Marketing Week*, 20 January 1992, 12. The earlier figure comes from Michael Doan, "262 Billion Dogfight for Your Leisure Spending," *U. S. News and World Report*, 26 July 1982, 47.

tise *Of Education.* Milton believed that the goal of education is "to know God aright, and out of that knowledge to love him, to imitate him, to be like him." With the Christian context thus established, he proceeded to outline his educational ideals, which were useful for life but also a preparation for leisure. Milton notes, as Aristotle and Plato had also observed, that the Spartans' educational system equipped their citizens for war but not for peace. He therefore outlined an educational plan that would prepare a person for both work and leisure. Milton's ideal students are expected to enjoy reading, music, and physical exercise. The educational process itself included times of work, of cultural enrichment, and of encounters with nature.

To transport this breadth of vision into our leisure time in the twentieth century is not easy. It requires a much higher ideal of leisure than most people today are prepared to accept. But for the Christian, it remains an ideal undergirded with abundant biblical warrant, as we will see later.

Further Reading

Sebastian de Grazia, *Of Time, Work, and Leisure* (1962).
John R. Kelly, *Leisure* (1982).
Witold Rybczynski, *Waiting for the Weekend* (1991).

8

"We *All* Know That the Puritans . . ."
The Original Protestant Ethic

How often have we heard a statement beginning with the glib assertion, "We *all* know that the Puritans . . ." Usually the discussion involves an equally glib use of the phrase "the Puritan ethic." The distortions are not limited to the secular world but have been imported into Christian circles as well. Like Nicodemus, who was a teacher in Israel and yet did not know the basics of the new birth, evangelical Protestants are often strangers to what is best in their own tradition. The purpose of this chapter is to set the record straight regarding the much maligned Protestant ethic.[1]

Six Fallacies about the Protestant Work Ethic

Many of the misconceptions about the original Protestant ethic can be traced to Max Weber's unjustifiably influential book entitled *The Protestant Ethic and the Spirit of Capitalism* (1930). Noting that the rise of middle-class trade occurred chiefly in Protestant countries, Weber argued that there was a connection between "the Protestant ethic" and "the spirit of modern capitalism."

1. For more on the subject than space allows here, see my book *Worldly Saints: The Puritans As They Really Were* (Grand Rapids: Zondervan, 1986).

Weber's main thesis, scantily supported with selective quotations from the Puritans, is a classic case of reading back into a movement features that arose two or three centuries later. Scholars have long since shown the inadequacy of Weber's book, showing that instead of the Protestant ethic influencing capitalism, the influence worked the other way: capitalism arose only by changing the original Protestant ethic.[2] Yet Weber's thesis continues to appeal to people who want to blame the ailments of today's work ethic on the Protestant movement. As a way into the subject of original Protestant ethic, therefore, I want to examine six fallacies or stereotypes of the Protestant ethic that are commonly accepted among those looking for a scapegoat.

Fallacy 1: Work Should Absorb Nearly All of One's Time.

The common stereotype is that the Protestant ethic led people to devote virtually all of their time to work. One modern writer, for example, describes New England Calvinism as "the tradition that life should be wholly devoted to work."[3]

The original Protestants, however, preached a clear message of moderation in work. The Puritan divine John Preston wrote, "Take heed of too much business, or intending it too much, or inordinately."[4] Richard Steele warned against moonlighting by saying that a person ought not to "accumulate two or three callings merely to increase his riches."[5] Similarly, Martin Luther wrote a letter to Philip Melanchthon in which he told him not to overwork and "then pretend you did it in obedience to God."[6]

The notion that the original Protestants reduced life to continual work is easily refuted by the sheer quantity of time they devoted to spiritual exercises. They set aside Sunday in its entirety for rest from work. They had daily worship in the home and attended midweek meetings. They were also avid readers on religious matters. Furthermore, they believed that recreation was "both needful and expedient," since it is impossible "for the body to be exercised in continual labors."[7]

2. Sources that show the inadequacy of the Weber thesis include these: Albert Hyma, *Christianity, Capitalism and Communism: A Historical Analysis* (Ann Arbor: George Wahr, 1937); A. M. Robertson, *Aspects of the Rise of Economic Individualism* (New York: Kelley and Millman, 1959); Forrester, *Christian Vocation*, 152–67; Robert W. Green, ed., *Protestantism and Capitalism: The Weber Thesis and Its Critics* (Boston: D. C. Heath, 1959); and Michael Walzer, *The Revolution of the Saints: A Study in the Origins of Radical Politics* (Cambridge, Mass.: Harvard University Press, 1965).

3. Max Kaplan, *Leisure in America: A Social Inquiry* (New York: John Wiley and Sons, 1960), 151.

4. John Preston, *The Saint's Qualification* (London: Nicolas Bourne, 1633), 208.

5. Richard Steele, *The Tradesman's Calling* (London: Samuel Sprint, 1684), 180.

6. Martin Luther, letter to Melanchthon; quoted in Ewald M. Plass, ed., *What Luther Says: An Anthology* (St. Louis: Concordia, 1959), 787.

7. William Burkitt, *The Poor Man's Help* (London: T. Parkhurst, 1701), 18.

Fallacy 2: Self-Interest Is the Motivation for Work.

Many of the misleading claims about the Protestant ethic have occurred when people impose modern attitudes toward work on the original Protestants. An example is the claim that the Reformers taught that people should work hard to get benefits for themselves. At stake here is the question of what constitutes the motivation and reward of work.

Did the original Protestant ethic make a self-interest a virtue? Hardly. Luther wrote that "work should . . . be done to serve God by it, to avoid idleness, and to satisfy His commandments."[8] He also spoke slightingly of people who "do not use their talents in their calling or in the service of their neighbor; they use them only for their own glory and advantage."[9]

John Preston said that we must labor "not for our own good, but for the good of others."[10] "'Every man for himself, and God for all,' is wicked," wrote William Perkins, "and is directly against the end of every calling or honest kind of life."[11] Richard Steele considered it a "sin and folly" when people aim "only at their wealth, ease, and honour; and not at the glory of God and the public good, as well as their own subsistence."[12] And the American Puritan John Cotton wrote that we must "not only aim at our own, but at the public good," with the result that a Christian will not think he has "a comfortable calling, unless it will not only serve his own turn, but the turn of other men."[13]

Fallacy 3: Getting Rich Is the Goal of Life.

Though solidly entrenched in the minds of many, the claim that the original Protestants regarded making money as the goal of life is one of the most absurd charges. The Reformers and Puritans did not despise money and earthly goods, but they certainly did not regard them as the goal of life.

Thomas Watson asserted that "blessedness . . . does not lie in the acquisition of worldly things. Happiness cannot by any art of chemistry be extracted here."[14] Another Puritan told his son, "Travail not too much to be rich. . . . He that is greedy of gain troubleth his own soul."[15]

---

8. Luther, sermon on the fourth petition of the Lord's Prayer; quoted in Plass, *What Luther Says*, 1494.

9. Luther, sermon on 1 Peter 4:8–11; in Plass, *What Luther Says*, 1497.

10. John Preston, *The New Covenant* (London: Nicolas Bourne, 1629), 178.

11. William Perkins, *A Treatise of the Vocations or Callings of Men*, in *Works* (London: John Haviland, 1631), 1:751.

12. Steele, *Tradesman's Calling*, 10.

13. John Cotton, *The Way of Life* (London: L. Fawne and S. Gellibrand, 1641), 439.

14. Thomas Watson, *The Beatitudes* (Edinburgh: Banner of Truth, 1977), 25.

15. Lord Montagu, as quoted by Lawrence Stone, *The Crisis of the Aristocracy, 1558–1641* (Oxford: Oxford University Press, 1965), 331.

Richard Baxter believed that it brings glory to God "when we contemn the riches and honour of the world," adding that "when seeming Christians are worldly and ambitious as others, and make as great matter of their gain, and wealth, and honour, it showeth that they do but cover the base and sordid spirit of worldlings with the visor of the Christian name."[16] Elsewhere we read that a person "must not aim at riches," and that "you have far more cause to be afraid of prosperity, than of adversity; of riches, than of poverty."[17]

The truth is that the Puritans were obsessed with the *dangers* of wealth. William Perkins claimed that "seeking of abundance is a hazard to the salvation of the soul," elsewhere commenting, "Let us consider what moved Judas to betray his master: namely, the desire of wealth."[18] "The experience of all ages has verified," wrote William Bates, "that none are exposed to more dangerous trials than the prosperous in this world," adding that prosperity inclines people "to an impious neglect of God."[19] Thomas Adams thought that "wealth and wickedness are near of kin."[20] Puritan scholar Edmund Morgan rightly comments that "the Puritans always felt more at ease when adversity made them tighten their belts."[21]

Fallacy 4: People Can Be Successful through Their Own Efforts.

In our day, the Protestant ethic is described as an ethic of self-reliance. The Reformers, runs the argument, believed that people can pull themselves up by their own bootstraps. The harder we work, the more money we will make. The final result is "the self-made person" that our own culture worships.

The stereotype is utterly baseless. The Protestant ethic is an ethic of grace, not merit. In fact, the whole theological bent of Protestantism opposes the idea of human merit before God. If salvation is by faith rather than works, how can one earn one's way?

Calvin thus asserts that "men in vain wear themselves out with toiling . . . to acquire riches, since these also are a benefit bestowed only by

16. Richard Baxter, *A Christian Directory*, in *The Practical Works of Richard Baxter* (Ligonier, Pa.: Soli Deo Gloria, 1990), 1:151.

17. John Preston, *A Remedy against Covetousness* (London: Michaell Sparke, 1632), 44; and Baxter, *Christian Directory*, in *Works*, 1:78.

18. William Perkins, *The Whole Treatise of the Cases of Conscience*, in *Works*, 2:125; and *An Exposition of the . . . Creed of the Apostles*, in *Works*, 1:193.

19. William Bates, *The Whole Works of the Rev. W. Bates* (Harrisonburg, Va.: Sprinkle, 1990), 2:207, 218.

20. Thomas Adams, *The Works of Thomas Adams* (Edinburgh: James Nichol, 1861), 2:407.

21. Edmund Morgan, "The Puritan Ethic and the American Revolution," in *Puritanism and the American Experience*, ed. Michael McGiffert (Reading, Mass.: Addison-Wesley, 1969), 185.

God."[22] And again, "Whenever we meet with the word 'reward' or it crosses our minds, let us realize that it is the height of the divine goodness towards us."[23] Luther was of the same opinion:

> When riches come, the godless heart of man thinks: I have achieved this with my labors. It does not consider that these are purely blessings of God, blessings that at times come to us through our labors and at times without our labors, but never because of our labors; for God always gives them because of His undeserved mercy.[24]

The American Puritan Cotton Mather said aphoristically, "In our occupation we spread our nets; but it is God who brings unto our nets all that comes into them."[25] Richard Bernard was of a similar opinion: "Riches are from God, and not by man; man cannot make himself rich by any means, if God's common blessing be not assistant thereto."[26] George Swinnock claimed that "the diligent hand of itself can do . . . nothing without the blessing of God."[27] Richard L. Greaves's massive survey of the primary sources reveals that the Puritans "asserted that no direct correlation exists between wealth and godliness. . . . Not riches, but faith and suffering for the sake of the gospel are signs of election."[28]

Fallacy 5: Wealth Is a Sign of God's Favor and Evidence of One's Salvation.

Modern scholars often claim that the original Protestants regarded wealth as a sign of God's favor. Tony Campolo, for example, claims that for the Puritans "prosperity became the evidence of a right relationship with God."[29] But where is the evidence? I know of none.

It will come as a shock to the debunkers of the Protestant ethic to learn that the original Protestants saw an *inverse* relationship between wealth and godliness. Given their position as an often persecuted minority, the early Protestants regarded persecution and suffering, not earthly success, as the most likely result of godly living.

22. John Calvin, commentary on Psalm 127:2, in *Commentary on the Book of Psalms*, trans. James Anderson (Grand Rapids: Eerdmans, 1949), 5:107.

23. Calvin, commentary on Luke 17:7, in *A Harmony of the Gospels Matthew, Mark and Luke*, trans. T. H. L. Parker (Grand Rapids: Eerdmans, 1972), 2:124.

24. Luther, exposition of Deuteronomy 8:17–18, in Plass, *What Luther Says*, 1495.

25. Cotton Mather, *Sober Sentiments*; quoted in Ralph Barton Perry, *Puritanism and Democracy* (New York: Vanguard, 1944), 312.

26. Richard Bernard, *Ruth's Recompense* (London: Simon Waterson, 1628), 384.

27. George Swinnock, *The Christian Man's Calling*, in *Works* (Edinburgh: James Nichol, 1868), 1:303.

28. Richard L. Greaves, *Society and Religion in Elizabethan England* (Minneapolis: University of Minnesota Press, 1981), 550.

29. Anthony Campolo, Jr., *The Success Fantasy* (Wheaton: Victor, 1980), 141.

Puritan Thomas Watson claimed that "true godliness is usually attended with persecution."[30] Baxter warned, "Take heed that you judge not of God's love, or of your happiness or misery, by your riches or poverty, prosperity or adversity."[31] Luther called "utterly nonsensical" the "delusion" that led people to conclude that if someone "has good fortune, wealth, and health, . . . behold, God is dwelling here."[32] Samuel Willard wrote, "As riches are not evidences of God's love, so neither is poverty of his anger or hatred."[33] Thomas Hooker said that "afflictions are no argument of God's displeasure . . . but the ensign of grace and goodness."[34] Richard Bernard claimed that "the Lord chooseth most of such as be poor for his people, . . . neither will the Lord make many of them rich, lest they should wax in their wealth proud and forgetful of God."[35]

With quotations like these in front of us, I trust that we can lay to rest the misconception that the Puritans regarded wealth as a sign of their election to salvation. That viewpoint came on the scene long, long after the Puritans and was mainly limited to a handful of famous businessmen such as John D. Rockefeller.

Fallacy 6: The Protestant Ethic Approved of All Types of Business Competition.

A final fallacy is that the Protestant ethic was the forerunner of modern business practices. In particular, the charge is made that the Protestant ethic approved of virtually any type of competition and profiteering that led to moneymaking. Here again is an example of a modern view being read back into what the Reformers and Puritans actually said.

The English Puritan John Knewstub spoke disparagingly of businessmen who "come to buying and selling as it were to the razing and spoiling of some enemy's city . . . where every man catcheth, snatcheth and carrieth away whatsoever he can come by."[36] When Baxter denounced economic abuses, the activities he deemed illegitimate included taking more for goods than they are worth, making a product seem better than it is, concealing flaws in a product, asking as high a price as one thinks he or she can get, and taking advantage of another person's need.[37] Sim-

30. Watson, *Beatitudes*, 259.

31. Baxter, *A Christian Directory*, in *Works*, 1:514.

32. Luther, exposition on Genesis 19:2–3, in Plass, *What Luther Says*, 1436.

33. Samuel Willard, *A Complete Body of Divinity*; quoted in Stephen Foster, *Their Solitary Way: The Puritan Social Ethic in the First Century of Settlement in New England* (New Haven: Yale University Press, 1971), 128.

34. Thomas Hooker, *The Christian's Two Chief Lessons* (London: P. Stephens and C. Meredith, 1640), 65.

35. Bernard, *Ruth's Recompence*, 129.

36. John Knewstub, *Ninth Lecture on the Twentieth Chapter of Exodus*, in *Elizabethan Puritanism*, ed. Leonard J. Trinterud (New York: Oxford University Press, 1971), 351.

37. Richard Baxter, *Christian Directory*, in *Works*, 1:833–35.

ilar lists of economic vices appear regularly in the writings of the British Puritans.[38]

On the American scene, Cotton Mather, stressed the virtue of honesty in business and prohibited such practices as concealing information from a customer, exaggerating the truth about a commodity, taking advantage of the weakness of a buyer, and manufacturing anything that is not "well wrought."[39] Then there was the celebrated case of Robert Keayne, a merchant of Boston whom the townspeople thought charged excessive prices. Keayne was brought to church trial, fined two hundred pounds by the magistrates, and nearly excommunicated.[40]

Summary

What is referred to as "the Protestant ethic" today is nearly the opposite of what the original Protestants actually advocated and practiced. Only when the religious conscience and theological framework had been removed did the original Protestant ethic acquire the traits that are mistakenly attributed to it.

What the Reformation Really Said

Exploring the original Protestant ethic is not a mere historical exercise. In listening to what the Reformation said about work we are also laying a foundation for what a Christian view of work should include today.

The Virtue of Work

The common stereotype about the Protestant ethic is right in one regard: it *did* assert the value of industrious work. Everywhere we turn in the writers and preachers of the Reformation era we hear a chorus of admonition that God created us to work. The original Protestants, however, did not advocate work because it was inherently meritorious but rather because it was God's appointed means of providing for human needs.

The Protestant tradition made much of work as a creation ordinance, already established by God for the human race before the fall. Luther noted that "man was created not for leisure but for work, even in the

38. For specimens, see Adams, *Works of Thomas Adams*, 1:16–17, 1:85–89, 2:243–49; and Perkins, *Works*, 1:770–71.

39. Cotton Mather, *A Christian at His Calling*, excerpted in *Puritanism and the American Experience*, ed. Michael McGiffert (Reading, Mass.: Addison-Wesley, 1969), 126.

40. John Winthrop's *Journal* contains the account; see *Puritanism and the American Experience*, 115–16.

state of innocence."[41] "Adam in his innocence had all things at his will," wrote Perkins, "yet then God employed him in a calling: therefore none must be exempted, but every man both high and low must walk in his proper calling."[42] The effect of viewing work as a creation ordinance and not as a result of the Fall was to dignify the concept of work. Work was regarded as a mark of being truly human.

Convinced that work bore God's approval, the Reformers extolled diligence in work as one of the primary virtues in the Christian life. The word *diligent* was, in fact, one of the Puritans' "value terms": "be diligent and industrious in the way of thy calling"; "be diligent in your callings"; "every man must do the duties of his calling with diligence."[43] Not to work diligently is to presume on God's providence. Luther expressed the idea with his usual vividness:

> God does not want to have success come without work. . . . He does not want me to sit at home, to loaf, to commit matters to God, and to wait till a fried chicken flies into my mouth. That would be tempting God.[44]

Thomas Watson agreed: "God will bless our diligence, not our laziness."[45]

Underlying this Protestant affirmation of the need to work was a sturdy realism about what it takes to sustain life in a fallen world. Work is "God's appointed means for the getting of our daily bread."[46] Again, "God has commanded us in the sweat of our brows to get our bread."[47]

Robert Bolton summarizes well the Protestant endorsement of the need to obey God's command to be diligent in work in his statement that a Christian must

> be diligent with conscience and faithfulness in some lawful, honest particular calling . . . not so much to gather gold and engross wealth, as for necessary and moderate provision for family and posterity: and in conscience and obedience to that common charge laid upon all the sons and daughters of Adam to the world's end.[48]

41. Luther, exposition on Genesis 2:14, in Plass, *What Luther Says,* 1994.
42. Perkins, *An Exposition of the . . . Creed of the Apostles,* in *Works,* 1:152.
43. Burkitt, *Poor Man's Help,* 16; Baxter, *Christian Directory,* in *Works,* 1:254; Perkins, 1:752.
44. Luther, exposition on Exodus 13:18, in Plass, *What Luther Says,* 1496.
45. Watson, *Beatitudes,* 257.
46. Baxter, *Christian Directory,* in *Works,* 1:376.
47. Joshua Moody, *A Practical Discourse Concerning the Choice Benefit of Communion with God;* quoted in Emory Elliott, *Power and the Pulpit in Puritan New England* (Princeton: Princeton University Press, 1975), 180–81.
48. Robert Bolton, *General Directions for a Comfortable Walking with God* (Ligonier, Pa.: Soli Deo Gloria, 1991), 77.

The Protestant Critique of Idleness

Corresponding to the Protestant praise of diligence in work was a steady stream of contempt for idleness and sloth. The social context for this contempt was the large number of privileged aristocracy and church-supported clerics that populated Europe at the time of the Reformation. "God doth allow none to live idly," wrote the English Puritan Arthur Dent in his influential book *The Plain Man's Path-way to Heaven*.[49] His fellow Puritan Robert Bolton called idleness "the very rust and canker of the soul."[50] Baxter agreed: "It is swinish and sinful not to labor."[51] "Idleness is a great sin, the nurse of all vice," wrote Richard Bernard.[52]

For the Reformers, work was both an individual responsibility and a social obligation. The drone was a recurrent Puritan image for idle people who live off others' work: "God hath commanded you some way or other to labour for your daily bread, and not live as drones on the sweat of others."[53] In a discourse against begging, Perkins asserted that "every man must live by the labor of his own hands, and feed upon his own bread."[54] Paul's command that people who do not work should not eat was frequently quoted, as in the statement by Cotton Mather that "for those who indulge themselves in idleness, the express command of God unto us is that we should let them starve."[55]

If social privilege is no excuse not to work, neither is so-called spirituality. Richard Steele claimed that "it is no way justifiable to neglect a man's necessary affairs upon pretense of religious worship."[56] His fellow Puritan Thomas Shepard gave this advice to a religious zealot who complained that spiritual thoughts distracted him while he was at work:

> As it is a sin to nourish worldly thoughts when God set you a work in spiritual, heavenly employments, so it is . . . as great a sin to suffer yourself to be distracted by spiritual thoughts, when God sets you on work in civil . . . employments.[57]

---

49. Arthur Dent, *The Plain Man's Path-way to Heaven* (London: Robert Dexter, 1601), 192.

50. Bolton, *General Directions*, 77.

51. Baxter, *The Catechizing of Families*, in *Works*, 4:129.

52. Bernard, *Ruth's Recompense*, 135.

53. Baxter, *A Christian Directory*, in *Works*, 1:115.

54. Perkins, *Cases of Conscience*, in *Works*, 2:144.

55. Cotton Mather, *Durable Riches;* quoted in Christopher Hill, *Society and Puritanism in Pre-Revolutionary England* (New York: Schocken Books, 1964), 186.

56. Steele, *Tradesman's Calling*, 86.

57. Thomas Shepard, *Certain Select Cases Resolved,* in *The Works of Thomas Shepard* (New York: AMS Press, 1967), 1:306.

What emerges from these typical comments is a deeply ingrained contempt for people who display an aversion to work.

The Sanctity of All Legitimate Types of Work

Another key element in the Protestant platform was a belief in the sanctity of all legitimate types of work. This conviction began with a thoroughgoing rejection of the dichotomy between "sacred" and "secular" work. Luther was the person who more than anyone else challenged the notion that clergymen, monks, and nuns were engaged in holier work than the housewife or shopkeeper. He wrote, "It looks like a small thing when a maid cooks and cleans and does other housework. But because God's command is there, even such a small work must be praised as a service of God far surpassing the holiness and asceticism of all monks and nuns."[58] Again, even though household work "has no appearance of sanctity . . . yet these very works in connection with the household are more desirable than all the works of all the monks and nuns," so that "seemingly secular works are a worship of God and an obedience well pleasing to God."[59]

The most important result of this outlook was to sanctify common work. It opened the door to regarding every task or job as important in God's eyes. William Tyndale said that if we look externally "there is difference betwixt washing of dishes and preaching of the word of God; but as touching to please God, none at all."[60] According to Perkins, "The action of a shepherd in keeping sheep . . . is as good a work before God as is the action of a judge in giving a sentence, or a magistrate in ruling, or a minister in preaching."[61] The principle underlying this attitude was stated succinctly by Baxter: "God looketh not only nor principally at the external part of the work, but much more to the heart of him that doth it."[62]

Obviously this view of work renders every task of intrinsic value and integrates every legitimate vocation or task with a Christian's spiritual life. It makes every job consequential by claiming it as the arena for glorifying God, and it provides a way for workers to serve God not only *within* their work in the world but *by* that work.

58. Luther, *Works*; quoted in Forrester, *Christian Vocation*, 148.
59. Luther, commentary on Genesis 13:13, in *Luther's Works*, ed. Jaroslav Pelikan (St. Louis: Concordia, 1960), 2:349.
60. William Tyndale, *The Parable of the Wicked Mammon*; quoted in Louis B. Wright, *Middle-Class Culture in Elizabethan England* (Chapel Hill: University of North Carolina Press, 1935), 171.
61. Perkins, *Vocations or Callings of Men*, in *Works*, 1:758.
62. Baxter, *Christian Directory*, in *Works*, 1:111.

The Protestant Doctrine of Calling or Vocation

At the very heart of the Protestant contribution to ideas about work is the idea of calling. Every Christian, said the Reformers, is called by God to serve him. To follow that call is to obey God.

The Reformers actually spoke of a double call by God, and this is important to our understanding of the Christian doctrine of vocation. The general call comes in the same form to every person and consists of the call to conversion and sanctification. Perkins explained, "The general calling is the calling of Christianity, which is common to all that live in the church of God. . . . [It] is that whereby a man is called out of the world to be a child of God."[63] This is the general context in which people perform their work. They are first of all called to be God's people. The Reformers' view of the primacy of the spiritual did not desert them when they came to theorize about work, and again we can see how thoroughly secularized the concept of calling became later on.

The particular calling, according to the Reformers, consists of the specific job and tasks that God places before us in the course of daily living. It focuses on a person's occupation, but it is not limited to that. It includes one's work and roles more generally. As Gustaf Wingren puts it in his book *Luther on Vocation*, "The life of the home, the relation between parents and children, is vocation, even as is life in the field of labor. . . . From this it is clear that every Christian occupies a multitude of offices at the same time, not just one. . . . All these are vocations."[64] Perkins described vocation as "a certain kind of life, ordained and imposed on man by God, for the common good," implying that vocation extends to all of life.[65]

Several important corollaries follow from the Protestant doctrine of vocation. Since God is the one who calls people to their work, the worker becomes a steward who serves God. Work ceases to be viewed only in itself and instead becomes an act of obedience and service to God. "Whatsoever our callings be," wrote a Puritan, "we serve the Lord Jesus Christ in them."[66] If "God himself is the author of every lawful calling,"[67] the worker becomes a steward, and his or her work an act of service and even worship to God. To perform one's tasks, in this view, is to work in the sight of God: do your work, advised Baxter, "as in

---

63. Perkins, *Vocations or Callings of Men*, in *Works*, 1:752.

64. Gustaf Wingren, *Luther on Vocation*, trans. Carl C. Rasmussen (Philadelphia: Muhlenberg Press, 1957), 5.

65. Perkins, *Vocations or Callings of Men*, in *Works*, 1:750.

66. John Dod and Robert Cleaver, *Ten Sermons. . .* ; quoted in Horton Davies, *Worship and Theology in England: From Cranmer to Hooker, 1534–1603* (Princeton: Princeton University Press, 1970), 66.

67. Perkins, *Vocations or Callings of Men*, in *Works*, 1:750.

[God's] sight, passing to his judgment, in obedience to his will."[68] Cotton Mather's advice was, "Let every Christian walk with God when he works at his calling, and act in his occupation with an eye to God, act as under the eye of God."[69]

Another practical result of the doctrine of Christian calling is that it leads to contentment in one's work. If one's work comes from God, one has a reason to accept it. Luther said, "Nothing is so bad . . . but it becomes sweet and tolerable if only I know and am certain that it is pleasing to God."[70] Calvin was of a similar opinion:

> In all our cares, toils, annoyances, and other burdens, it will be no small alleviation to know that all these are under the superintendence of God. . . . This, too, will afford admirable consolation in following your proper calling. No work will be so mean and sordid as not to have a splendor and value in the eye of God.[71]

In the original Protestant ethic, the doctrine of vocation or calling combined a cluster of related ideas: the providence of God in arranging human work, work as the response of a steward to God, and contentment with one's tasks. John Cotton's advice about work sums it up: "Serve God in thy calling, and do it with cheerfulness, and faithfulness, and a heavenly mind."[72]

Work as Service to God and Society

A main emphasis of the original Protestant ethic was to delineate the motivations and rewards of work. The rewards of work were overwhelmingly conceived as spiritual and moral. Work glorified God and benefited society. William Perkins sounded the keynote:

> The main end of our lives . . . is to serve God in the serving of men in the works of our callings. . . . Some man will say perchance: What, must we not labor in our callings to maintain our families? I answer: this must be done: but this is not the scope and end of our lives. The main end of our lives is to do service to God in serving of man.[73]

According to John Preston, "Our aim must be God's glory and the public good."[74] And Richard Steele advised, "Direct all to the right end, the

---

68. Baxter, *Christian Directory*, in *Works*, 1:97.
69. Mather, *Christian at His Calling*, in *Puritanism*, 127.
70. Luther, *The Estate of Marriage*, in *Luther's Works*, 45:49.
71. Calvin, *Institutes of the Christian Religion*, 3.10.6, trans. Henry Beveridge (Grand Rapids: Eerdmans, 1972), 2:35.
72. Cotton, *Way of Life*, 450.
73. Perkins, *Vocations or Callings of Men*, in *Works*, 1:757.
74. Preston, *Remedy against Covetousness*, 44.

honour of God, the public good as well as your private commodity, and then every step and stroke in your trade is sanctified. You are working for God, who will reward you to your heart's content."[75]

Although the Reformers and Puritans generally believed that one should remain loyal to one's calling and avoid casual changes in occupation, they did not uncritically accept the vocational structure of their day.[76] Virtually every Protestant writer on the subject spoke of "lawful" or "warrantable" or "honest" callings, implying that some occupations did not measure up to the standard of Christian morality. The original Protestants' grasp of the moral and spiritual goals of work provided a standard by which to judge the choice of a vocation. As William Ames wrote,

> It is not enough that one should simply work: He must work for what is good, Eph. 4:28. Quietly and diligently let him follow an occupation which agrees with the will of God and the profit of men, 1 Thess. 4:11, 12; 2 Thess. 3:12.[77]

A group of Puritan ministers that met in Boston in 1699 agreed that no occupation "is lawful but what is useful unto human society."[78]

In a similar vein, Baxter urged people to

> Choose that employment or calling . . . in which you may be most serviceable to God. Choose not that in which you may be most rich or honourable in the world; but that in which you may do most good, and best escape sinning.[79]

75. Steele, *Tradesman's Calling*, 92.

76. The charge is made by Paul Marshall, "Vocation, Work and Jobs," in *Labour of Love: Essays on Work*, ed. Josina Zylstra (Toronto: Wedge, 1980), 12–14. On the contrary, Baxter wrote that "the first and principal thing to be intended in the choice of a trade or calling for yourselves or children is the service of God and the public good. . . . Some callings are employed about matters of so little use . . . that he that may choose better should be loathe to take up with one of these, though possibly in itself it may be lawful" (*Christian Directory*, in *Works*, 1:377). Calvin's commentary on 1 Corinthians 7:20 explains what he means by his cautions against easily leaving one's occupation for another; Calvin said Paul "only wishes to correct the thoughtless eagerness which impels some to change their situation without any proper reason. . . . He does not lay it down that each person must remain in a certain way of life, once he has adopted it; but, on the other hand, he condemns the restlessness which prevents individuals from remaining contentedly as they are." Cotton Mather wrote, "When a man is become unfit for his business, or his business becomes unfit for him, unquestionably he may leave it; and a man may be otherwise invited sometimes justly to change his business. . . . But many a man, merely from covetousness and from discontent throws up his business" (*A Christian at His Calling*, in McGiffert, *Puritanism*, 127).

77. William Ames, *The Marrow of Theology*, ed. John D. Eusden (Boston: Pilgrim, 1968), 322.

78. Cotton Mather, *Magnalia Christi Americana* (New York: Russell and Russell, 1967), 2:270.

79. Baxter, *Christian Directory*, in *Works*, 1:114.

If "two callings equally conduce to the public good," added Baxter, "and one of them hath the advantage of riches and the other is more advantageous to your souls, the latter must be preferred."[80] The Protestant emphasis on the moral and spiritual ends of work was not merely idealistic theory; it had a practical influence on how people viewed their work.

Moderation in Work

In addition to providing a balanced Christian view of the goal and rewards of work, the Protestant work ethic aimed at an ideal of moderation in work. Moderation involves a golden mean between opposite extremes. This is what the Protestant ethic proclaimed in theory.

On the one side, the Protestant ethic avoided idleness and laziness. "Certainly God curses laziness and loafing," said Calvin, who went on to denounce "idlers and good-for-nothing individuals who live by the sweat of others."[81] Two "damnable sins" that Perkins rebuked were "idleness, whereby the duties of our callings ... are neglected or omitted," and "slothfulness, whereby they are performed slackly and carelessly."[82]

On the other side, the Protestant ethic condemned excessive devotion to work and wealth. English Puritan Philip Stubbes wrote, "So far from covetousness and from immoderate care would the Lord have us that we ought not this day to care for tomorrow, for (saith he) sufficient to the day is the travail of the same."[83] John Cotton urged moderation in work with the statement that although the Christian must "labor most diligently in his calling, yet his heart is not set upon these things."[84] According to Richard Steele, "Diligence walks between [the] extremes" of (on the one hand) "idleness and carelessness ... and on the other hand immoderate carking and slavish drudging."[85]

Since attitudes toward work and wealth have always been closely intertwined, we might note that the Protestant affirmation of moderation extended to possessions as well as work. Perkins denounced "excessive seeking of worldly wealth, when men keep no measure or moderation."[86] Mather spoke out against people's "insatiable desire after land

---

80. Ibid., 377.

81. Calvin; quoted in Andre Bieler, *The Social Humanism of Calvin*, trans. Paul T. Fuhrmann (Richmond: John Knox, 1961), 45.

82. Perkins, *Vocations or Callings of Men*, in *Works*, 1:752.

83. Philip Stubbes, *The Anatomy of the Abuses in England*; quoted in Tawney, *Rise of Capitalism*, 216.

84. Cotton, as quoted by Perry Miller, *The New England Mind: The Seventeenth Century* (Cambridge, Mass.: Harvard University Press, 1939), 42.

85. Steele, *Tradesman's Calling*, 77.

86. Perkins, *A Godly and Learned Exposition upon Christ's Sermon in the Mount*, in *Works*, 3:163.

and worldly accommodations . . . only so that they might have elbow-room enough in the world."[87] Steele called it "a sin most repugnant to contentedness" when a person shows "an unsatiable desire of riches; when a man will be rich, or else thinks he cannot be happy."[88]

It is in this context of setting boundaries to work that we can understand Protestant sabbatarianism, which was the particular preoccupation of the English and American Puritans. For them, Sunday observance was part of social action. This explains why not all sabbatarians were Puritans. The reason national and local governments of the time were so zealous in passing and enforcing sabbath laws was that without it some employers would have forced people to work seven days a week.

Sunday observance protected workers who (in Baxter's words) "would be left remediless under such masters as would both oppress them with labour, and restrain them from God's service."[89] Arthur Hildersham said that Sunday observance was especially necessary for hardworking people who were in danger of having their hearts "corrupted and glued to the world."[90] A modern authority on the Puritans claims that "in the seventeenth century there was only one way in which the industrious sort could be protected from themselves: by the total prohibition of Sunday work."[91]

Summary

The Protestant work ethic, rightly so-called, is almost the opposite of what people today take it to mean. Starting from the assumption that work is a virtue and idleness a vice, the original Protestants asserted the sanctity of all legitimate types of work, viewing work as the response of a steward to a call from God. Service to God and society was viewed as the ultimate goal of work, which is to be undertaken with a sense of moderation. These ideas about work are not simply specimens in a historical museum; they remain a standard to guide Christian thinking and practice today.

The Protestant Ethic Today

Is the Protestant ethic alive today? It shows signs of revival, though as yet there is no visible articulation of its comprehensive vision on

87. Mather, *Magnalia Christi Americana*, 2:324.
88. Steele, *Tradesman's Calling*, 177.
89. Baxter, *Catechizing of Families*, in *Works*, 4:129.
90. Arthur Hildersham, *CLII Lectures Upon Psalm LI*; quoted in Hill, *Society and Puritanism*, 175.
91. Hill, *Society and Puritanism*, 152.

work. We see plenty of vestiges of a secularized version of the Puritan ethic in which success is the goal of work and the impetus for a good deal of overwork. We also find bits and pieces of the original Protestant ethic in Christian circles, especially in the lay movement noted in chapter 16.

The most systematic articulation of the tenets of the original Protestant view of work that I have seen is Pope John Paul II's encyclical *On Human Work*, published in 1981.[92] The Puritans would have loved the document, right down to its arbitrary italicizing. Since the Catholic tradition fares poorly in the historical orientation of my book, I want to balance the picture by documenting how thoroughly the official Catholic position has changed in the latter twentieth century.

The dominant impression that one derives from the pope's sixty-six-page booklet is the conviction that work carries tremendous dignity. Work "is a fundamental dimension of man's existence on earth" (5). It "has ethical value of its own" (16). Work "corresponds to man's dignity" and "expresses this dignity and increases it" (23). Through it a person "not only transforms nature" but "also achieves fulfillment as a human being" (23).

What reasons are adduced for this enthusiastic endorsement of work? The same reasons that the Reformers and Puritans adduced. In pragmatic terms, work is "an obligation, . . . a duty, on the part of man" (39). It is such "both because the Creator commanded it and because of his own humanity, which requires work in order to be maintained and developed" (39). Through work "man must earn his daily bread" (5).

Important theological reasons buttress this practical reason, as the encyclical ranges over exactly the same biblical and doctrinal data that the original Protestants made so much of. The Pope insists on rooting his "gospel of work" in the Bible, from which he repeatedly quotes. "The source of the church's conviction" in regard to work "is above all the revealed word of God" (11). The Church thinks of human beings not only in the light of human reason "but in the first place in the light of the revealed word of the living God" (11).

The biblical foundation of the human dignity of work comes from Genesis 1–3. From it we learn that man was made in "the image and likeness of God Himself" and placed in the earth to subdue it (5). "From the beginning therefore" people are "called to work" (5). The God who created people in his image gave people a mandate to subdue the earth, and in carrying out this mandate "every human being reflects the very action of the Creator of the universe" (12) and "shares by his work in

92. John Paul II, *On Human Work* (Boston: Daughters of St. Paul, 1981). For an analytic critique of the encyclical, see Miroslav Volf, "On Human Work: An Evaluation of the Key Ideas of the Encyclical *Laborem Exercens*," *Scottish Journal of Theology* 37 (1984):65–79.

the activity of the Creator" (57). After the Fall, "God's fundamental and original intention with regard to man . . . was not withdrawn or cancelled out even when man, having broken the original covenant with God," found that work was transformed by the curse into toil (22).

The dignity of human work as cooperation with God "was given particular prominence by Jesus Christ" (59), who "was Himself a man of work" and "belongs to the 'working world'" (59). In his parables of the kingdom, Jesus "constantly refers to human work" (60). Furthermore, "the books of the Old Testament contain many references to human work" (60), and the teaching and example of Christ in regard to work find "a particularly lively echo in the teaching of the Apostle Paul" (60).

All of this means that there is no cleavage between sacred and secular spheres of life. In speaking out "on work from the viewpoint of its human value and of the moral order to which it belongs," the church is fulfilling "one of her important tasks within the service that she renders to the evangelical message as a whole" (56). "Even by their secular activities" Christians can assist one another "to live holier lives," and "in this way the world will be permeated by the spirit of Christ" (59).

One practical result of this orientation is that common work carries full dignity and importance in God's sight. The value of work depends not primarily on "the kind of work being done" but "on the one who is doing it" (16). "Participation in God's activity" reaches even to "the most ordinary everyday activities" (58).

The encyclical places special emphasis on work within the family. The work of the mother, because it is unpaid and often lowly, needs to be protected from stigma. It "will redound to the credit of society" to free mothers for "the need that children have for care, love and affection in order that they may develop into responsible, morally and religiously mature and psychologically stable persons" (46–47). For this to happen, society will need to "make it possible for a mother—without inhibiting her freedom, without psychological or practical discrimination, and without penalizing her as compared with other women—to devote herself to taking care of her children" (47).

All of these ideas about work constitute a "spirituality of work" (61) in which work is placed in relation to one's spiritual walk with God. Work is something that "the whole person, body and spirit, participates in" (56). In order for "the work of the individual human being" to be "given the meaning which it has in the eyes of God," and to enable work to enter "into the salvation process," an "inner effort on the part of the human spirit, guided by faith, hope and charity" is required (56). The message of the church in regard to work should be one that "will help all people to come closer, through work, to God, the Creator and Redeemer, to participate in His salvific plan for man and the world and to deepen their friendship with Christ in their lives by accepting, through faith, a living participation in His threefold mission as Priest, Prophet and King" (56–57). As for the suffering that toil often entails, "the Christian finds in human work a small part of the Cross of Christ" and accepts it in the "spirit of redemption" (63).

This is the official Catholic view of work today. The original Protestants would have been very pleased. Protestants would do well to take the encyclical seriously.

Further Reading

R. H. Tawney, *Religion and the Rise of Capitalism* (1926).
Robert S. Michaelsen, "Changes in the Puritan Concept of Calling or Vocation," *New England Quarterly* 26 (1953): 315–36.
Christopher Hill, *Society and Puritanism in Pre-Revolutionary England* (1964).
Leland Ryken, *Worldly Saints: The Puritans As They Really Were* (1986).

Of course there is no substitute for reading the Puritans at first hand. Several key Puritan texts have been excerpted in modern anthologies:

John Cotton, *Christian Calling*, 319–27, in vol. 1 *The Puritans*, revised edition, ed. Perry Miller and Thomas H. Johnson (1963).
Cotton Mather, *A Christian at His Calling*, 122–27, in *Puritanism and the American Experience*, ed. Michael McGiffert (1969).
William Perkins, *A Treatise of the Vocations or Callings of Men*, 35–59, in *Puritan Political Ideas, 1558–1794*, ed. Edmund S. Morgan (1965).

9

"Honest Mirth and Delight"

Did the Puritans Ever Play?

"Puritanism is the haunting fear that someone, somewhere, may be happy." So thought H. L. Mencken, who tried to debunk the Puritans.[1] Thomas More, a Catholic contemporary of William Tyndale, who often is considered the first Puritan, gave the opposite assessment. He found the Protestant religion of Tyndale overly indulgent. He described its adherents as people who "loved no lenten fast" but instead "eat fast and drink fast and lust fast in their lechery."[2]

Puritanism, we are told today, "damages the human soul, renders it hard and gloomy, deprives it of sunshine and happiness."[3] Such a charge would have come as quite a surprise to the Quaker George Fox, a contemporary of the Puritans who despised their "ribbons and lace and costly apparel," as well as their "sporting and feasting."[4]

Did the Puritans Outlaw Fun?
Examining Some Common Charges

The Protestant movement has been even more ridiculed and misrepresented for its attitude toward leisure than for its ideas about work.

1. H. L. Mencken; quoted in Ralph Barton Perry, *Puritanism and Democracy* (New York: Vanguard, 1944), 239.
2. Quoted by C. S. Lewis, "Donne and Love Poetry in the Seventeenth-Century," in *Seventeenth Century Studies Presented to Sir Herbert Grierson* (Oxford: Oxford University Press, 1938), 74.
3. Langdon Mitchell; quoted in Perry, *Puritanism and Democracy*, 240.
4. George Fox, *Journal* (London: J. M. Dent and Sons, 1924), 151.

The Puritans have taken the brunt of the attack, so I will accordingly speak of "the Puritans" in this chapter. I will begin by assessing the accuracy of some common charges.

Charge 1: The Puritans Were Opposed to Fun.

Untrue. Against the modern debunkers' charges that Puritanism damages the human spirit, we may place statements such as these by the Puritans themselves: "God would have our joys to be far more than our sorrows;"[5] Christians "may be merry at their work, and merry at their meat";[6] "there is a kind of smiling and joyful laughter . . . which may stand with . . . the best man's piety";[7] "joy suits no person so well as a Christian."[8] William Bradshaw wrote that it is the purpose of Satan to persuade us that "in the kingdom of God there is nothing but sighing and groaning and fasting and prayer," whereas the truth is that "in his house there is marrying and giving in marriage, . . . feasting and rejoicing."[9]

Charge 2: The Puritans Did Not Allow Sports or Recreation.

This charge is largely false. The more scholars learn about the Puritans, the more questionable these older views of their hostility to recreation become. The best source of information is Hans-Peter Wagner's study entitled *Puritan Attitudes towards Recreation in Early Seventeenth-Century America*.[10] His research shows that the Puritans enjoyed such varied sports as hunting, fishing, bowling, reading, music, swimming, skating, and archery. Richard Sibbes, the famous British Puritan, said regarding recreations that Christians should "enjoy them as liberties, with thankfulness to God, that allows us these liberties to refresh ourselves."[11] William Burkitt wrote that

> God has . . . adjudged some diversion or recreation . . . to be both needful and expedient. . . . A wise and good man . . . is forced to . . . let religion choose such recreations as are healthful, short, recreative, and proper, to refresh both mind and body.[12]

5. Richard Baxter, *The Saints' Everlasting Rest* (Westwood, N.J.: Revell, 1962), 182.
6. Richard Rogers, *Seven Treatises*; quoted in Irvonwy Morgan, *The Godly Preachers of the Elizabethan Church* (London: Epworth, 1965), 143.
7. Richard Bernard, *The Isle of Man* (London: Edward Blackmore, 1630), unpaginated material at end of book.
8. Burkitt, *Poor Man's Help*, 22.
9. William Bradshaw, *A Marriage Feast* (London: Fulke Clifton, 1620), 14.
10. Hans-Peter Wagner, *Puritan Attitudes towards Recreation in Early Seventeenth-Century America* (Frankfurt: Verlag Peter Lang, 1982).
11. Richard Sibbes, *King David's Epitaph*, in *The Complete Works of Richard Sibbes* (Edinburgh: James Nichol, 1863), 6:507.
12. Burkitt, *Poor Man's Help*, 18.

Cotton Mather preached a sermon on "how to employ the leisure of the winter for the glory of God."[13] John Downame encouraged moderate indulgence in "walking in pleasant places, conferences which are delightful without offence, poetry, music, shooting, and such other allowable sports as best fit with men's several dispositions for their comfort and refreshing."[14] Most telling of all was a parliamentary act of 1647, when the Puritans controlled Parliament, that decreed that every second Tuesday of the month was to be a holiday when all shops, warehouses, and places of business were to be closed from eight in the morning until eight in the evening for the recreation of the workers.[15]

Charge 3: The Puritans Passed Laws Prohibiting Some Forms of Recreation.

This is true, but it does not represent opposition to recreation in principle. The modern stereotype of the Puritans is based on misreadings of the evidence.

The Puritans rejected all sports on Sundays and selected sports at all times. Their rejection of sports on Sunday was based on their view that the entire day was to be devoted to spiritual activities, chiefly worship and rest from the ordinary concerns of the week. They rejected other sports on moral grounds. These included games of chance, gambling, bear baiting, horse racing, and bowling in or around taverns. By modern standards, some of their prohibitions seem frivolous, such as their outlawing the game of shuffleboard.[16]

If there is any defense of the Puritans on these matters, it is that small concessions can lead to larger issues when placed in the context of one's general lifestyle, and often this context is concealed from us at this late date. Among other considerations, the Puritans were wary of games, idleness, and carousing that occurred in or around taverns. The positive principles that their prohibitions were designed to protect include the good use of time, the virtue of hard work, and self-control.

Charge 4: The Puritans Abolished Many of the Holidays That Had Prevailed in the Middle Ages.

True. Under medieval Catholicism the number of holy days grew to as many as 115 days per year, not counting Sundays.[17] The Puritans re-

13. Wagner, *Puritan Attitudes*, 14.

14. John Downame, *The Christian Warfare*; quoted in Stephen Foster, *Their Solitary Way: The Puritan Social Ethic in the First Century of Settlement in New England* (New Haven: Yale University Press, 1971), 106.

15. Percy Scholes, *The Puritans and Music in England and New England* (London: Oxford University Press, 1934), 110–11.

16. Max Kaplan, *Leisure in America: A Social Inquiry* (New York: John Wiley and Sons, 1960), 151.

17. Kelly, *Leisure*, 57.

jected such days on religious grounds, and whatever leisure elements they contained went as well. We should remember that social conditions were changing as society became less and less rural, so the loss of church holidays would have occurred for economic reasons quite apart from the Puritan movement.

What the critics fail to mention is that the Puritans had their own religious activities that often took the place of Catholic holy days. One was the rigorous keeping of Sunday as a day of rest and worship. Also, the Puritans loved visiting and feasts. The idea of celebrating the American Thanksgiving Day was vintage Puritanism, and we might note that the original thanksgiving celebration lasted at least three days.[18] In fact, the Puritans made a regular practice of calling their own family days of thanksgiving, to which they usually invited friends and neighbors. Consider the following entry from a Puritan diary of such an event:

> We had a solemn day of thanksgiving at my house for my wife's and son's recovery; my son Eliezer began, Mr. Dawson, John proceeded, I concluded with preaching, prayer; we feasted 50 persons and upwards, blessed be God.[19]

One Puritan minister's diary indicates that he attended anywhere from forty-seven to sixty-four such days of thanksgiving in a typical year.[20]

We should also note that Puritan New England celebrated events that have since dropped out of the calendar. Days of festivity were set aside for ordinations of ministers, lecture days, election days, training days, commencement days for courts, and graduation days for colleges.[21] Wedding celebrations were yet another occasion for holidays.

Charge 5: The Puritans Had a Negative Attitude toward Culture and the Arts.

This is only partly true. Their bad reputation rests partly on a misreading of the evidence. For example, it is well known that the Puritans removed all artwork and organs from their churches. However, they were objecting to Catholic worship and ceremony, not to music and art themselves.[22] In fact, after removing organs and paintings from

18. Wagner, *Puritan Attitudes*, 14.

19. Oliver Heywood, *Diary*; quoted in Horton Davies, *The Worship of the English Puritans* (Westminster: Dacre, 1948), 282.

20. Davies, *Worship*, 283.

21. Wagner, *Puritan Attitudes*, 18.

22. The best source to consult is Percy Scholes, *The Puritans and Music in England and New England*. Other helpful sources include these: Joseph Crouch, *Puritanism and Art:*

churches, the Puritans often bought them for private use in their homes.[23] John Cotton wrote a treatise stating the usual objections to musical instruments in church, but he went on to say that he did not "forbid the private use of any instrument of music."[24] Oliver Cromwell removed an organ from an Oxford chapel to his own residence at Hampton Court, where he employed a private organist. When one of his daughters was married, Cromwell engaged a 48-piece orchestra to accompany the dancing.[25] While confined to prison for preaching, John Bunyan not only wrote fictional stories but secretly made a flute out of a chair leg.

On the negative side, although the Puritans fostered religious literature, they had a distressingly hostile view toward other forms of literature.[26] It is to their discredit that they closed the theaters at a time when Shakespeare was common fare, though even here we should remember that the objections were partly political and moral, not necessarily extending to the act of reading plays. It is also necessary to distinguish between "low-brow" Puritans and educated Puritans. The latter were thoroughly saturated in classical literature and were, in fact, the earliest translators of the classics into English.[27]

Charge 6: The Puritans Took the Color Out of Life by Wearing Drab, Unfashionable Clothes.

Untrue. The Puritans dressed according to the fashions of their class and time. It is true that black carried connotations of dignity and formality (as it does today) and was standard for clothes worn on Sundays and special occasions.

_____

Inquiry into a Popular Fallacy (London: Cassell, 1910); Edward Dowden, *Puritan and Anglican: Studies in Literature* (London: Kegan Paul, 1910); Roland Frye, *Perspective on Man: Literature and the Christian Tradition* (Philadelphia: Westminster, 1961), 171–79; Lawrence Sasek, *The Literary Temper of the English Puritans* (New York: Greenwood, 1969); Sacvan Bercovitch, *The American Puritan Imagination* (Cambridge: Cambridge University Press, 1974); Robert Daly, *God's Altar: The World and the Flesh in Puritan Poetry* (Berkeley: University of California Press, 1978); John Wilson, "Calvin and the Arts," *Third Way*, 2, no. 2 (1978): 3–5; Barbara K. Lewalski, *Protestant Poetics and the Seventeenth-Century Religious Lyric* (Princeton: Princeton University Press, 1979); Emory Elliott, ed., *Puritan Influences in American Literature* (Urbana: University of Illinois Press, 1979); Alan Sinfield, *Literature in Protestant England, 1560–1660* (London: Croom Helm, 1983); E. Beatrice Boston, *John Bunyan: Allegory and Imagination* (London: Croom Helm, 1984).

23. Scholes, *Puritans and Music*, 6.

24. Ibid., 5.

25. Ibid.

26. For information about the Puritans' negative attitudes toward literature, see Sasek, and Russell Fraser, *The War Against Poetry* (Princeton: Princeton University Press, 1970).

27. See C. H. Conley, *The First English Translators of the Classics* (New Haven: Yale University Press, 1927).

The Quaker George Fox, a contemporary of the Puritans, paints quite a different picture of them from the modern conception. As I noted at the beginning of this chapter, Fox condemned their "ribbons and lace and costly apparel." Surviving inventories of clothes show the popularity of russet, various shades of orange-brown, red, blue, green, yellow, and purple.[28]

Summary

Most of the modern charges against the Puritans are either untrue or exaggerated. They tend to be based on the Puritans' bias against selected *manifestations* of leisure activities that were acceptable to the Puritans *in principle*. Within their religious and moral framework, the Puritans engaged in a healthy range of leisure activities.

Puritan Contributions to Leisure

Out of the mixture of good and bad attitudes toward leisure that we find among the Puritans, it is not hard to extract the positive contributions they made. These same principles will make a reappearance in Part 5. Because this chapter ends by crititicizing the Puritans' utilitarian defense of leisure, I want to accentuate here the most attractive features of their leisure theory.

A Religious Context for Leisure

When the Puritans spoke of leisure, they placed it in a spiritual context of receiving a gift from God. The result is some of the most heartwarming statements about the need for leisure and about how we should receive it that one will find in the history of writing on the subject.

According to the Puritans, leisure is not simply an impersonal phenomenon in our lives: it is a gift of God, who is its source. Thomas Adams thus called God "the giver" of the delights of leisure.[29] Thomas Gataker said regarding the delights of life that "the godly man hath them as favours bestowed on him by God."[30]

Several corollaries follow. One is the good conscience with which we can enjoy leisure. The Puritans' favorite term for a conscionable activ-

28. John Demos, *A Little Commonwealth: Family Life in Plymouth Colony* (New York: Oxford University Press, 1970), 53–54.

29. Thomas Adams, *The Works of Thomas Adams* (Edinburgh: James Nichol, 1861), 3:134.

30. Thomas Gataker, *The Joy of the Just* (London: Fulke Clifton, 1623), 18.

ity was "lawful," with the adjective "honest" running a close second. Leisure and recreation emphatically bore that stamp of approval. Richard Baxter, for example, asserted that "no doubt some sport and recreation is lawful, yea needful, and therefore a duty to some men."[31] Thomas Adams said that "men may eat and drink even to honest delight,"[32] while Gataker claimed that "no man may eat his meat with more delight, or use his honest recreations and disports with more comfort, . . . than the godly man may."[33] The effect of statements like these is to provide an atmosphere of good conscience that is a prerequisite to any full enjoyment of an activity.

Another corollary of believing that God is the source of leisure is that it opens the way for leisure to be received as a gift with gratitude to the giver. Richard Bernard thus said that "the creatures of God" (the Puritan term for the delights of life in this world) are to be "received with thanksgiving."[34] For Gataker the right frame of mind for enjoying leisure activities is to be "heartily thankful to God for them."[35]

At stake also is the view of God that emerges from this general drift of thought. According to Adams, "Let no teacher make the way to heaven more thorny than God himself made it and meant it. . . . The world hath ways enough to vex us; we need not be our own tormentors."[36] "Christ Jesus is no enemy to honest mirth and delight," wrote William Bradshaw; if he had been, "surely then would not Christ have been so often invited to feasts as he was; or if he had, he would not have frequented them so often."[37] Recreation is one of God's mercies to the human race—evidence of his desire that we have not only life but abundant life: "The merciful God is pleased, out of his bounty, not only to allow his creatures what is for necessity, but also what is for delight."[38]

Most attractive of all is the Puritan conviction that God wants us to have leisure and recreation and that, in fact, it gives him pleasure when we enjoy these delights. Adams expresses it best: "Our lawful pleasures are his pleasures."[39] For Gataker, the pleasures that God gives us are "effects and fruits of his love," which "doth exceedingly improve [the godly person's] joy and delight in them: since it is the giver oft that joyeth a man more than the gift."[40] For Bradshaw, an assurance of God's

31. Baxter, *Christian Directory*, in *Works*, 1:386.

32. Adams, *Works of Thomas Adams*, 3:134.

33. Gataker, *Joy of the Just*, 18.

34. Richard Bernard, *Ruth's Recompense* (London: Simon Waterson, 1628), 202–3.

35. Gataker, *Joy of the Just*, 18.

36. Adams, *Works of Thomas Adams*, 3:134.

37. William Bradshaw, *A Marriage Feast* (London: Fulke Clifton, 1620), 13–14.

38. George Swinnock, *The Christian Man's Calling*, in *The Works* (Edinburgh: James Nichol, 1968), 1:289.

39. Adams, *Works of Thomas Adams*, 3:134.

40. Gataker, *Joy of the Just*, 18.

presence in our leisure actually increases the delight: "The servants of Christ . . . are more merry when he sits at table with them."[41]

Religious Activities as Part of Leisure

I am not at all certain that the Puritans would have approved of putting religious activities under the heading of leisure, but there is a sense in which they put religious activities in the place where others put ordinary recreations. Leisure is typically defined partly in terms of its ability to refresh, to provide a break from the everyday routine, to draw a boundary around the acquisitive aspects of life. By such standards, many of the Puritans' religious activities and exercises infused an element of godly leisure into their lives.

For example, Puritans prized "Christian conference," by which they meant conversation with Christians of like mind that left the conversers refreshed. John Winthrop records in his diary a "conference with a Christian friend or two," adding that "God so blessed it unto us, as we were all much quickened and refreshed by it."[42] An extension of this desire for social interaction was the Puritans' love of dinners and social meals.

The Puritan Sabbath also had a dimension of leisure to it. It set a limit to the acquisitive urge. In fact, William Ames distinguished between proper and improper Sunday activities on the basis of whether they represented a break from weekday work. Inappropriate activities were "those which concern our wealth and profit."[43] Nicholas Bownde similarly argued that we cannot attend to God's business if we are encumbered with worldly business on Sunday.[44]

Refusal to Exempt Leisure from Spiritual and Moral Standards

Another great strength of the Puritans was their refusal to exempt leisure from spiritual and moral considerations. The discussion and practice of leisure in our own century is conducted by most people in an amoral atmosphere in which religious implications are considered irrelevant. This secular spirit has invaded the leisure of many Christians as well.

41. Bradshaw, *Marriage Feast*, 14.
42. John Winthrop, *Winthrop Papers*; quoted in J. Sears McGee, *The Godly Man in Stuart England: Anglicans, Puritans, and the Two Tables, 1620–1670* (New Haven: Yale University Press, 1976), 196.
43. William Ames, *The Marrow of Theology*, ed. John D. Eusden (Boston: Pilgrim, 1968), 299.
44. Nicholas Bownde, *The Doctrine of the Sabbath*; quoted in James T. Dennison, *The Market Day of the Soul: The Puritan Doctrine of the Sabbath in England, 1532–1700* (Lanham, N.Y.: University Press of America, 1983), 39.

The Puritans can stand as a corrective. They expected leisure pursuits to measure up to the criterion of being "lawful." William Perkins, for example, listed four religious and moral principles by which to judge leisure: (1) recreations must be "of the best report"; (2) they must be "profitable to ourselves and others; and they must tend also to the glory of God"; (3) their purpose must be "to refresh our bodies and minds"; and (4) their use "must be moderate and sparing" of time and "of our affection."[45] There is something potentially legalistic about such a list, but its virtue is that it applies religious standards to leisure pursuits.

The same concern for morality in leisure underlies some of the Puritan prohibitions of selected recreations. Dennis Brailsford's history of sport in England correctly ascribes Puritan strictures to moral reasons, noting Puritan "attacks on dancing, for its carnality; on football, for its violence; on maypoles for their paganism; and on sports in general for their despoliation of the Sabbath."[46] The Puritans objected to bear baiting and cock fighting as being cruel to animals and dangerous. They disliked sports at taverns because of the drunkenness and low moral standards that usually prevailed at such places. They objected to plays and fictional romances because of the immoral behavior portrayed in some of them.

Even if we disagree with where the Puritans drew the line, we can commend them for applying Christian moral standards to leisure activities.

Moderation in Leisure

While affirming leisure itself, the Puritans were aware that it could be pursued in excess. It could, for example, take too much of a person's time, as Increase Mather noted: "For a Christian to use recreations is very lawful, and in some cases a great duty, but to waste so much time in any recreation . . . as gamesters usually do at cards and dice, and tables, is heinously sinful."[47] Cotton Mather similarly preached that "moderate recreations . . . are more than a little healthful and useful," but warned that

the most harmless recreations may become very culpable and hurtful for want of observing proper rules with regard to time, place, company, manner. . . . God expects that in everything you . . . act under the governance of reason and virtue, and accordingly that you . . . be always sparing of [di-

45. William Perkins, *The Whole Treatise of the Cases of Conscience,* in *Works* (London: John Legatt, 1631), 2:142.

46. Dennis Brailsford, *Sport and Society Elizabeth to Anne* (London: Routledge and Kegan Paul, 1969), 130.

47. Increase Mather, *Testimony against Several Profane and Superstitious Customs* (London: n.p., 1687), 17.

versions], that you time them well, regulate them prudently, make them give place to business, make them subserve religion.[48]

The Puritans urged moderation not only in the time devoted to recreation but also the money spent on it.[49]

The Ideal of Christian Culture

The stereotype of the Puritans as uneducated and uncultured people is unsupportable. They were highly educated. Moreover, their education gave them an acquaintance with classical culture. At their best, the Puritans valued what I will call Christian culture, including culture that by God's common grace expresses truth and beauty even when produced by non-Christians.

There is evidence that the Puritans favored intellectual and cultural leisure pursuits over physical recreation.[50] The Puritans were great readers, for example, and the study of literature in public schools can be traced back to Puritan schools.[51] Puritan writers of imaginative literature include such giants as Edmund Spenser, John Milton, John Bunyan, and Edward Taylor. Music was also valued by educated Puritans, as Percy Scholes's book *Music in Puritan England and New England* abundantly shows.

The home in which John Milton was raised illustrates the Puritan ideal of Christian culture. Milton's father, who had been put out of his home and permanently disinherited when his Catholic father found him reading an English Bible in his room, was sufficiently accomplished at music to have several of his compositions published. There was an organ in the home. Milton himself was thoroughly acquainted with music and literature during his years at home and college. With the advantage of an upbringing like this, it is perhaps no surprise that Milton could write later in life that "we . . . have need of some delightful intermissions, wherein the enlarged soul . . . may keep her holidays to joy and harmless pastime."[52] Among Milton's poetic tributes to leisure are Sonnet 20 inviting a friend to supper, and his twin poems *L'Allegro* and *Il Penseroso*, which are a catalog of English pleasures that breathe a holiday spirit.

48. Cotton Mather, *Winter-Meditations*, in Wagner, *Puritan Attitudes*, 61.
49. Baxter, *Christian Directory*, in *Works*, 1:387.
50. See Wagner, *Puritan Attitudes*, 86–94, and Scholes, *Puritans and Music*.
51. See Roland Frye, *Perspective on Man: Literature and the Christian Tradition* (Philadelphia: Westminster, 1961), 171–79.
52. John Milton, *Tetrachordon*, in *Complete Prose Works* (New Haven: Yale University Press, 1959), 2:597.

Where the Puritans Failed in Regard to Leisure

Despite much that is positive about the Puritans' attitude toward leisure, the overall picture remains unsatisfactory. Three main failings can be discerned.

A Legalistic Approach to Leisure

The first item for concern about the Puritans' attitude toward leisure is the number of rules with which they surrounded leisure activities. As already noted, the Puritans expected leisure activities to measure up to moral and spiritual standards. But the number of such rules was sometimes so great that the effect was to undermine the Puritans' theoretic endorsement of leisure.

Richard Baxter, for example, devised a list of eighteen qualifications to govern a Christian's choice of leisure.[53] It must be for the ends of serving God and helping us "in our ordinary callings and duty." Recreation must not be profane or obscene, and it must not harm others. Sports are unlawful that "occasion the multiplying of idle words about them." Furthermore, if a person chooses a "less fit and profitable" leisure pursuit "when a better might be chosen, it is . . . sin." The net result of such stipulations is to instill an aura of suspicion about leisure, even though theoretically it is "lawful."

There is a positive side to the Puritans' preoccupation with regulating leisure that should be noted. At least they dignified leisure with conscious choice and credited it with having a moral effect on a person's life. Even though Dennis Brailsford's survey of sport in England paints a largely negative picture of the Puritans' influence on physical sports in English society, he nonetheless concludes regarding Puritanism that "one of its great strengths was that it did ask questions about [recreation's] role and purpose. . . . Just to ask 'what is physical fitness *for?*' was a decisive contribution to the history of physical education."[54]

Being Suspicious of Leisure

The number of rules with which the Puritans circumscribed leisure suggests a related problem. The Puritans were simply too uneasy about leisure. They frequently conveyed the impression of "looking for trouble" as they considered the leisure activities that people pursued in their society. William Burkitt devotes one paragraph to endorsing recreation, followed by nine paragraphs of cautions.[55]

53. Baxter, *Christian Directory,* in *Works,* 1:387.
54. Brailsford, *Sport and Society,* 157.
55. Burkitt, *Poor Man's Help,* 18–20.

The closing of the theaters is a prime example of Puritan uneasiness about leisure. Puritan objections to attending plays encompassed a wide range of arguments that are notably lacking in substance. They included such claims as these: theaters contributed to the spread of plagues; there was danger that the scaffolding of the playhouses might collapse; male actors wore women's clothing and impersonated female characters; attending plays competed with church attendance; it is hypocritical for players to act a role other than their real-life identity; plays appeal to the most sensual people and are repugnant to the "best and wisest persons"; plays were of pagan origin; plays are not associated with godly persons in the Bible; plays have harmed "thousands of young people"; and on and on. The truth is, I believe, that the Puritans were simply uneasy about attending theaters; it did not quite fit their lifestyle and values. They were therefore quick to latch onto any argument against attending theaters.

The same Puritan uneasiness about recreation is evident in other leisure activities that they prohibited. A New England law, for example, ordered constables to "search after all manner of gaming, singing and dancing" and to report "disordered meetings," even when they occurred in private homes.[56] This is similar in tone to a Connecticut law that prohibited "the game called shuffleboard . . . whereby much precious time is spent unfruitfully."[57] The general Puritan tendency was to assume the worst about a leisure activity and to ban it if it carried either the appearance or potential for immorality.[58]

A Utilitarian Attitude toward Leisure

Although the Puritans were not opposed to leisure in principle, their defense of leisure was essentially utilitarian. Leisure was good because it made work possible. It was not valued for its own sake, or viewed as a celebration of life or an enlargement of the human spirit. One Puritan wrote that "recreation belongs not to rest, but to labor; and it is used that men may by it be made more fit to labor."[59] Recreation "serveth only to make us more able to continue in labour," wrote William Perkins.[60] Sibbes called recreations "whettings to be fitter for our call-

56. Records cited by Foster Rhea Dulles, *America Learns to Play: A History of Popular Recreation, 1607–1940* (New York: Appleton Century, 1940), 6.

57. Ibid.

58. For a thorough survey of Puritan commentary that documents this ambivalence (theoretic endorsement, actual mistrust) toward leisure, see Bruce C. Daniels, "Sober Mirth and Pleasant Poisons: Puritan Ambivalence toward Leisure and Recreation in Colonial New England," *American Studies* 34 (1993):121–137.

59. Francis White; quoted in Wagner, *Puritan Attitudes*, 45.

60. Perkins, *A Treatise of the Vocations or Callings of Men*, in *Works*, 1:775.

ings."[61] According to Richard Rogers, the end of our recreations is "to be the fitter to the duties of our calling."[62] For Richard Steele, the purpose of recreations is that "men may be more fitted for their general and particular callings."[63]

This utilitarian leisure ethic was a result of the Puritans' overemphasis on work, and it was closely tied to the question of time. If work is the best use of time, then leisure becomes a frivolous waste of time. The condemnation of time wasting is a major theme throughout Puritan preaching and writing. Baxter equated "pastimes" with "time wasting" and rejected the very word as "infamous."[64] He therefore advised,

> Keep up a high esteem of time and be every day more careful that you lose none of your time. . . . And if vain recreation, dressings, feastings, idle talk, unprofitable company, or sleep be any of them temptations to rob you of any of your time, accordingly heighten your watchfulness and firm resolution against them.[65]

If all of one's time is to be devoted to something useful, leisure will obviously fare poorly. This is often what happened in the Puritans' utilitarian ethic.

Realistically speaking, how much leisure will emerge from a milieu in which the leaders say things like these:

> Let your business engross the most of your time. . . . Be stirring about your business as early as tis convenient. Keep close to your business, until it be convenient you should leave it off.[66]

> Keep thyself in the constant employments of thy calling, and spend not one quarter of an hour in idleness, and allow not leisure to thy thoughts, so much as to think of thy drink and pleasures; much less to thy body to follow it.[67]

Time and work were the fuel that ran the engine of the Puritan ethic. In those rare moments when the engine was not running, leisure was allowed. Puritan paranoia about the dangers of idleness works against the spirit of liberation at the heart of leisure—a spirit expressed by Bertrand Russell's "praise of idleness" and G. K. Chesterton's ideal of being free to do nothing.[68]

61. Sibbes, *King David's Epitaph*, 507.

62. Richard Rogers, *Seven Treatises* (London: Thomas Man and Robert Dexter, 1603), 374.

63. Steele, *Tradesman's Calling*, 70.

64. Baxter, *Christian Directory*, in *Works*, 1:244.

65. Ibid., 1:468.

66. Cotton Mather, *A Christian at His Calling* (Boston: Samuel Sewall, 1701), 48–49.

67. Baxter, *Christian Directory*, in *Works*, 1:328.

68. Bertrand Russell, *In Praise of Idleness and Other Essays* (London: Allen and Unwin; 1935); Chesterton, "On Leisure," in *Generally Speaking*, 111.

Summary

Although the Puritans did not reject leisure in theory, and although they enjoyed many leisure pursuits (especially the more intellectual types such as reading), their practice often revealed a general distrust of leisure. Their extensive rules showed their uneasiness about leisure, and they made their leisure ethic an appendage to their work ethic.

Further Reading

Percy Scholes, *The Puritans and Music in England and New England* (1934).
Hans-Peter Wagner, *Puritan Attitudes towards Recreation in Early Seventeenth-Century New England* (1982).
Leland Ryken, *Worldly Saints: The Puritans As They Really Were* (1986).

PART 4

Inadequate Solutions

10

Hoping for the Best but Not Achieving It

Contemporary Secular Thinking about Work and Leisure

The general structure of this book is a movement from the problems of work and leisure in our world to a consideration of biblically grounded solutions. Before looking at what the Bible says, I want to take a wide-angle view at what secular and Christian thinkers are saying about work and leisure today.

I have called these ideas "inadequate solutions," but this does not mean that current thinking is totally wrong. Some good ideas and practices are floating around in our society. Nor do I mean that all individuals are on the wrong path in regard to work and leisure. It is the general trends of thought which, while not totally wrong, are demonstrably inadequate.

The Secular Context

I came to do my research for this book already conversant with what the Protestant tradition and the Bible said about work and leisure. What struck me most forcibly about contemporary writing on the subject was its secularism, by which I mean its absence of religious reference.

One obvious result is that the agenda of secular writers omits a lot that Christians want to see discussed. Secular time use studies act as though Christian service and worship are nonexistent. The weekend has emerged as a major theme among popular writers on leisure, but one looks in vain for any awareness that people might go to church on Sunday and regard it as a holy day rather than simply a day off from work. Secular writers betray an ignorance or lack of interest in how the weekly schedule of Christians differs from what prevails in society at large.

Loss of Transcendent Authority

A more important result of the secular ground rules for discussing work and leisure is the loss of any transcendent authority to authenticate the claims that writers make. Through the centuries, Christian solutions to the problems of work and leisure have rooted themselves in the Bible. The result, from the Reformation onward, has been a prophetic sense of authority to pronouncements that the Church has made about work and leisure. By contrast, contemporary secular writing offers nothing more than the voice of human opinion. Pronouncements that once carried the force of a moral imperative seem little more than thoughts to ponder, devoid of any sense of authority. The average person pays no attention whatever to what the experts on work and leisure are saying. Indeed, most of them do not read enough to even know that experts are theorizing on these subjects.

When God dropped out of consideration, the sense of vocation that undergirded attitudes toward work for at least two centuries also evaporated. The very concept of calling implies that there is a God who calls. The chasm between the Protestant view of calling and secular attitudes toward work cannot be bridged. It is no wonder that a recovery of the Christian doctrine of work in our day is virtually synonymous with a recovery of the doctrine of vocation.

Dominance of the Social Sciences

The lack of a prophetic voice is reinforced by the way in which almost all of the current secular writing on work and leisure is done by social scientists, broadly defined. The result is an abundance of descriptive data, but almost no attempt at prescriptive solutions. Surveys of people's attitudes and practices are abundant in this empirical approach. The data is useful in diagnosing current problems and needs in regard to work and leisure, but it offers no clear pathway out of the problems that are diagnosed.

Again the contrast to the Christian past is striking. In the Protestant tradition, beginning in the sixteenth century and continuing today, almost all of the writing on work and leisure has been done by preachers and theologians. What they have had to say carries the authority of the Bible behind it, and lay people have taken notice.

Confused Goals

The bias toward description rather than prescription means that we have a lot of information about what people actually *do* in regard to work and leisure, but no balancing exhortation on what they *should* do. As I have read this material I have been reminded of Albert Einstein's view that we live in a day of perfect means and confused goals. The Christian tradition has had a lot to say about what work and leisure are *for*. Contemporary secular thinking has little to say on the matter. It tells us *how* people work and play but not *why*.

The contemporary vacuum will emerge at once if we simply set it beside its opposite from the past. Here, for example, is a typical statement by Martin Luther:

> If you ask an insignificant maidservant why she scours a dish or milks the cow she can say: I know that the thing I do pleases God, for I have God's word and commandment.[1]

Here is a prophetic voice appealing to a transcendent authority on *why* people should work and *how* they should work in light of that reason. The contemporary spirit would replace this with a Harris poll on how people *feel* about their work.

This is not so much an inadequate solution as a failure to produce a solution. The contemporary problems surrounding work and leisure require a great deal more than a descriptive survey of where we stand. That is where the secular spirit and social science orientation of current thinking have let us down.

The Attack on the Work Ethic

One of the most persistent trends on the secular scene is an assault on the work ethic, also called "the Protestant ethic." The attack often comes from leisure theorists, though it is not limited to them.

What we need to do, claims one source, is "escape from the shackles of the work ethic."[2] Another says "The Work Ethic no longer fits the needs of the hour."[3] We are also told that "what we need is a non-work ethic,"[4] and that we must "renounce the false notions of the dignity of

1. Martin Luther, exposition of 1 Peter 2:18–20, in *What Luther Says*, 1500.
2. Ivor Clemitson and George Rodgers, *A Life to Live: Beyond Full Employment* (London: Junction Books, 1981), 174.
3. Roger Clarke, *Work in Crisis: The Dilemma of a Nation* (Edinburgh: Saint Andrew, 1981), 189.
4. Lord Ritchi-Calder, "Education for the Post-Industrial Society, " in *Continuing Education for the Post-Industrial Society*, ed. N. Costello and M. Richardson (Milton Keynes: Open University Press, 1982), 16.

work, the necessity of work, self-fulfillment through work, and . . . the duty to work."[5] And in case we have missed the point: "it appears . . . that society, both individually and collectively, would be happier, would be more harmonious and would have fewer problems if the work ethic were either destroyed or reconstructed."[6]

Two ideas are often encompassed within this attack on the traditional work ethic. One is a prevailing (though usually unstated) presupposition that leisure is good and work as we know it bad. The other is the quest for a scapegoat.

The Priority of Leisure

Certainly the bias among leisure theorists is that leisure is good and work is bad. The bias is a response to a genuine problem: the well-documented trend toward longer working hours and less leisure time. It is only natural that leisure enthusiasts see a strong work ethic as the obstacle to their program.

Offering leisure as a substitute for the traditional work ethic is inadequate, however, because it is unrealistic. Work is the means for sustaining life. In fact, we need to grant priority to work, not because work is more noble or more worthy than leisure, but because it comes before leisure. Work is necessary to maintain our physical existence and well-being. We must work before we have the resources to play.

Furthermore, work gives meaning to leisure. By itself, leisure quickly palls and loses its point. When seen as a contrast to work and a reward for it, leisure assumes its proper meaning and refreshment value. The solution to an overly greedy work ethic is not to starve it but to balance it with a complementary leisure ethic.

The Search for a Scapegoat

Concomitant with recognizing that work has claimed too large a share of people's time and energy is the quest for a scapegoat. Almost uniformly, theorists find what they are looking for in "the Protestant ethic" or "the Puritan ethic"; a variant is to speak of the "icy waters of Calvinism." The real issue that deserves analysis is why some scholars have been so eager to believe Max Weber's thesis in *The Protestant Ethic and the Spirit of Capitalism*.

Two fallacies undermine the critics' case. First, the work ethic they ascribe to the original Protestants is not what they advocated. In many cases it is the opposite. Instead of urging an end to the Protestant ethic,

---

5. A. J. Veal, *Leisure and the Future* (London: Allen and Unwin, 1987), 26–27.

6. Clive Jenkins and Barrie Sherman, *The Leisure Shock* (London: Eyre Methuen, 1981), 15.

those who are discontent with current overwork or lack meaning in work would do better to urge a return to the original Protestant ethic. Such ideals as working to serve God and society, work as stewardship to God, moderation in work, and regarding work as only one of a person's callings in life are not inimical to leisure. On the contrary, leisure depends on our having a work ethic like this.

Second, searching for a scapegoat is a way of evading responsibility for our society's own worst attitudes and practices. The original Protestant ethic has been gone for three centuries. To blame our own warped attitudes toward work on something that has no direct connection with them is to live in a dream world. It is time for the secular world to acknowledge that it is to blame for what had happened since the Protestant work ethic was stripped of its theological core.

Worshiping Work

At the opposite pole from the undervaluing of work that leisure theorists display is the worship of work by a majority of people in Western societies. These people do not have a healthy work ethic. They overvalue work and value it for the wrong reasons. Numerically they dominate the scene.

Advertising as an Index to Contemporary Work Attitudes

The biggest influence on contemporary attitudes toward work, and the best index to them, is modern advertising. Not that it gives us pictures of work. Quite the contrary, its usual strategy is to give us images of a utopia of leisure and self-indulgence.

The reason for the influence of advertising on the modern work ethic is that it makes us want more goods and services. It does not tell us that we have to work like slaves to acquire what is dangled in front of us. We are smart enough to draw that conclusion for ourselves. The prevailing work ethic that modern advertising has created can be called either the *acquisitive ethic* or the *consumer ethic*.

The weakness of the consumer ethic is that it values work for the wrong reason. Its ability to motivate people to work is often impressive, but it motivates people to work for goals that are inferior to the service of God and society, and it tends to make people work too much. Moreover, the consumer goals for which people work cannot be satisfied. The writer of Ecclesiastes recognized this when he observed that "he who loves money will not be satisfied with money, nor he who loves wealth, with gain. This also is vanity" (Ecclesiastes 5:10). Indeed it is. The human appetite for goods is insatiable, and the goods themselves do not satisfy us permanently or at our deepest level of need. The secular solution that motivates people to work hard to enable them to acquire things ends up destroying workers.

The Success Ethic

The consumer ethic is coupled with the *success ethic* and the *career ethic*. These value work as the means toward attaining success, with one of the signs of success being a rising and prestigious career. To achieve success, workers must deny themselves, their families, and their friends. They also usually have to assume a competitive spirit that tramples other people on the way to success.

A new ingredient to the mix is the *feminist work ethic* that has taken the work world by storm in the last two decades. The biggest branch of feminism claims for women the rights and opportunities that have traditionally been open only to men. Many of these opportunities have been in the world of work. For these feminists, the goal is to beat men at their own game, or at least to claim an equal share of the rewards of work.

The inadequacies of this feminist work ethic are multiple. One is that it has only served to enlarge the scope of overwork and stress to encompass a larger segment of the population. This does not mean that women should be denied equal opportunity with men. But if the success ethic *itself* is a problem, then extending its domain compounds the problem instead of solving it.

A natural consequence of an acquisitive view of work is that non-paid work is not highly regarded. The homemaker's work has been the biggest loser. The feminist claim might be right (though the case has not been proven) that the homemaker's work and role did not receive its due in the pre-feminist era, but there can be little doubt that this role has suffered an eclipse in dignity as feminism has gained in ascendancy. Several years ago when Barbara Bush spoke at Smith College, a New England women's college, there was a mass exodus of students from the auditorium when she stood up to speak, in protest of the fact that Mrs. Bush has devoted her life to being a housewife and supporting her husband's career rather than pursuing her own career.

Summary

The dominant work ethic in the Western world today is economically based. It values work as a stepping stone to the acquisition of either goods or prestige. The deficiencies of this work ethic are that it is sometimes insufficient to motivate people to their best work, it induces many people to overwork, it devalues unpaid work, and it ignores more enlightened motivations and rewards for work.

False Hopes

Another factor in current secular thinking is that proposed solutions raise false hopes for work and leisure. These solutions beckon us to an illusory world and are sometimes openly sentimental in their appeals.

Romantic Nostalgia

My research for this book uncovered an undertow of romantic nostalgia for a rural past when people lived close to nature. This simpler past is offered as a solution to the problems of both work and leisure.

In regard to work, farming is idealized as an antidote to the problems of industrial work. In place of specialized labor in which workers do only one thing, farmers do everything that farm work entails. Farmers also see the products of their labor. The picture often painted is one of contented farmers standing in their fields or riding in their air-conditioned tractors.

Speaking as someone who grew up on a farm, I must say that this romantic view of farm work bears little resemblance to reality. Farm work has more than its share of sheer drudgery. Our problem today is that we picture farm work from the vantage point of never having done it. Furthermore, there simply are not enough farms available for this to be a viable solution for more than an infinitesimal segment of the population.

Leisure theorists also idealize the rural past. They speak glowingly of a time when people enjoyed more leisure than they do today. After all, there was no cleavage between the place of work and play, as there is in an urban situation.

Speaking again from my farm background, I would simply ask: What play? On a farm one is never free from the setting of work; the moment one looks out the kitchen window one sees the place of work. Moreover, people who live on farms today do pretty much what their city counterparts do when they have time for leisure: they either jump in the car to find entertainment in town or they plop down in front of the television in their living room.

The romantic view, like the Marxist view, is entirely too eager for easy answers that would convince us that the problems of work are essentially external and therefore they can be solved by changing the externalities of work.

The Utopian Impulse

Another leading theme among those who write on work is that institutional change is the solution to the problems of work. Faced with the problems of industrial work, these people offer an overhaul of the social and economic structures as the hope for reform. I call this the utopian impulse because it envisions an institutional key to ushering in the good society.

The most common institutional solution, especially among British thinkers, is socialism. Again and again I have read books about the modern problems of work that wind their way toward a socialist solution in the final pages.

The utopian impulse is not wrong, but it is inadequate. While it is a good impulse to assume that things may be done either better or worse and to work toward doing them better, the hope that institutional change will solve our social problems overlooks the way in which people and situations in a fallen world foul up all human institutions. Furthermore, if institutional changes could deliver on their promises, they would have established a track record of success by now. But all that the utopian designers have produced is pockets of improved work situations.

Furthermore, our jobs are only part of the work that we do. All the unpaid work that we do is left unaccounted for in the utopian scheme. Taking the car to the mechanic and then sitting in the waiting room, painting the house, and doing the dishes are not problems with the structure of society. They are problems of the individual worker and need to be addressed as such.

Finally, the Christian faith does not share the utopian faith in institutions as the key to a changed society. Instead it places its hope in transformed individuals and their attitudes. Jesus' Sermon on the Mount is in one sense a utopian vision of the good society. Where does it place its hope? Not in institutions but in personal morality and values. The Bible is more interested in the worker than in work and its institutional forms. Utopian dreams overlook the fact that human institutions are comprised of individual humans. The utopian premise that institutions somehow can stand apart from people and impose improvement on them from a position of superiority is contrary to all that history tells us.

Nevertheless, Christians should support all possible efforts to improve the conditions and management structures of work. The second half of Lee Hardy's book *The Fabric of This World* is full of good ideas.[7] But we need to acknowledge that structural theories promise more than they can deliver. They cannot solve the fundamental problems of work. The suggestions they make to employers are excellent; the problem is that most of us are not employers. While we can commend the methodological improvements that utopian thought articulates and sometimes implements in a limited sphere of work, therefore, we have

7. Hardy, *Fabric of This World*.

to remain clearsighted about the ways in which the utopian impulse holds out a false hope for most of the problems of work and leisure.

Waiting for the Weekend

The leisure counterpart to the socialist hope is the emphasis on the weekend. A survey of recent articles on the subject of leisure shows the degree to which the secular world is pinning its hopes for adequate leisure on the weekend. The fullest treatment is in Witold Rybczynski's book *Waiting for the Weekend*. The author documents how societies throughout history have found their own ways of institutionalizing leisure, correctly noting that "the weekend is our own contribution."[8]

There is much that is appealing to Christians about the institution of the weekend. It offers many possibilities for enrichment in leisure. There is something accurate about Rybczynski's comparing the weekend to sacred space, protected by rituals from the workaday world. Yet we should be critical of its secular attempt to achieve what only Christian faith can provide. Nor can the weekend suffice to provide enough leisure for most people. In middle-class circles, Saturday is perhaps the busiest work day of the week as people catch up on the chores they have not had time to do during the week. The weekend offers a lot of potential for leisure, but it cannot fulfill the expectation that is increasingly being put on it. It is not unusual to answer the question, "What did you do on the weekend?" with the deflated reply, "The usual."

Individualism and Self-Fulfillment

Critics of the social scene are in general agreement that the dominant spirit of today is one of individualism and self-fulfillment. To understand the phenomenon better, we can put it into its historical context by tracing the history of the work ethic during the past five centuries.[9]

Where We Came From

Modern attitudes toward work began with the *Protestant ethic* of the sixteenth and seventeenth centuries. Work was viewed as a calling in which the worker served God. Hard work was a virtue and idleness a vice. The goals of work were spiritual and humanitarian—work glorified God and served humanity.

8. Rybczynski, *Waiting for the Weekend*, 33.
9. My brief history builds on Michael Maccoby, *The Leader* (New York: Simon and Schuster, 1981), 23–54; and David L. McKenna, *Love Your Work!* (Wheaton: Victor, 1990), 35–43.

The Protestant ethic was succeeded by the *entrepreneurial ethic.* Industriousness was still valued, but it occurred in a spirit of self-reliance rather than God-reliance. The spiritual ends of work were replaced by economic and personal goals. The worker no longer relied on God's providence but on his or her own skills and thrift. The *immigrant ethic* ran a parallel course in America, though its goal was not personal gratification so much as improved social and financial opportunities for the next generation.

As the economic system became concentrated in large corporations, the *career ethic* took over where the entrepreneurial ethic had left off. The economic motivation for work was replaced by a desire for success in an organization. The self-reliant worker gave way to the person devoted to fitting into an organization's goals and demands. Conformity supplanted rugged individualism as the prime virtue in the workplace.

Where We Have Arrived: The New Individualism

The evolution of the work ethic ends with the *ethic of self-fulfillment.* It is the predictable manifestation of the individualism and self-absorption of our day. The streams that fed the new ethic included the seventies phenomenon known as the "me generation" and the demand for rights and entitlement that has been a dominant social force in the last quarter of our century.

As with the entrepreneurial ethic and career ethic, the worker in search of self-fulfillment is primarily interested in what he or she can get from work. But the rewards are no longer primarily measured in financial or career terms. Instead workers want a nurturing work environment, time for family and leisure, security, job satisfaction, and self-realization.

Two good sources on the impact of the self-fulfillment movement are Daniel Yankelovich's book *New Rules* and Robert Bellah's *Habits of the Heart.*[10] Yankelovich's surveys revealed that beginning in the 1970s Americans began asking that work meet criteria of personal fulfillment. According to Yankelovich, workers have become less willing to sacrifice their families for their jobs. They want variety on the job. They want to contribute to the decisions made at work. They want work to carry inherent satisfaction instead of putting up with it for the sake of external benefits.

The new ethic is more Christian in its value structure than crass materialism and careerism. The fly in the ointment is that it presupposes a more ideal world than we actually live in. A lot of work simply does

---

10. Daniel Yankelovich, *New Rules: Searching for Self-Fulfillment in a World Turned Upside Down* (New York: Random House, 1981); Bellah *et al., Habits of the Heart.*

not carry its own reward. Some form of external motivation is needed—motivation like the assurance that one is pleasing God and serving others. The ethic of self-fulfillment is generally healthy for one's leisure, but in order for work to thrive, both on and off the job, a good deal of self-sacrifice is required. Again we find a development that contains much that is good but which is still inadequate to solve the problems of work and leisure.

Wishful Thinking

Many proposed solutions to the problems of work and leisure are unrealistically optimistic in their assumption that people's attitudes and the conditions of work will simply improve if a good solution is put on the table. Francis Schaeffer defines this kind of romanticism as a viewpoint that offers optimistic answers on an inadequate basis.[11] I have read numerous books that offer a helpful diagnosis of what is going on in our society only to escape into sentimental and utopian optimism when they come to propose solutions. The solutions themselves sound great, but—to anticipate my criticism of them—they do not take into account the realities of a fallen world, and they fail to explain what will empower people to behave as the visionaries claim they will. The following three examples illustrate the phenomenon that I call wishful thinking.

The authors of a book entitled *A Life to Live* contrast the work ethic with a *life ethic*.[12] The terms in which they describe this life ethic are impressive. It is "concerned with the full development of human beings and human potential." It refuses to see "a person's only and major contribution to society as being made through his or her employment," preferring instead to judge a person's value in terms of the whole range of human roles that the person fills. A life ethic "is about wholeness" and therefore obliterates the cleavage between work and leisure. In this ethic, work is "understood as creative activity" and not as "a curse laid upon a recalcitrant and disobedient race." The life ethic is concerned "with the development of human beings, with wholeness, with freedom and liberation from oppression, with equality." And how will all this be achieved? Through the socialist platform of the Labour Party in England. "Life ethic socialism" is "the only credible and humane choice. . . . Only then will there be a chance that the future can be a blessing not a curse."

11. Francis A. Schaeffer, *The God Who Is There* (Chicago: InterVarsity Press, 1968), 46. Schaeffer, in fact, often used this definition of romanticism in his lectures.
12. Clemitson and Rodgers, *A Life to Live: Beyond Full Employment*, cited above.

Daniel Yankelovich hopes an *ethic of commitment* is the goal toward which the "new rules" are leading contemporary society. This ethic combines parts of the traditional ethic and the tendencies of the ethic of self-fulfillment. It "shifts the axis away from the self . . . toward connectedness with the world." The commitment itself is vaguely conceived: it "may be to people, institutions, objects, beliefs, ideas, places, nature, projects, experiences, adventures and callings." The new ethic of commitment will preserve such traditional values as political freedom and the pursuit of material comfort. But it will enlarge the scope of common virtues, finding room for "a more caring attitude," the ability to view life "as an adventure as well as an economic chore," and "a larger place for the awe, mystery and sacredness of life."

How will it all come about? It will require two "distinct steps" to "develop an ethic of commitment." The first step is for individuals to change their "strategy for self-fulfillment" from a preoccupation with inner needs and desires to an awareness that "self-fulfillment requires commitments" and that "the expressive and sacred can only be realized through a web of shared meanings that transcend the self." In short, individuals will need to effect "changes in consciousness—in self-conception and attitude." Second, individuals will need to have their personally revised consciousness supplemented by "clear and distinct signals from the larger society—from political leadership, the mass media, institutional leadership . . . and from informal interchange of views with friends and neighbors." We can be inspired by the fact that "Americans have a history of responding well to signals about society's changing rewards and constraints."

Whereas Yankelovich hopes to salvage at least part of the impulse toward self-fulfillment, the authors of *Habits of the Heart* are very critical of it. The repeated moral norm for them is a vaguely defined *community ethic*. If only people will give up their quest for self-fulfillment and devote themselves to society, American society might survive after all. In fact, without "the transformation of which we speak," there "may be very little future to think about at all."

The authors speak optimistically about "reconstituting the social world." Work is a linchpin in the vision of a new society. In fact, "a change in the meaning of work and the relation of work and reward is at the heart of any recovery of our social ecology." In the new order, people will regard work "as a contribution to the good of all and not merely as a means to one's own advancement." People will be able "to make vocational choices more in terms of intrinsic satisfactions." Work "that is intrinsically interesting and valuable is one of the central requirements for a revitalized social ecology." There will be "a revival of crafts." Excellence in work will be "a primary form of civic virtue."

And what will empower the new order and prompt people to reform their attitudes and institutions? In a manner akin to the authors of *A Life to Live*, who believe that voting for the Labour Party will usher in a new age, the authors of *Habits of the Heart* commend "the proposals of the proponents of the Administered Society and Economic Democracy." Beyond that, we simply must hope for transformation:

> Such a change involves a deep cultural, social, and even psychological transformation that is not to be brought about by expert fine-tuning of economic institutions alone. On the contrary, at every point, institutional changes, educational changes, and motivational changes would go hand in hand.[13]

Here is utopian idealism in its pure form. It fails to deal with the facts of a global workplace in which the world faces a shrinking number of full-time, permanent jobs and an increasing number of potential workers.

Summary

What all three of these examples have in common is an unfounded optimism about the current physical, social, and moral conditions in our world. They overrate people's moral ability to change themselves. The lofty ideals that these authors mention are worthy, but the means that they offer for achieving them are illusory. I return also to my earlier point that by pinning their hopes solely on social rather than individual moral transformation, these proposed solutions have an "all or nothing" effect. They are powerless to help individual workers make sense of their work in lieu of the structural shifts that are envisioned. In these schemes, individuals are powerless to change their habits and attitudes until the revolution comes.

Also, these authors are concerned almost exclusively with work, to the neglect of leisure. Their visions of a new society have virtually nothing to say about people finding joy and meaning in their leisure time.

Finally, the tendency of secular solutions is to set themselves up as a substitute religion. The terms in which they are couched are quasi-religious. Reading these platforms is like reading a secular sermon. The final appeal of *A Life to Live* is couched in terms of the words of Moses in Deuteronomy 30:19, where Moses claims to have set life and death before the people and urges them to "choose life." Yankelovich likewise uses religious terminology in his vision of an improved society, speaking, for example, of "reverential thinking" as a feature of the ethic of commitment. Of course the traditional Christian concepts get reinterpreted in secular terms. The authors who urge their readers to "choose

---

13. Bellah, et al., *Habits of the Heart*, 289.

life" substitute voting for a liberal political party for the Old Testament understanding that to "choose life" meant to obey God's moral and spiritual laws. The authors of *Habits of the Heart* claim that "a calling links a person to the larger community." At some secondary level this is true, but the primary meaning of calling is that it links the individual to God, the one who calls. Again the authors have emptied a traditional idea of its religious content and resorted to semantic mysticism.

Making Sense of the Secular Scene

What sense are Christians to make of all this? There is much that is perplexing about the secular scene, but I will hazard some conclusions.

We can begin with the premise of common grace—the grace that God distributes generally on the human race, endowing all people, regenerate and unregenerate alike, with a capacity to find truth. The secular sources are most helpful to Christians in their analysis of the problems surrounding work and leisure and their assembling of the social realities of work and leisure in today's world. This chapter has dealt with the solutions that the secular world proposes.

Here the secular sources are of very limited usefulness. The goals that they offer are for the most part worthy ones. Christians can agree that we need to find a balance between work and leisure, between private fulfillment and social concern, between personal and family goals. These goals, however, are shortcircuited to avoid any inclusion of God and human spiritual aspirations. Secular sources do not comment on the ultimate goals and rewards of work and leisure.

The most glaring omission in secular thinking on work and leisure concerns the question of how we as individuals and as a society can effect the changes that the evidence emphatically tells us need to be made. This leads us to the question of how much change we can expect from unconverted people. The answer would seem to be that we should not hope for too much. Enlightened self-interest might lead some people to elevate leisure to a more prominent position in their lives, to work diligently but not excessively, to look upon their work as a service to others. But without the transcendent authority of God's Word to command certain changes, and without the transforming power of God's Holy Spirit to effect moral and spiritual change, and without the glory of God as an overriding goal, the change will be generally minimal.

If one excises the biblical data that I will cover in Part 5, not much remains to be said about solutions to the problems of work and leisure. At first glance this sounds terribly provincial, but since it has logic and experience behind it Christians should not shrink from drawing the conclusions that naturally follow. If Christians cannot change the world in regard to work and leisure they can at least work toward solutions in their own lives and be models among their acquaintances. Christians as a group can also represent the corporate church in the eyes of a secular world.

11

Missed Opportunities and Wrong Messages

The Church's Failure

Again I need to begin with a disclaimer: In saying that the church in our century has dropped the ball regarding work and leisure I do not mean to deny that Christians have contributed significantly to these topics. A renaissance of sorts may even be occurring. But if so, the message has not made enough of the rounds, as evidenced by a scarcity of published materials and a prevailing ignorance of thinking among the typical churchgoer.

Silence and Gaps

The most obvious failing of the church in regard to work and leisure is that it has simply not said enough about these topics. The number of secular books and articles far outnumbers those written from a Christian perspective. When I came to integrate the data of the secular sources with the Christian faith, I often found myself working in a vacuum.

The lack of books and articles on work and leisure from a biblical perspective might indicate a more important gap: the failure of pastors to address the subjects of work and leisure from the pulpit. Most Christians have little reason to regard their work and leisure as a religious issue; judging by what they hear on Sunday, God is not terribly interested in their work and leisure. One survey found that more than ninety percent of churchgoers had never heard a sermon that applied biblical principles to everyday work issues.[1] This is in sharp contrast to the Reformation era, when work was one of the most frequent sermon topics (even when it did not constitute the main point of the sermon). Most Christians today would not be able to define the doctrine of vocation. Nor would they be able to speak precisely about the goals and rewards of work. And as for a Christian view of leisure, most Christians have never given it a second thought.

Leisure: The Subject of Neglect in the Church

Of the books and articles that Christians have written, another gap at once emerges: when the church *has* turned its attention to work and leisure, almost all of its attention has been devoted to work. Leisure is the subject of neglect in the Christian church in this century.

Many churchgoers would be surprised to be told that one can think Christianly about leisure. We should not assume that the person in the pew believes that leisure is good and something that can glorify God. Commitment to work, to achievement, to utilitarianism, and to service runs strong in Christian churches. Leisure usually gets lost in the shuffle.

Of course the opposite situation also exists. Some Christians are so busy pursuing leisure activities that they are seldom or never available to do the work of the church. Television and sports have made the Sunday evening service obsolete in many churches. In such cases the church needs to preach a message of moderation in leisure and balance in the Christian life. But this message is as scarce as the endorsement of legitimate leisure.

Ignoring the Secular Sources

If the church is going to lead people to higher ground in regard to work and leisure, it will need to relate a Christian perspective to what the secular world is saying about work and leisure, partly because it has diagnosed the problems correctly and partly to counteract its erroneous conclusions. But the church is virtually silent on the matter. Above all, Christian thinkers on work and leisure need to expose the shallowness and faulty value system that underlie most people's attitudes toward work and leisure today, and to construct a Christian view of work and leisure that addresses the prevailing attitudes and behavior. But Chris-

1. Douglas Sherman and William Hendricks, *Your Work Matters to God* (Colorado Springs: NavPress, 1987), 16.

tians have not been encouraged to live countercultural lives. The result is that they mainly mimic the attitudes and practices of the surrounding secular society in regard to work and leisure. The other peril in ignoring what secular sources tell us is that the Christian community fails to benefit from the social science data that can provide a helpful diagnosis of the problems that need to be solved.

Failure to Acknowledge the Increased Challenge for Christians

The church has not been courageous in confronting the problems that the Christian faith itself generates in regard to work and leisure, especially the latter. One of these problems is that the Christian life possesses qualities that are antithetical to leisure. They include a sense of duty and "oughtness," seriousness, service, and self-denial. Leisure, on the other hand, presupposes such qualities as legitimate self-indulgence, self-satisfaction, and self-fulfillment.

There are, in other words, two sides to the Christian life that are on a collision course and need to be reconciled. The church has not had the nerve to wrestle with finding rapprochement between these conflicting forces. Its general tendency has been to implicitly side with the ascetic side and starve the need for leisure. Individual Christians have sometimes taken the opposite approach, ignoring the claims of duty in deference to the equally Christian ideal of rest and leisure. Christians would benefit from a carefully reasoned strategy for reconciling the two sides in this perennial tension.

Also, Christians are uniquely called to pursue certain activities. Christian living involves time commitments for prayer, devotional reading, church attendance, Bible studies, committee work, volunteer work in the church or for Christian or community agencies, and so forth. The inevitable result is that these activities take time away from potential leisure time and increase the time spent at the obligatory end of the time scale. The problems of overwork and inadequate leisure thus tend to be heightened for Christians.

Then, too, there is the Christian imperative to serve those in need. This places further strain on the weekly time budget and is reinforced by a bias that favors self-discipline and self-sacrifice, which often translates into a distrust of pleasure or enjoyment. A study of evangelical Protestants noted that they "have tended to value productive or constructive activities in their leisure (e.g., volunteer work, working around the house, taking courses, and gardening)."[2] To this we can add the duty that Christians feel toward contributing a portion of their money to religious

2. Hunter, *Evangelicalism*, 52.

causes, thereby decreasing the amount of money available for leisure and perhaps increasing the need for additional income.

God also commands a day of rest. Yet Sunday must feel leisurely and relaxed in order to rank as a day of worship and rest from work. For many conscientious workers in the church, Sunday is not a day of rest. It is a day of physical and emotional exertion that leaves them drained. We need to respect the principle of leisure in Sunday observance, especially leisure in the sense of feeling free from the obligations of life.

The net result of all this is to make the impulse toward overwork and the time famine for leisure even more acute for Christians. By failing to be forthright about how certain features of the Christian life affect the weekly schedules of church members, the church has cut off the possibility of finding solutions. Before we can solve a problem we need to understand it.

Lost Opportunities at a Solution

Part of the cost of not considering the problems just mentioned is that we have thereby missed opportunities to address them. Christian obligations also contain within them the seeds of a partial restoration of leisure. After all, one of the standard ways to define leisure is in terms of its ability to refresh, to provide a break from everyday routine, to draw a boundary around the acquisitive aspects of life. Many of the religious activities cited above can be nudged at least into the realm of semi-leisure, if we can think of them in terms of refreshment rather than duty.

Solutions for the Privileged

For a growing minority of Christians, the failures that I have noted do not apply. Books and articles *are* being written on a Christian perspective on work and leisure. Workshops and study groups exist. Organizations are starting to put together series of books and tapes.

These are encouraging developments. Yet most of the efforts have been slanted toward the economically and socially privileged segment of the Christian world, especially successful business and professional people. This is perhaps the only place to start. After all, these are the people who have the time and money to attend workshops.

But if the church is going to speak to the needs of Christians generally, the scope will have to broaden considerably. Business and professional people are not the only ones who need to make sense of their work and leisure in Christian terms. People who work with their hands and care for the home and children and cannot afford the time or money to attend plush retreats are also in need of a doctrine of work and leisure. For the most part, they are not being recognized.

Never the Twain Shall Meet

A final inadequacy is the failure of Christians to discuss work and leisure together. The books on work usually contain a token chapter on leisure. Those on leisure acknowledge work with an obligatory chapter on it. This is no way to find a solution to the problems of work and leisure.

Work and leisure together make up our lives and compete for our time. To solve the problems of either one will require us to devote equal attention to both of them. When we discuss only one without the other we end up viewing one as the impediment to the other. The Bible joins work and leisure. It is time for Christian discussions to do the same.

Summary

My discussion has been a litany of accusations. Compiling it was not a pleasant task. Yet much can be gained by confronting our failures. Silence can be broken. Gaps can be filled. The time has come to do both. Christians are generally strangers to what is best in their own religious tradition in regard to work and leisure. It is time to introduce them to that tradition, beginning with the Bible.

Theological Aberrations

Another area where the church has failed in regard to work and leisure is that it has perpetuated bad theology. Perhaps it has been the *victim* of bad theology. In either case, the church has refrained from speaking on work and leisure, or it has sent the wrong message in regard to them. In naming these theological aberrations I will make no attempt to refute them. Part 5 is designed to do that. My purpose is mainly to describe the attitudes and explain how they fail to solve the problems of work and leisure.

The Sacred-Secular Heresy

While we tend to associate the sacred-secular dichotomy with medieval Catholicism, the truth is that it has never been absent from the Christian church since then. Protestantism has its own versions of the idea.

It surfaces most overtly in the concept of "full-time Christian service." That phrase is used to cover people whose livelihood consists of employment by a church, a missionary organization, or a parachurch organization. People who move from such jobs to the other type of work are regularly subjected to statements about their having left "full-time Christian service." A distinction between clergy and laity invariably creeps into this scheme, with the former elevated and the latter denigrated.

The sacred-secular dichotomy not only divides *people* on the basis of their vocations. We also internalize the division and begin to think of our *activities* in terms of the dichotomy. When we do this we operate on the premise that some aspects of our life are spiritual, and others are not. Worshiping God and praying are sacred activities. Working on the job and playing are not.

It is obvious that such a theological outlook provides no Christian solution at all to the problems of work and leisure. Its whole tendency is to exempt work and leisure from spiritual considerations. The result is that people behave pretty much like unbelievers in their pursuit of work and leisure. They also view their work and leisure as lacking the dignity and significance that they should possess.

The Two-Story View of the Universe

Another theological aberration is to divide the earthly and the heavenly into separate spheres. In this model, God is in heaven and we are on earth. Since God is the center of our spiritual lives, the logical conclusion is that our spirituality involves our moments of conscious communication with God in prayer, worship, listening to sermons, and reading religious books and articles. The remainder of life is lived "down here." In the two-story universe, God is not much interested in these lesser things. Two possible responses follow. One is to conclude that if God is only mildly interested in our daily routine of work and leisure, they are not worthy of our best thought and effort. The other is to conclude that we are free to pursue earthly pursuits outside of spiritual directives and play by the rules of a secular world. "Business is business," people conclude. And, we might add, "play is play."

The antidote to the two-story view of reality is to view reality quite literally as a *universe*—as one world. It is to say, in the words of the hymn, "This is my Father's world," and to claim it for him, both in our individual lives and in society.

The Body-Soul Dichotomy

Another division that has crept into some people's theology is that between body and soul. This is the old Docetic and Gnostic heresy of the superiority of the spiritual over the physical. The body is regarded as either unworthy or the chief instigator of what is evil. Accordingly, it is either something of no consequence, or it is something that we should actively deny and suppress. In either case, work and leisure are devalued. They might simply be done half-heartedly, or they might become the arena of penance in which people work hard and forego leisure as a form of self-punishment. In the body-soul dichotomy, the activities of the soul merit our attention and nurture. The goal of life is to have as little to do with the physical as possible and as much to do with the spiritual as a human can manage.

The results for work and leisure are of course negative. As Wendell Berry notes, "It is impossible to see how good work might be accomplished by people who think that our life in this world either signifies nothing or has only a negative significance."[3] Play, as we could imagine, is viewed as absolutely frivolous.

The Ceaseless Evangelism Model

Another theological premise that has had a strong life in Protestant circles is the view that evangelism is the only supremely worthy goal of Christians. "Saving souls" is the purpose of our lives. It is also the primary message that the church should proclaim. Other aspects of life are at best peripheral, or, more likely, active obstacles to what God has put us here for.

If evangelism is our only worthy activity, our work can hardly claim much thought or allegiance. The less of it we do the better, for then we are freed to do our real task. And as for leisure, it is unworthy of a spiritually minded Christian, who might better spend the time and money in evangelizing unbelievers.

The One-Kingdom View of Life

Similar to the "ceaseless evangelism" view of the Christian life is the view that Christians have only one calling: to be members of God's spiritual kingdom. This is in contrast to the Puritans, who believed that Christians have both a general calling (living the holy life) and particular callings (our work and roles in the world). It also runs counter to a very long theological tradition (stretching back through Calvin and Luther to Augustine) that embraces the idea of "the two kingdoms," in which Christians are viewed as living in both God's kingdom and an earthly kingdom that they are called to infuse with the values and ethics of the heavenly kingdom.

The one-kingdom theory shrinks the playing field. Here is a statement of the theory:

> Nowhere in the New Testament is human work regarded as "divine vocation." God does not call people to be doctors, lawyers, or truck drivers. . . . Tent-making was only incidental to what God had called [Paul] to do.

3. Wendel Berry, *Sex, Economy, Freedom, and Community* (New York: Pantheon Books, 1992), 109–10.

. . . There is but one call in the Scriptures—to be a child of God and to behave as such.[4]

While this viewpoint is not a theological disaster, it is simply inadequate. It falsifies how we actually live our daily lives. Regeneration of
soul does not remove us from our lives of work and play in the physical
and social worlds and transport us into a spiritual kingdom. By removing one of the two kingdoms from view this theological model makes
integration between the two impossible. No attempt is made to let
work and leisure be governed by Christian principles. If work and leisure are themselves only incidental, they end up being devalued.

Summary

It is not my purpose here to refute these common theological viewpoints. That they continue to exist in churches and institutions is un-
disputed. Their effect on work and leisure is negative. They are part of
the church's inadequate solutions to the problems of work and leisure.

Buying into the Secular Scene

The silence of the church, combined with the theological inadequacies just noted, lead Christians to ape the attitudes of a secular society
much of the time. In the absence of encouragement to adopt distinctly
Christian attitudes toward work and leisure, Christians sometimes
view their work with disdain, sometimes overvalue it, often do not
take time for leisure, and much of the time do not consecrate their
work, time, or leisure to God. As a result Christians lapse into secular-
ity by default.

Sometimes, though, the church actively appropriates a secular view
and gives it a religious cast. Two examples have been prominent.

The Time Management Movement

The time management movement has been a major phenomenon in
both Christian and secular circles. Its chief target has been business and
professional people. Its goal is to increase the efficiency in people's lives
so they can get more done and feel less harried. These goals, though
limited in scope, are laudable. As I critique the concept of time management, I am concerned not only with the workshops and books on
the subject, but also with the general orientation toward time repre-

4. Henlee H. Barnette, *Christian Calling and Vocation* (Grand Rapids: Baker, 1965),
63, 79.

sented by the movement. This is an orientation that people can share even if they have never attended a workshop or followed the advice of a book on the subject.

The view that dominates the time management movement is that time is a quantity. Its rigid division of time into units is designed to enable people to control their time more fully. Behind this attempt sometimes lies the view that people are not subject to creaturely limitations. Indeed, sometimes the ideal person is pictured as almost godlike. What is in danger of getting lost is the view of time as a quality in which the crucial question is not how much a person gets done but whether in a given activity a person has been all that he or she can be.

Another danger is that time management is really part of the success ethic in which the goal is to achieve as much as possible in terms of one's career, income, or social standing. The movement is oriented toward professional people who want to be successful. Its tendency is not to question whether the values and lifestyle of busy and successful people are Christian but to assume that they are. Having assumed that a successful life is the correct one, people then channel their efforts into salvaging that lifestyle and making it as Christian as possible. This is not always invalid, but sometimes it is. The time management movement has tended to accept the success ethic instead of encouraging people to question it. People are not encouraged to consider whether they should try to do less, or change jobs, or simplify their lifestyle.

Closely related to this is the preoccupation with goals. Examining one's goals, arranging them according to priorities, and dividing one's time accordingly are central to time management. But as Robert Banks notes, "While the time management approach urges people to define their goals, it does not encourage them to think whether these goals ultimately lie outside the purely secular understanding of life," with the result that the approach "generally encourages people to adapt more to their present situation rather than to challenge or transform it."[5]

The time management movement also ties in heavily with the individualism of our society. Its focus is usually the busy and successful person. A person's time problems are assumed to be personal ones. Solutions are equally personal. As Banks diagnoses the situation, "Generally speaking, time problem solving is left to the individual, with only an occasional reference to other people or the Christian community."[6]

Another thing that the Christian time management movement shares with the secular world is its preoccupation with work. While the movement may pay lip service to finding time for leisure, it does not achieve that end. Doing so would, indeed, fit in well with the concept

5. Robert Banks, *The Tyranny of Time: When 24 Hours Is Not Enough* (Downers Grove, Ill.: InterVarsity, 1983), 163.
6. Ibid.

of managing and scheduling one's time. But the movement itself is oriented toward helping successful professionals maintain their success. Time management can itself become a compulsion. Someone has said that "obsession with time management and productivity and schedules and busyness is . . . just as much slavery as another person's compulsion to abuse alcohol or indulge in pornography."[7]

Summary

To say that the time management concept is an inadequate solution to the problems of work, leisure, and time is not to say that it is totally bad. Managing one's time is good stewardship. There is, however, more to the problem than this, and people who adopt time management premises often fail to look beyond this: to view work and leisure as a calling from God, to work and play in an awareness of the goals of these activities, to inquire exactly how we can work and play in a moral way. Time management helps people find time for everything, but it does not enrich how they go about these things once they have found a time for them. In general, the movement promises more than it can deliver.

The Gospel of Prosperity

A more serious deviation from biblical Christianity is the gospel of prosperity. Its most visible examplars are several radio and television preachers. Some prominent businessmen and a few dynamic lecturers have also helped to proclaim the optimistic news that God wants believers to be fabulously wealthy and successful.[8]

The movement is based partly on a theology of success. Adherents quote verses from the Bible that promise success to God's people. A sampling from a book entitled *God's Will Is Prosperity* yields the following examples.[9] Psalm 112:3 says regarding the righteous person that "wealth and riches are in his house." Jesus said that "there is no one who has left house, [family], or lands, for my sake and for the gospel, who will not receive a hundredfold now in this time" (Mark 10:29–30). That verse, combined with Jesus' picture of a hundredfold yield in the parable of the sower, leads to "the hundredfold return" principle in which God can be trusted to reward believers with material prosperity if they exercise extraordinary faith. The teaching of the parable of the talents is that the person who is faithful in a little will eventually be

7. Ben Patterson: quoted in Ron R. Lee, "Downtime without the Guilt," *Marriage Partnership*, Fall 1994, 42.

8. For an overview of the movement, see Cynthia R. Schaible, "The Gospel of the Good Life," *Eternity*, February 1981, 21–27.

9. Gloria Copeland, *God's Will Is Prosperity* (Tulsa: Harrison House, 1978).

put in possession of much (Luke 16:10), including expanded material goods and financial resources.

There are at least three criticisms of how the prosperity gospel handles the Bible. It quotes selectively, overlooking balancing comments about suffering and sacrifice being the lot of the believer. It often quotes out of context, or incorrectly applies a biblical statement to refer to material prosperity, or extracts principles from biblical statements that do not refer to material success. It also overlooks the social context of the subsistence economy of Bible times in which the standard of what constituted "wealth" fell far short of even a modest lifestyle in the Western world today.

In the prosperity gospel, biblical data is liberally supplemented by elements of the secular success ethic and pop psychology. Except for the religious terms that are sprinkled into the message, the viewpoint is no different from the secular world's pursuit of wealth and success. It is the language of earthly ambition and success, supplemented by religious sentiment.

The gospel of success covers a great deal more than work and leisure.[10] In regard to those subjects, however, we can say that the gospel of prosperity glorifies work at the expense of leisure and makes ambition the motivation for a strenuous work ethic. The chief goals of work are prestige in a career and the accumulation of wealth.

I have already suggested the Puritan aversion to this kind of thinking, and the remainder of this book will provide a theological critique of it. In brief, the gospel of prosperity does not preach the "whole counsel of God," it provides an inadequate goal and motivation for work, it devalues leisure, and it values work for the wrong reasons.

Let's Play "Blame the Puritans"

I noted in the previous chapter that secularists searching for a scapegoat usually blame the Protestant ethic, but Christians who are critical of the prosperity movement often do the same thing. Tony Campolo ends a good critique of the gospel of success by resorting to the usual "let's blame the Puritans" ploy, undermining his credibility in the process.[11] He cites that old favorite, Max Weber's *Protestant Ethic and the Spirit of Capitalism*, which he claims is the result of "careful historical analysis." Weber's book is actually a slender volume that selectively quotes a few Puritan sources and ignores the major themes of these writers. Campolo's particular claim is that the early Protestants regarded material success as proof that they were saved and therefore worked ceaselessly to be-

10. A specimen book is Robert A. Schuller, *Just Because You're on a Roll . . . Doesn't Mean You're Going Downhill* (Old Tappan, N.J.: Revell, 1990).

11. Anthony Campolo, Jr., *The Success Fantasy* (Wheaton: Victor, 1980), 141.

come rich. But the Puritans never preached such a gospel of success. They regarded *good works* (the biblical "fruit of the Spirit"), not successful *work* and its financial rewards, as evidence of regeneration, just as Christ told us to judge people by their works.

A question worth asking is why some Christians are so anxious to find a scapegoat. Christians have enough real foes to combat that they do not need to fabricate ones. The Puritan movement has been off the scene for 300 years. Modern preachers of the prosperity gospel emphatically do not quote the Puritans for support. In the meantime, the effect of statements like Campolo's is to make sure that Christians remain ignorant of what is best in their own tradition.

Summary

The gospel of success is the most blatant (but not the only) example of people adopting views of work and leisure from the secular world and giving them a religious cast. The prosperity gospel accepts the premises of a secular success ethic and inflames Christians' urge for success by claiming that it is part of the life of faith. It ignores what the Bible says about suffering for the sake of Christ and avoiding the snares of worldly-mindedness.

Further Reading

Anthony Campolo, Jr., *The Success Fantasy* (1980).
Robert Banks, *The Tyranny of Time* (1983).
Douglas Sherman and William Hendricks, *Your Work Matters to God* (1987).

PART 5

Recovering the Lost Keys:
What the Bible Says about Work and Leisure

12

What Does God Do All Day?
God at Work and Play

For the ancient Greeks, the life of most of the gods was a life of celestial loafing, interrupted only by occasional amorous excursions or councils to determine the affairs of the human race. Homer describes Olympus, "the gods' abiding place," as "unshaken for ever. There are no beating winds or drenching rain; no snow falls there, but the clear sky spreads cloudless, over it a white radiance floats; there the blessed gods are happy all their days."

By contrast, the God of the Bible is a veritable dynamo of work and activity, and equally a devotee of purposive rest and leisure. The classic Sunday-schooler's question, "What does God do all day?" actually requires a long answer, for the truth is that God does a lot.

God at Work

Many who have written on the subject of work trace the biblical data back to the curse that befell work after the Fall in Genesis 3. Others trace it back to the work that God gave Adam and Eve in Paradise, as narrated in Genesis 2. Actually the biblical view of work goes back even further to the work of God as narrated in Genesis 1.

God the Worker

Work in the Bible begins with God's work of creation. This creative work is obviously not toil. It is more like the exuberance of an artist. It is joyous, self-expressive, and energetic, unencumbered by the need to overcome obstacles or wrestle the physical elements into a finished product.

Yet the activity of God in creating the world must be considered work. For one thing, we read that after the six days of creation "God finished his work which he had done, and he rested on the seventh day from all his work which he had done" (Genesis 2:2). In the actual account of creation, moreover, God rests from his creative work after each day, setting up a rhythm of work and rest or leisure.

The work that God did when creating the world is described in human terms. God becomes a cosmic gardener who planted a garden in Eden (Genesis 2:8). He formed Adam from the dust of the ground (Genesis 2:7) and made woman from the rib of Adam (Genesis 2:21–22). It is obvious from such actions that in the Bible's creation story God is preeminently a craftsman. Psalm 19:1 says that "the firmament proclaims his handiwork." Psalm 8:3 pictures the heavens as the work of God's fingers. Note additionally the sheer energy that the verbs in the creation story convey. As we move through the kaleidoscope of actions that God performed, we read that he *separated, made, called, set, formed,* and *planted.* In short, he was very busy with the work of creation.

God's work did not stop with the creation of the world but continues throughout history. God neither slumbers nor sleeps but is always busy protecting his people (Psalm 121). If early Genesis portrays God as a cosmic gardener busy planting a garden, Psalm 104:10–22 extends that picture to God's providing for nature like a gardener who waters and nurtures plants. Psalm 107 describes God's acts of rescue: God is known "for his wonderful works to the sons of men" (vv. 8, 15, 21, 31). The works of God as described in the Bible fall into the categories of creation, providence, judgment, and redemption.

In the New Testament, Christ, too, is a worker. He was a carpenter until the age of thirty. During his public ministry he spoke repeatedly of his work. "We must work the works of him who sent me," Jesus said (John 9:4). His food was "to do the will of him who sent me, and to accomplish his work" (John 4:34). "My Father is working still, and I am working," Jesus told the Jews (John 5:17).

"The God of the Bible," Paul Minear aptly notes, "is preeminently a worker."[1] What is the significance of this? It at once lends sanction and dignity to the very idea of work. Robert Banks says we know from the

---

1. Paul S. Minear, "Work and Vocation in Scripture," in *Work and Vocation: A Christian Discussion,* ed. John Oliver Nelson (New York: Harper and Brothers, 1954), 44.

Bible's portrait of God as worker "that God is highly interested in work, that God understands the possibilities and frustrations of work, . . . that the world of work is not strange to God."[2]

There is an important link between how the human race regards its work and how it regards its deity. I noted earlier that the Greeks regarded ordinary work with contempt. Not surprisingly, when they imagined the golden age of innocence that had once existed, they pictured a world in which neither gods nor people had to work. According to Hesiod, for example, "At the beginning the generations of men lived on the earth far removed from evils of difficult toil. . . . Men of the Golden Age used to live like gods . . . free from cares, from labour and from grief."[3] Someone has noted that "a glance at a [biblical] Concordance will show by the very frequency of mentions of work throughout the Old Testament that the Greek idea of the indignity of work has no place whatever there."[4]

What the Image of God as Worker Tells Us

The biblical image of God as worker is foundational to our thinking about both God and work. The former is the focus of Robert Banks's book *God the Worker: Journeys into the Mind, Heart and Imagination of God*. Banks explores the images of God as composer and performer, metalworker and potter, garmentmaker, gardener, farmer, shepherd, tentmaker, and builder. The very fact that the Bible uses images of human work to describe God's work shows us that analogies exist between them. In the words of Banks, "Analogies between God's activity and human work teach us something dependable about both."[5]

Logically then, the work of God, even though it is unique, is a model for human work. It affirms that work is good and Godlike in principle. The work of God is creative, orderly, and constructive. It is universal, benefiting people and all creatures. It declares the very nature of God and bears his imprint or signature. Human work can do no better than emulate God's work. In the words of Pope John Paul II, "Man ought to imitate God, his Creator, in working, because man alone has the unique characteristic of likeness to God."[6]

God's work in creating and controlling the world also tells us something about the arena within which human work has meaning. When God finished his work of creation, he "saw everything that he had made, and behold, it was very good" (Genesis 1:31). This world that

---

2. Robert Banks, *God the Worker* (Sutherland, Australia: Albatross Books, 1992), 386.

3. Hesiod, *Works and Days*; quoted in W. R. Forrester, *Christian Vocation* (New York: Charles Scribner's Sons, 1953), 121.

4. Forrester, *Christian Vocation*, 131.

5. Banks, *God the Worker*, 394.

6. Pope John Paul II, *On Human Work*, 58.

God made and declared good is the God-given sphere in which people do their work. If "the earth is the Lord's and the fullness thereof, the world and those who dwell therein" (Psalm 24:1), then people's ordinary work in the world can be God's work.

By removing all stigma from the material world, the Christian doctrine of creation also takes away the reproach that other traditions have placed upon earthly work. The Christian doctrine of creation renders any dichotomy between the earthly and the sacred impossible. The world has value to God and therefore to his creatures who live and work in it. In a discussion of how Christianity views the physical creation as good in principle, Wendell Berry correctly claims that "by our work we reveal what we think of the works of God."[7]

The Image of God in People

According to the Bible's creation story, the God who works made people in his image (Genesis 1:26–27). No doubt many things make up this resemblance between God and his human creatures. But one obvious similarity between God and people made in his image is that both are workers. This link between God's work and humanity's work is made explicit in the fourth commandment of the Decalogue:

> Six days you shall labor, and do all your work. . . . For in six days the Lord made heaven and earth, the sea, and all that is in them (Exodus 20:9, 11).

People work because the God who created them in his image works. Human work has meaning partly because it expresses the divine image in people.

It follows that human work should share the nature of God's work. God worked not because he had to but because he wanted to. The song of the elders around God's throne stresses this: "thou didst create all things, and by thy will [KJV: for thy pleasure] they . . . were created" (Revelation 4:11). Dorothy Sayers wrote in a famous essay exploring the implications of the divine image in people that work should

> be thought of as a creative activity, undertaken for the love of the work itself; and . . . man, made in God's image, should make things, as God makes them, for the sake of doing well a thing that is well worth doing. . . . Work is the natural exercise and function of man—the creature who is made in the image of his Creator.[8]

7. Berry, *Sex, Economy, Freedom, and Community*, 109.
8. Dorothy L. Sayers, "Why Work?" in *Creed or Chaos?* (New York: Harcourt, Brace, 1949), 46, 53.

The Pope's encyclical on work makes the same point: "Man, created in the image of God, shares by his work in the activity of the Creator."[9] This is identical to the view of Elton Trueblood, who believes that work "becomes holy, because it is by toil that men can prove themselves creatures made in God's image. . . . If God is the Worker, then men and women . . . must be workers, too. They are sharing in creation when they develop a farm, paint a picture, build a home or polish a floor."[10]

God and People as Joint Workers

To the ideas of God as worker and people as created in his image we must add the concept of God's work and humanity's work as a cooperative partnership. At first this may seem out of place, but the Bible claims that it is possible. Of course God is sovereign, so no concept of human equality with God is envisioned. Human work itself cannot exist outside God's control, so the modern notion of the self-made person is an impossibility. But people can become junior partners with God, carrying on his delegated work in dependence on him.

Psalm 127:1 articulates this possibility: "Unless the Lord builds the house, those who build it labor in vain." We should notice first that work itself is not disparaged here. Human labor is declared futile only when it is done apart from God's assistance. Furthermore, work itself is insufficient; what matters is the attitude of the worker toward God. That attitude, we infer, must be one of dependence, service, and worship. From this humble stance human work has dignity as a cooperative effort with God. God works through the worker, transforming human labor into something exalted, even spiritual.[11]

The blend of human and divine work also appears in Psalm 90:16–17:

> Let thy work be manifest to thy servants,
>   and thy glorious power to their children.
> Let the favor of the Lord our God be upon us,
>   and establish thou the work of our hands upon us,
>   yea, the work of our hands establish thou it.

Again we find that the work of God is bigger than human work. As the writer of Ecclesiastes reflects, "Consider the work of God; who can make straight what he has made crooked?" (Ecclesiastes 7:13). But within this acknowledgment of God's sovereignty over the worker's life people can legitimately pray that the God who himself works will establish or bless the work of their hands.

9. Pope John Paul II, *On Human Work*, 57.
10. Elton Trueblood, *Your Other Vocation* (New York: Harper and Brothers, 1952), 64.
11. For insightful commentary on this verse from Psalm 127, I commend the discussion of Minear, "Work and Vocation," 40–44.

A biblical pattern for this divine-human cooperation in work can be found in the rebuilding of the wall of Jerusalem as recounted in the Book of Nehemiah. The project rested partly on human effort: "all the wall was joined together to half its height. For the people had a mind to work" (Nehemiah 4:6). When Nehemiah's enemies tried to divert him from his work, his response showed the importance he attached to the physical work of building a wall: "I am doing a great work and I cannot come down. Why should the work stop while I leave it and come down to you?" (6:3).

But Nehemiah's work was more than a human effort. When enemies tried to frighten the workers, saying to themselves that "their hands will drop from the work," Nehemiah prayed, "But now, O God, strengthen thou my hands" (Nehemiah 6:9). When the work was finished, moreover, Nehemiah offered an assessment that echoed his earlier commendation of the people because they "had a mind to work." The enemies were afraid, Nehemiah wrote, "for they perceived that this work had been accomplished with the help of our God" (6:16). All human work is accomplished with the help of God, whether or not the worker acknowledges the help of God.

Luther's concept of vocation made much of this human-divine cooperation in work.[12] According to Luther, when we carry out our vocation in faith to God and obedience to his commands, God will work through us. Such a view of work saves us both from the paralyzing fear of human ineffectiveness and from the arrogance of human achievement. We have no ability that God has not given to us. When we submit ourselves to God, our work becomes God's work. Luther observed that God's blessings

> at times come to us through our labors and at times without our labors, but never because of our labors; for God always gives them because of His undeserved mercy. . . . He uses our labor as a sort of mask, under the cover of which he blesses us and grants us what is His, so that there is room for faith.[13]

In our day, John Stott has written,

> This concept of divine-human collaboration applies to all honorable work. God has so ordered life on earth as to depend on us. . . . So whatever our work, we need to see it as being . . . cooperation with God. . . . It is this that glorifies him.[14]

12. See the discussion by Gustaf Wingren, *Luther on Vocation,* trans. Carl C. Rasmussen (Philadelphia: Muhlenberg Press, 1957), 123ff.

13. Martin Luther, exposition on Deuteronomy 8:17–18, as excerpted in *What Luther Says,* 1495.

14. John Stott, "Reclaiming the Biblical Doctrine of Work," *Christianity Today,* 4 May 1979, 37.

In a similar vein, the Pope's encyclical on work asserts as an ideal "that man's work is a participation in God's activity," an awareness that "ought to permeate . . . the most ordinary everyday activities."[15] Elton Trueblood wrote that what the Christian view of work adds to the satisfaction of simply doing a job well is "the sense of joy that comes to a believer who is convinced that, humble as he is, he is a partner of the Living God, helping minutely in the work of creation."[16]

Summary

Throughout the Bible, God is portrayed as an extremely active worker. In itself, this affects how we view human work. If God works, work is good and necessary. It is as simple as that. God's work is a model for human work, showing us that human work in the world is worth doing in a purposive, enjoyable, and fulfilling manner. But God is more than a model for us to follow; God allows us to work with him in such a way that it can be said that "we are God's fellow workers" (1 Corinthians 3:9).

Divine Leisure

Does God play? The Bible does not explicitly say so, but it describes activities by God that correspond to what we mean by play. God is therefore as much a model for human leisure as for work. As Augustine put it, in both our working and our resting God is "the pattern which we are to follow."[17]

The Rest of God

Just as work can be traced back to God's activity in Genesis 1, so can leisure. Some theologians even claim that God's creation of the world was play. I cannot agree. The Bible calls it work. But in Genesis 1 God rested as well as worked. After each day of creation he contemplated and (we infer) enjoyed what he had created, pronouncing it "good."

After the individual days of creation, each punctuated at the end by rest, there came the grand finale—an entire day of rest. Here is how the Bible describes it:

15. Pope John Paul II, *On Human Work*, 58.
16. Trueblood, *Your Other Vocation*, 63.
17. Augustine; quoted in Robert A. Markus, "Work and Worker in Early Christianity," in *Work: Christian Thought and Practice*, ed. John M. Todd (Baltimore: Helicon Press, 1960), 22.

Thus the heavens and the earth were finished, and all the host of them. And on the seventh day God finished his work which he had done, and he rested on the seventh day from all his work which he had done. So God blessed the seventh day and hallowed it, because on it God rested from all his work which he had done in creation (Genesis 2:1–3).

We tend to think that God created the world in six days and that the seventh day was a cessation of God's activity of creation, but Jewish scholar Abraham Heschel suggests that "it took a special act of creation to bring [the Sabbath] into being, . . . the universe would be incomplete without it."[18]

What are we to make of God's devoting a day to rest? Later in history it became the model and sanction for setting aside a day for believers to worship God. But we should not too hastily conclude that this was its original meaning. Certainly God did not worship on the seventh day. The Genesis account itself simply stresses the idea of cessation from labor.

The truth is that the exact origins of the Old Testament Sabbath are veiled in mystery. Setting aside one day in seven as a religious day is at least as old as the exodus from Egypt (see Exodus 16), but it is not clear whether it stretches back beyond that point. Some theologians believe that "originally the Sabbath was characterized merely by the prohibition of all work."[19]

We do not, of course, have to choose *between* rest and worship in our interpretation of Sabbath rest. The more one explores the matter, the more apparent it becomes that a Christian view of leisure must incorporate the experience of worship. Not that the two are identical, but leisure and worship have important things in common, including cessation from work and refreshment of spirit.

What, then, does God's rest from work say about leisure? It affirms leisure by drawing a boundary around human work and acquisitiveness. Like God's rest, leisure frees us from the need to produce and allows us instead to enjoy what has already been made. It has within it the quality of "letting go" of the utilitarian urges that occupy us in the world of getting and spending (to use William Wordsworth's evocative phrase). Josef Pieper is right in saying that leisure is the possession "of those who are open to everything; not of those who grab and grab hold, but of those who leave the reins loose . . . almost like a man falling asleep."[20] In leisure, as in God's rest after creation, there is an element

18. Abraham Heschel, *The Sabbath: Its Meaning for Modern Man* (New York: Farrar, Straus and Giroux, 1951), 23.

19. A. Alt; quoted in Johnston, *Christian at Play*, 88–89. Johnston notes others who agree with this view of the prehistory of the Sabbath.

20. Pieper, *Leisure the Basis of Culture*, 28.

of celebration of what has been accomplished and of knowing that for the moment work is unnecessary and, in fact, inappropriate. Kenneth Woodward puts it well: "For Jews and Christians, the essence of leisure was time off for the timeless—for thanking God for what has been freely given and not produced by human labor."[21]

Another thing that we can infer from God's rest after creation is that it was more than emptiness or idleness. Such rest has the positive quality of joy and satisfaction. It is linked, moreover, with contemplation, specifically of nature, artistry, and beauty. Having completed his work of creation, God "saw everything that he had made, and behold, it was very good" (Genesis 1:31). It would of course be arbitrary to say that this is the extent of what our leisure should consist of, but at the very least it sanctions contemplative and aesthetic forms of leisure. Even in a technological age, leisure remains a primary means by which people renew their contact with nature.

There is, finally, an aspect of refreshment or re-creation in God's rest. We learn this from Exodus 31:17, where Sabbath observance is said to be "a sign for ever between me and the people of Israel that in six days the Lord made heaven and earth, and on the seventh day he rested, and was refreshed." Here the rest of God is defined, not as something God did, but by its function of refreshment, so we again can see a divine model for human rest and leisure.

The motifs of Sabbath and rest extend throughout the Bible, as Paul Heintzman delineates with admirable clarity.[22] The biblical concepts of Sabbath and rest, writes Heintzman, are descriptive of what leisure may be. One dimension of the analogy is quantitative, establishing a rhythm to life that prescribes a minimum quota of rest and leisure to balance the rigors of work. The other is qualitative, encompassing such things as peace, joy, well-being, relief from the burden of work, and contentment of body, soul, and mind.

The Example of Jesus

Like the Old Testament emphasis, Jesus exemplified the need to follow God's lead in punctuating work with rest. Throughout his extraordinarily busy public years, Jesus found time to retreat from work. Consider this typical scenario:

---

21. Kenneth L. Woodward, "What Is Leisure Anyhow?" *Newsweek*, 26 August 1991, 56.

22. Paul Heintzman, "Implications for Leisure from a Review of the Biblical Concepts of Sabbath and Rest," in *Christianity and Leisure: Issues in a Pluralistic Society*, ed. Paul Heintzman, Glen Van Andel, and Thomas Visker (Sioux Center, Iowa: Dordt College Press, 1994), 17–34.

> Immediately he made his disciples get into the boat and go before him to
> the other side, to Bethsaida, while he dismissed the crowd. And after he
> had taken leave of them, he went up on the mountain to pray. And when
> evening came, the boat was out on the sea, and he was alone on the land
> (Mark 6:45–47).

The Gospel of Luke gives us similar pictures of Jesus going to the
mountains to pray (Luke 6:12; 9:28).

Jesus prescribed the same pattern for his disciples, as we see from an
incident in the Gospel of Mark:

> The apostles returned to Jesus, and told him all that they had done and
> taught. And he said to them, "Come away by yourselves to a lonely place,
> and rest a while." For many were coming and going, and they had no lei-
> sure even to eat. And they went away in the boat to a lonely place by
> themselves (Mark 6:30–32).

These passages from the Gospels are important to our understanding
of leisure. They show that Jesus did not reduce life to ceaseless work
and evangelism. By his own example, God draws a boundary to every
type of work—even the work of proclaiming the gospel and helping
needy people.

The event that makes the point most memorably is the story of
Mary and Martha (Luke 10:38–42). The story features contrasting personality types—types that psychologists today call Type A and Type B.
Martha is the activist, preoccupied with the work that needs to be done
in order to get a meal on the table. Jesus criticizes her spirit as one that
is "anxious and troubled about many things." Mary, by contrast, chose
to retire, at least temporarily, from the obligations of work. Jesus commended her for having "chosen the good portion."

Resting with God

Earlier in this chapter we observed how the Bible affirms the possibility of viewing ourselves as actually working with God. To this we
should add the even less familiar possibility of resting with God.

The Old Testament implicitly makes a link between God's rest and
our rest in Sabbath observance. To begin, the creation story in Genesis
contains a hint that the rest of God was not a once-only event. Genesis
2:3 tells us, "So God blessed the seventh day and hallowed it, because
on it God rested from all his work which he had done in creation." Unlike the other days of creation, this one lacks the concluding formula
"and there was evening and there was morning," suggesting that the
rest continues. Furthermore, God's delighted contemplation of the perfection of his new creation is something that remains appropriate.

There is thus a logic to Augustine's suggestion that although humans experience work and rest in succession, God "is always at work and yet always at rest."[23]

If God continues to rest in the sense of contemplating and enjoying the perfection of his work, the fourth commandment can be viewed as an invitation to join God in his divine leisure. In the Old Testament God calls the Sabbath "a perpetual covenant" between himself and his people, "a sign for ever between me and the people of Israel that in six days the Lord made heaven and earth, and on the seventh day he rested, and was refreshed" (Exodus 31:16–17). The Sabbath, moreover, is a foretaste of the heavenly rest that believers share with God.

But the idea of sharing God's rest goes beyond observing the Sabbath. William Still's discussion of physical and emotional rest roots it in the redemptive work of Christ.[24] In its most profound manifestation, rest is part of what the Old Testament calls *shalom*—the peace and fulfillment that God offers to people who trust in him. It is a state of soul, not simply free time or physical inactivity. This peace finds its ultimate manifestation in the redemptive work of Christ that offers us salvation from sin and inner peace even when external circumstances are distressful. The basis of physical and emotional relaxation for the Christian "is a mind set at rest from all possible care by God through Christ."[25] The command to "rest in the Lord" (Psalm 37:7 KJV) does not prescribe something that we do apart from God; it is a resting that we do *with* God.

Summary

If God works, he also rests. If he prescribes work for the human race, he also prescribes rest. Although rest from work does not by itself constitute leisure, it is a prerequisite for leisure and an ingredient of it. But an analysis of the biblical concepts of Sabbath and rest shows that they are more than an absence of work. They are filled with people doing things and experiencing a quality of life that also characterize human leisure. If God rested from his work and was refreshed by it, we can do the same.

God at Play

That God rested is common knowledge. To say that God plays will seem to most people a harder case to make. But the Bible makes it possible for us to speak of the play of God.

23. Augustine; quoted in Markus, "Work and Worker," 23.
24. William Still, *Rhythms of Rest and Work* (Aberdeen: Gilcomston South Church, 1992).
25. Still, *Rhythms*, 21.

God at Play in Creation

A good starting place is to contemplate the plants and animals that God created. Can we imagine anyone producing them without an element of playfulness? Think of the elephant and hippopotamus: could someone without a sense of humor fashion them? And what about the sheer exuberance of shapes, colors, and textures in plants: could anyone create them without a sense of playfulness?

A passage in the Book of Proverbs (8:30–31) confirms our reflections. As a way of praising the divine origin of wisdom, the writer develops a creation story in which wisdom, personified as a woman, pictures herself as being present when God created the world. Some translators believe that Wisdom is portrayed as "a child without a care," the "vivacious playmate of God and man, with heaven and earth as her playground."[26] A translation from the Jewish Publication Society reflects a similar understanding:

> Then I [Wisdom] was by Him, as a nursling;
> And I was daily all delight,
> Playing always before Him,
> Playing in His habitable earth,
> And my delights are with the sons of men.[27]

The Jerusalem Bible translation is similar:

> I was by his side, a master craftsman,
>   delighting him day after day,
>   ever at play in his presence,
> at play everywhere in his world,
>   delighting to be with the sons of men.

The general intention of the passage is to make play an active ingredient in God's world both at its creation and subsequently.

A parallel passage can be found in Psalm 104, which catalogs the provisions that God has created nature to supply. One of these is play or sport. God is said to have created the leviathan "to sport [NIV, frolic]" in the sea (v. 26). Here, too, we find a brief affirmation of an important aspect of leisure—the impulse to abandon oneself in play in the world God has made for the provision of his creatures and for his own pleasure (Revelation 4:11). In the description of Behemoth (possibly the hippopotamus or the elephant) in the book of Job, we see a picture of the mountains "where all the wild beasts play" (40:20).

26. William McKane, *Proverbs: A New Approach* (Philadelphia: Westminster, 1970), 357.

27. Proverbs 8:30–31, translation of the Jewish Publication Society of America; quoted in W. Gunther Plaut, *Book of Proverbs: A Commentary* (New York: Union of American Hebrew Congregations, 1961), 113–114.

The Playfulness of Jesus

The sayings of Jesus display a playfulness and humor that tell us something important about the divine temperament. This has been documented at fullest length in Elton Trueblood's small classic *The Humor of Christ*.[28] Trueblood sets out "to challenge the conventionalized picture of a Christ who never laughed . . . by reference to deeds as well as to words." Rejecting the "assumption that Christ never joked," Trueblood shows that the sayings and parables of Jesus show continuous humor. The most characteristic form of that humor was the giantesque—the hilarious exaggeration, the preposterous fantasy, the "Texas story, which no one believes literally, but which everyone remembers." Trueblood's final conclusion relates to the subject of God at play: "If Christ laughed a great deal, as the evidence shows, and if He is what He claimed to be, we cannot avoid the logical conclusion that there is laughter and gaiety in the heart of God."

There is present in the humor of Christ the same spirit that underlies much leisure. That spirit is characterized by such qualities as nonseriousness, a letting go of formality and inhibition, high-spiritedness, and spontaneity. We can legitimately speak of the fun impulse evident in Jesus' humor, and we know that a main purpose of leisure is simply to have fun. The lightheartedness of Jesus is all the more noteworthy because he was also the man of sorrows, acquainted with grief.

Summary

The accounts that the Bible gives us of God's creation of the world and Jesus' life and personality suggest that God is playful as well as serious. And if he made a world in which Wisdom and Leviathan can play, his human creatures may do the same.

Further Reading

Alan Richardson, *The Biblical Doctrine of Work* (1952).
Wade H. Boggs, *All Ye Who Labor* (1962).
Robert K. Johnston, *The Christian at Play* (1986).
John C. Haughey, *Converting 9 to 5* (1989).
Robert Banks, *God the Worker* (1992).
Paul Hintzman, "Implications for Leisure from a Review of the Biblical Concepts of Sabbath and Rest," in *Christianity and Leisure: Issues in a Pluralistic Society* (1994), 17–34.

28. Elton Trueblood, *The Humor of Christ* (New York: Harper and Row, 1964).

13

"And It Was Very Good"

Work and Play in the Created Order

Essential to an understanding of Christian doctrine is its scheme of history. History began with God's creation of the world and life before the Fall of the human race. This is the moral and spiritual norm against which we can measure human activity in history.

Of course the Fall altered the conditions of human life in the world, making possible the perversion of what had once been good. But even in a fallen world the redemption of human life in all its spheres remains a possibility. And such redemption—such progress, we might call it— is in reality a return to what had been there from the beginning. T. S. Eliot said that the end of human exploration is "to arrive where we started / And know the place for the first time."[1]

To see what work and leisure should be for Christians we need to journey back to the Garden. There we will recognize work and leisure as they truly are for the first time.

Work as God Intended It

The first words that Adam speaks in Milton's epic poem *Paradise Lost* express gratitude for God's wonderful provisions given to the human race. Conspicuous among the provisions for which Adam praises

1. T. S. Eliot, *Little Gidding.*

God is daily work in the Garden. How can work be part of God's wonderful provision? we are inclined to ask. The Bible provides an answer.

Work as a Creation Ordinance

According to the Bible's story of creation, God himself prescribed work for the human race as part of his provision for human well-being. Having created people, God commanded, "Let them have dominion . . . over all the earth" (Genesis 1:26). To rule the earthly order in this way obviously involves work.

The usual term applied to God's command is *the creation mandate.* Two things are implied by this term. To call it a *creation* ordinance denotes that God was here declaring how he had created the world and correspondingly how he intended human life to be lived. To call God's statement a *mandate* implies that it has the force of a command that people are obliged to obey.

As interpreted by Christian theologians, the command to have dominion over the earth is more than an agricultural command. It does, of course, involve the control and nurture of the physical environment. But it is also a *cultural mandate*—a command by God to perform the tasks of culture and civilization as well as till the ground.

The very fact that God commanded such work shows that human work is part of the divine plan for history. Work is a human necessity in the eyes of God. Alan Richardson notes in *The Biblical Doctrine of Work* that

> the teaching of the Old Testament on the subject of work may be summed up by saying that it is regarded as a necessary and indeed God-appointed function of human life. Since to labour is the common lot of mankind, it is important that men should accept it without complaining and thus fulfil with cheerful obedience the intention of the Creator for human existence. . . . The basic assumption of the biblical viewpoint is that work is a divine ordinance for the life of man. As such it falls within the sphere of . . . natural law.[2]

To suggest that work has the character of a natural law is a logical inference from the way in which the Genesis account links human work with God's creation of the world. Like gravity, work is one of the "givens" of the world God created. We can legitimately speak of work as a natural duty and right of the human race. It is a natural law for human existence and an expectation that God has laid on the human race as part of the created order.

2. Alan Richardson, *The Biblical Doctrine of Work* (London: SCM, 1952), 21–22.

Psalm 104 confirms this. It is a nature psalm that praises the provisions God has made for his creation. The section devoted to the sun and moon (vv. 19–23) focuses on the natural rhythm of day and night that orders the activities of people and animals. "When the sun rises," we read, "man goes forth to his work and to his labor until the evening." The point is clear: work is as much a part of the natural order as the rising of the sun. The corollary of this is that failure to work, whether through a person's choice or circumstances beyond one's control, is abnormal and unnatural.

To regard work as a creation mandate and a natural law invests it with dignity. To work is to carry on God's delegated task for his creatures, making the fullness of creation fuller. This, in turn, supplies one of several proper motivations for work. In the words of Wade Boggs,

> this is the reason man should work today—not merely to make a living, not to gain luxuries, nor to "succeed" in the eyes of the world—but because it is God's plan for man to subjugate the earth. . . . Such an interpretation of daily work enables us to realize that our contribution, however small it may appear, fits into God's pattern for developing the world. . . . All honorable work, no matter how insignificant before men, offers some opportunity to subdue this earth to God's will.[3]

Pope John Paul concurs: "in carrying out this mandate, man . . . reflects the very action of the Creator of the universe," with the result that work "expresses [human] dignity and increases it."[4]

Work in Paradise

According to the classical tradition, work entered the world as a curse and punishment. It did not exist in the Golden Age that preceded ordinary history. The biblical tradition is sometimes misrepresented as having the same attitude. One need not read long to find statements like these cropping up:

> Christian theology, of course, ascribes the necessity for work to Adam's fall.[5]

> In Christian theology [work] was God's punishment for the sin of Adam.[6]

---

3. Wade H. Boggs, *All Ye Who Labor* (Richmond: John Knox, 1962), 13.
4. Pope John Paul II, *On Human Work* (Boston: Daughters of St. Paul, 1981), 12, 23.
5. Melvin Kranzberg and Joseph Gies, *By the Sweat of Thy Brow* (New York: G. P. Putnam's Sons, 1975), 219.
6. Nels Anderson, *Dimensions of Work: The Sociology of a Work Culture* (New York: David McKay, 1964), 83.

Certainly, the distrust of and disdain for work are rooted in the begin-
nings of the Judaeo-Christian religious tradition. We are told that "man's
first disobedience," as Milton put it, resulted in the curse of work.[7]

These are misconceptions. According to Genesis 2:15, work was part
of God's perfect provision in Paradise: "The Lord God took the man and
put him in the garden of Eden to till it and keep it." McCurley and Reumann rightly call attention to the order of events in Genesis 2: "Note
the order of the created things: the man, then the garden. The man was
not made to work the garden of God, as in other creation stories. Rather
the garden was made by God . . . for the man."[8]

The original Protestants made much of this verse, and rightly so. It
shows that work is part of God's original purpose for human life. Idleness is not the goal of human life, contrary to the Greek view of the
state of innocence as endless leisure. Life in Paradise remains the pattern of what God intended—and intends—for the human race. The Puritan John Robinson wrote, "God, who would have our first father, even
in innocency . . . to labour . . . would have none of his posterity lead
their life in idleness."[9]

John Milton's portrayal of life in Paradise (*Paradise Lost*, book 4)
is true to the spirit of biblical teaching and at the same time epitomizes the Puritan view of work. Milton repeatedly emphasizes that
work in Paradise was not only pleasant but also necessary. Someone
who made a thorough comparison of Milton's paradisal vision with
the visions of earlier writers found that to portray work as not only
pleasurable but also necessary was "the most strikingly original feature of Milton's treatment."[10] There is no better summary of the biblically based Protestant work ethic than these words of Adam to Eve
in Milton's poem:

> Man hath his daily work of body or mind
> Appointed, which declares his dignity,
> And the regard of Heaven on all his ways.[11]

Here, in kernel form, is the original Puritan ethic: work is appointed
by God, is the arena within which people live as stewards under

7. Lee Braude, *Work and Workers: A Sociological Analysis* (New York: Praeger,
1975), 5.

8. Foster R. McCurley and John H. Reumann, "Work in the Providence of God," in
Work As Praise, ed. George W. Forell and William H. Lazareth (Philadelphia: Fortress,
1979), 30. This essay provides a good overview of the biblical data on work.

9. John Robinson, *Observations of Knowledge and Virtue*; quoted in Richard Reinitz,
ed., *Tensions in American Puritanism* (New York: John Wiley and Son, 1970), 66.

10. J. M. Evans, *Paradise Lost and the Genesis Tradition* (Oxford: Oxford University
Press, 1968), 249.

11. John Milton, *Paradise Lost*, Book 4, lines 618–620.

God's oversight, and is part of the dignity that God has conferred on the human race.

Augustine is also good on the subject.[12] He theorized that work in Paradise did not suffer from the cleavage between striving and rest that characterizes life for us. Adam and Eve's work was not laborious but filled with the repose of innocence. Adam experienced work that was "not only free from labour but even endowed with delight of soul."

The Fruitfulness of Work in a Perfect World

The Bible not only teaches that work is part of God's intention for people in the created order; it also hints at its purpose: fruitfulness and enjoyment. We catch a glimpse of this in Isaiah's picture of work in the new creation that is coming:

> They shall build houses and inhabit them;
>   they shall plant vineyards and eat their fruit.
> They shall not build and another inhabit;
>   they shall not plant and another eat;
>   for like the days of a tree shall the days of my people be,
>   and my chosen shall long enjoy the work of their hands.
> They shall not labor in vain (Isaiah 65:21–23).

In a fallen world, part of the curse of work is that it is often fruitless (see Deuteronomy 28 for a picture of the curse of fruitless work). But this was not the intention. By the same token, work can be redeemed from the curse.

Summary

A biblical understanding of work reaches back to the very beginning of the world. When God created people and placed them in a perfect garden, work was part of his provision to give life meaning. It can still have that purpose today.

Leisure in the Created Order

It is fairly well known that God established work as a creation ordinance. It is not so well known that rest from work is equally a creation ordinance.

12. Augustine's views on work before the Fall are succinctly summarized by Robert A. Markus, "Work and Worker in Early Christianity," in *Work: Christian Thought and Practice*, ed. John M. Todd (Baltimore: Helicon Press, 1960), 22–23, from which I have taken my account.

Rest as a Commandment

The Bible teaches that God's rest from work on the seventh day of creation sets a pattern for human life. Early in Old Testament history the seventh day of the week became the Sabbath, a day of rest from work.

Eventually the God-ordained rhythm of work and rest was codified in the fourth commandment of the Decalogue. Part of this commandment states:

> Remember the sabbath day, to keep it holy. Six days you shall labor, and do all your work; but the seventh day is a Sabbath to the Lord your God; in it you shall not do any work . . . for in six days the Lord made heaven and earth, the sea, and all that is in them, and rested the seventh day; therefore the Lord blessed the sabbath day and hallowed it (Exodus 20:8–11).

Here the Sabbath has become a holy day of worship, while retaining the idea of resting and ceasing from work. The way in which the fourth commandment links the observance of the Sabbath with creation gives it the force of a creation mandate, making leisure (like work) something that God put into the very fabric of human well being in this world.

As elaborated in the Mosaic ceremonial laws, the Sabbath command shows that God has prescribed times when people make a complete halt from utilitarian activities. God does not intend human life to be totally governed by utilitarian ends. The Sabbath is a letting go of the acquisitive urge represented by daily work. Leonard Doohan rightly says that "people who refuse to rest on the Sabbath or reject genuine sabbatical living are those who trust in their own strength rather than God's grace."[13]

The fourth commandment also suggests that God's pattern for human life is a rhythm between work and rest. Neither work nor leisure is complete in itself. Each takes its meaning from the other. In prescribing a day of rest, the fourth commandment also commands us to work. Here is the integration of work and rest in a harmonious cycle that is essential to a Christian view of leisure. Modern leisure theorists call for an end to the work ethic. The Christian reply is that we do not need an end to our work ethic but an insistence on the equal importance of a leisure ethic.

Other biblical passages reinforce the idea that God provides for rest from work as part of the good life. The annual feasts of the Old Testament calendar were days away from work. For example, on the first and seventh days of the feast of unleavened bread, as well as the day of first

13. Leonard Doohan, *Leisure: A Spiritual Need* (Notre Dame: Ave Maria, 1990), 46.

fruits, the Israelites were commanded to "do no laborious work" (Numbers 28:18, 25, 26). When the Israelites entered the promised land, they were commanded not to till their land and vineyards in the seventh and fiftieth years (Leviticus 25).

It is evident, then, how profoundly the idea of rest was embedded in the Hebrew consciousness. We catch the echo of this consciousness in a passage from the New Testament Book of Hebrews (Richard Baxter elaborates on the passage in his devotional classic *The Saints' Everlasting Rest*):

> So then, there remains a Sabbath rest for the people of God; for whoever enters God's rest also ceases from his labors as God did from his. Let us therefore strive to enter that rest (Hebrews 4:9–11).

This picture of striving to enter into rest leads me to note an important implication for the topic of this book: we do not think of heaven as a place where we work but as a place where we rest from our labors. For all its inherent goodness, work does not carry on into eternity or heaven. Rest does, and it is experienced as the reward and consummation of work.

God's Nonutilitarian Creation

Another avenue for seeing how God intended leisure to be part of the created order is to ponder the nature of the world God created. God did not create a purely utilitarian world. He created a world in which much exists for the sake of beauty, delight, and refreshment. From a utilitarian viewpoint, God did not have to create a world filled with colors and symmetrical forms; he could have made everything a drab gray. He could have made trees whose leaves do not turn color in the fall or a world in which all flowers are brown.

At the heart of God's creation is something extravagant and gratuitous, going beyond what is strictly needed for survival. Someone has commented that the lilies that Jesus told us to contemplate "are lazy lilies, occupying space amid the common field grasses for no reason other than that it pleases God. Can we appreciate God's creative prodigality?"[14] God made provision for the quality of human life, not simply its survival. He is the God who came that people "may have life, and have it abundantly" (John 10:10). At its best, leisure is part of the human quest for the abundant life.

14. Virginia Stem Owens, "On Praising God with Our Senses," in *The Christian Imagination*, ed. Leland Ryken (Grand Rapids: Baker, 1981), 379.

God's Prescription of Nonutilitarianism

Just as God created a world that contains more than what is useful, he infused the same quality of nonutilitarianism into human life. The garden that God planted for Adam and Eve was more than utilitarian. We read that "out of the ground the Lord God made to grow every tree that is pleasant to the sight and good for food" (Genesis 2:9). The perfect environment for human life satisfied a dual criterion: it was both functional and artistic. The conditions for human well-being have never changed from that moment in Paradise.

Further endorsement of the nonutilitarian emerges from the nature psalms of the Psalter. The Old Testament attitude toward nature was, in the words of C. S. Lewis, "a delight which is both utilitarian and poetic."[15]

Psalm 104 furnishes a typical example. On the one hand, this psalm displays a farmer's attitude toward nature in which everything in the natural world is good for something. The streams, for example, "give drink to every beast of the field" (vv. 10–11). But even here the things that nature produces go beyond what is strictly needed for survival. The purpose of wine is "to gladden the heart of man," and oil is "to make his face shine" (v. 15) as part of a ritual of festivity. If one reason the trees exist is so "the birds of the air [may] have their habitation" in them, there is also the gratuitous fact that the birds "sing among the branches" (v. 12).

Jesus' Discourse about the Lilies

A similar picture of how God intends human life to be lived free from the tyranny of the utilitarian emerges from Jesus' famous discourse against anxiety (Matthew 6:25–34). The overall message of the discourse is that people must set a curb to the human impulse to be acquisitive and to reduce life to ceaseless striving. The specific areas to which Jesus extends his commands are food and clothing. Jesus conducts his persuasive argument by appealing to created nature. He tells us to take a look around us at the birds and lilies.

As for the birds of the air, "they neither sow nor reap nor gather into barns, and yet your heavenly Father feeds them" (v. 26). The birds, in other words, are free from the utilitarian striving and anxiety that trouble human life.

Even more important for our thinking about leisure is Jesus' comment about the lilies: "Consider the lilies of the field, how they grow; they neither toil nor spin; yet I tell you, even Solomon in all his glory

15. C. S. Lewis, *Reflections on the Psalms* (New York: Harcourt, Brace and World, 1958), 77.

was not arrayed like one of these" (vv. 28–29). Here, too, we are warned not to be preoccupied with the utilitarian side of life.

But more is suggested by Jesus' great aphorism commanding us to "consider the lilies of the field." Here is a call to observation and contemplation, as the antithesis of a mercenary and acquisitive lifestyle. Jesus' command also implies a concern for the quality of our sensory and artistic life. It calls us to something as nonproductive as delighting in something beautiful.

A Christian View of Beauty

Leisure incorporates more than the enjoyment of beauty, but it certainly includes the experience of beauty. My journeys through the history of aesthetics have led me to conclude that the fate of leisure has been closely connected to the attitude of various civilizations toward beauty. This is not surprising, since beauty is essentially something we enjoy rather than use. The beauty of a sunset or flower has no use other than to be beautiful to the glory of God and the delight of people. What, then, does the Bible say about beauty?

We have already noted that God made a beautiful as well as functional world and that he planted a garden that contained "every tree that is pleasant to the sight." Psalm 19 praises the world of nature for its beauty: "The heavens are telling the glory of God; and the firmament proclaims his handiwork" (v. 1). There is here no impulse to harness nature for useful ends. Instead we find a contemplation of nature in a spirit of worship.

The Bible even treats beauty as one of God's perfections. David "asked of the Lord . . . to behold the beauty of the Lord" (Psalm 27:4). Ezekiel described how God bestowed his beauty upon Israel: "Your renown went forth among the nations because of your beauty, for it was perfect through the splendor which I had bestowed upon you, says the Lord God" (Ezekiel 16:14). Beauty belongs to God; it needs no utilitarian defense beyond that.

Elsewhere in the Bible beauty merges with worship. The Old Testament worshiper could declare regarding God that "strength and beauty are in his sanctuary" (Psalm 96:6). From the King James Bible we have inherited the evocative idea of "the beauty of holiness" (e.g., Psalm 29:2). The implication is that beauty, though nonutilitarian, has value in itself. The embellished priestly garments of Aaron and his sons were "for glory and for beauty" (Exodus 28:2).

What does this biblical endorsement of created beauty say about leisure? It reinforces a general biblical theme of attaching value to things and activities that are not strictly useful. This overall biblical affirmation, rooted in the kind of world that God created, opens the way for leisure, which shares the same quality of being beyond what is utilitarian.

Summary

A Christian theory of leisure is rooted in the nature of the world that God created and in human nature as created by God to live in that order. At the heart of God's creation is something gratuitous—an exuberant going beyond what is strictly necessary to maintain life. Knowing that people are by nature acquisitive, God put curbs to the acquisitive urge.

These curbs are of two types. One is the system of prescriptions that God gave to the human race—prescriptions to set aside one day in seven for rest from work, for example, and to participate in annual festivals. The other curb to labor is the allurements to take time off that God built into the created order, like the example of nature's nonutilitarian abundance, or the beauty in the world and culture that make people want to take time for them, or the human impulse to relax and let go.

In Jesus' discourse against anxiety, he told us to take a look around us and within us. God created both people and their world in such a way as to make this a *natural* thing to do unless our values have gone awry.

Further Reading

The best source to read to get a feel for unfallen work and leisure is Book 4 of John Milton's epic poem *Paradise Lost.*

Other sources include these:
Josef Pieper, *Leisure the Basis of Culture* (1952).
Alan Richardson, *The Biblical Doctrine of Work* (1952).
Wade H. Boggs, *All Ye Who Labor* (1962).
Leland Ryken, *The Liberated Imagination* (Wheaton: Harold Shaw, 1989).

14

After the Fall

Work and Leisure in a Fallen World

T he first three chapters of Genesis are the Bible's story of origins. Together these chapters form a triad whose phases are God's creation of the cosmos, God's provision for human life, and the Fall of the human race and the world from its original innocence. Each of these phases tells us important truths about work and leisure as we practice them in our own lives. This chapter focuses on what became of work and leisure in the wake of human disobedience to God.

By the Sweat of Your Brow: Work as a Curse

We have seen that work was an important part of God's perfect provision for the human race in its state of innocence. Work gave purpose to life in Paradise. The fall of the human race did not bring work into the world. Instead it perverted something that was and remains good in principle.

Work in the Fall: A Curse Pronounced

The new development to arrive on the scene with the Fall was not work itself, as is often claimed, but the shift in work's being a blessing to its being a curse, as pronounced by God:

> cursed is the ground because of you;
>> in toil you shall eat of it all the days of your life;
> thorns and thistles it shall bring forth to you;
>> and you shall eat the plants of the field.
> In the sweat of your face
>> you shall eat bread
> till you return to the ground (Genesis 3:17–19).

We should note several things about this key passage. First, the Fall changed work but did not cancel work as a duty imposed by God on the human race. God still commanded Adam and his posterity to work. As Pope John Paul stated in his encyclical on work, "God's original intention with regard to man . . . was not withdrawn or canceled out even when man, having broken the original covenant with God, heard the words: 'In the sweat of your face you shall eat bread.'"[1]

Second, the Fall did not introduce work into the world. Work as a blessing was already present. The new element is that work has now become a curse. It is, more specifically, a punishment that people bear as a burden. Something that was originally good has been perverted from its original perfection.

In other words, work has become toil—something that must be accomplished against the hostility of the environment in which work occurs. Work originally served a purpose of human fulfillment, but it is now a source of frustration. W. R. Forrester comments that "man was meant to be a gardener, but by reason of his sin he became a farmer."[2] Work in a fallen world has the character of striving against forces that resist the worker's efforts. As twentieth-century British poet William Butler Yeats puts it in his poem "Adam's Curse," "It's certain there is no fine thing / Since Adam's fall but needs much labouring."

The mention of thorns and thistles in the biblical text suggests something more than the sheer laboriousness of work in a fallen world. William Still notes that in the wake of the curse work consists of "undoing rather than of constructing and edifying."[3] This, too, is part of the curse of work—that it lacks the creativity that we long for in our work and instead assumes the quality of caretaking and even protecting the physical and social order from the inroads of chaos.

In the story of the Fall, woman's pain in childbearing (Genesis 3:16) parallels the curse of the toil to work (v. 17). Forrester comments that the Hebrew word for toil and pain in these verses is the same, adding, "It is worth noting how in language after language the same word is used for toil and child-bearing, e.g., 'labour' and 'travail.'"[4]

1. Pope John Paul II, *On Human Work*, 22.
2. Forrester, *Christian Vocation*, 130.
3. Still, *Rhythms of Rest and Work*, 6.
4. Ibid., 129.

Work after the Fall

The Book of Ecclesiastes is a powerful commentary on the curse that work can be in a fallen world. It contains haunting pictures of the emptiness and futility of work "under the sun," that is, work pursued in a fallen world apart from God and spiritual values. These negative sections of Ecclesiastes are a virtual anatomy of what goes wrong with work.

When the speaker attempts to find satisfaction in acquiring more and more goods (2:1–10) he reaches a dead end: "Then I considered all that my hands had done and the toil I had spent in doing it, and behold, all was vanity and a striving after wind" (2:11). Here, expressed with poetic eloquence, is the rat race of work.

In addition to pursuing the acquisitive path, the Preacher undertook a quest to find meaning in work itself, only to admit failure in the end:

> I hated all my toil in which I had toiled under the sun. . . . What has a man from all the toil and strain with which he toils beneath the sun? For all his days are full of pain, and his work is a vexation; even in the night his mind does not rest (2:18, 22–23).

The book of Ecclesiastes here expresses in universal terms what all of us have experienced in our own lives. The interviews that Studs Terkel conducted for his book *Working* tell us in detail what the writer of Ecclesiastes alludes to in proverbs. The Christian doctrine of the Fall explains what lies behind the phenomenon of unfulfilling work. The curse God pronounced to Adam still echoes in our ears.

A troubled student once asked me whether work should not always be inherently fulfilling for a Christian; should we feel guilty when work is burdensome to us? The effect of the Fall on work is that work is not always inherently rewarding. In fact, God pronounced a curse on it. Many of the tasks we perform in a fallen world are inherently distasteful and wearisome. At this point the original Protestant ethic lets us down. Those who preached and wrote on the subject of work overrated it, acting as though it were not cursed at all.

The Abuses of Work

Not only did work become drudgery as a result of the Fall; it also became subject to abuse. The evidence comes from two sources. We can simply listen to the news and look around us to see that work has become perverted. One abuse is aversion to work. The opposite abuse is overwork, destructive to both worker and family. Labor is often forced upon people to their detriment and to the dishonest gain of those who exploit the worker. Some work is dishonest or immoral, and much of it is directed to produce goods and services that are useless or ignoble. In a discussion of "the problem of work," Miroslav Volf covers such issues as unemployment, discrimination in the workplace, dehumanization, exploitation, and ecological crisis.[5]

The rest of the Bible expands on the picture of the vices that became associated with work after the Fall. One is idleness or sloth, which the writer of Proverbs sarcastically stigmatizes with the epithet "sluggard" (e.g., Proverbs 6:6–11). Another vice is overwork, which the writer of Psalm 127 renders memorable in his metaphor of "eating the bread of anxious toil" in a description of people who wear themselves out by rising up early and going to sleep late (v. 2). The sin of self-reliance was denounced by Moses in his farewell discourse: "Beware lest you say in your heart, 'My power and the might of my hand have gotten me this wealth.' You shall remember the Lord your God, for it is he who gives you power to get wealth" (Deuteronomy 8:17–18).

Economic abuses rank high in the Old Testament prophets' troubled vision of what has gone awry in their society. Observe, for example, the vices that Amos castigates in a single short passage:

> Hear this, you who trample upon the needy,
>   and bring the poor of the land to an end,
> saying, "When will the new moon be over,
>   that we may sell grain?
> And the sabbath,
>   that we may offer wheat for sale,
> that we may make the ephah small and the shekel great,
>   and deal deceitfully with false balances,
> that we may buy the poor for silver
>   and the needy for a pair of sandals,
>   and sell the refuse of the wheat?" (Amos 8:4–6).

This is a nightmare of unscrupulous moneymaking, exploitation of the poor by the rich, greed, the acquisitive spirit gone wild, and a valuing of work over God-ordained rest. The indictment has just as much to say to us as it did when Amos uttered it.

Summary

Work neither began nor ceased with the Fall of the human race; it simply took a different shape. It became a curse rather than an unmitigated blessing. This is simply a "given" of life as we know it. The Bible is thoroughly realistic about work and its capacity for perversion.

But of course the whole thrust of biblical religion is to offer a solution to the problems occasioned by sin. Work can be redeemed, even in

5. Volf, *Work in the Spirit*, 25–45.

a fallen world. Anything that helps us to overcome the effects of sin on work is part of this redemption. Work itself retains some of the quality of a curse, but the attitude of the worker can transform it.

Leisure in a Fallen World

Leisure also has been affected by the Fall. Human sinfulness is at least as evident in the world of human leisure as it is in the world of work. We get a few pictures of this in the Bible, but abundant evidence emerges when we simply look around at what people are doing in their leisure time.

In human history, leisure has always had the potential to degenerate into immorality. A brief list of such degraded leisure pursuits appears in Galatians 5, where Paul mentions some of the things that make up "the works of the flesh," including immorality, impurity, licentiousness, drunkenness, carousing, "and the like" (5:19–21). There is something inherently self-indulgent about leisure in that it is something with which we reward ourselves. This is not necessarily bad, but it can always cross the line into self-centered indulgence. For the rich farmer in Jesus' parable, this is exactly what happened. Having earned the means for leisure, the farmer became self-indulgent in his hedonism, as captured by his inner dialogue: "Soul, you have ample goods laid up for many years; take your ease, eat, drink, be merry" (Luke 12:19). God pronounces this leisure enthusiast a fool for his complacent and worldly-minded hedonism.

Ecclesiastes expands the biblical picture of unfulfilling leisure. In a manner similar to that of the rich farmer in Jesus' parable, the speaker said to himself, "Come now, I will make a test of pleasure; enjoy yourself" (2:1). This quest to find satisfaction in pleasure took the Preacher partly in the direction of work and acquisition, but also into the realms of leisure and entertainment: "I searched . . . how to cheer my body with wine. . . . I bought male and female slaves, and had slaves who were born in my house. . . . I got singers, both men and women, and many concubines, man's delight" (2:3, 8). This hedonist could even claim, "Whatever my eyes desired I did not keep from them; I kept my heart from no pleasure," searching for it both "in all my toil" and in leisure, "my reward for all my toil" (2:10).

But the quest to find satisfaction in leisure and pleasure "under the sun" reached a dead end: "Behold, all was vanity and a striving after wind" (2:11). Here is a picture of the emptiness that characterizes many people's leisure time—a frantic attempt to find satisfaction in a whirl of leisure pursuits that ends in weariness of spirit. Adam and Eve did not have the same problem in Paradise.

It is tempting to think that the leisure problems just noted characterize only the gross and flagrant leisure pursuits. But the abuse of leisure can also happen to the cultured and refined. Cultural activities have the same potential to degenerate that life in the local bar does.

The prophet Amos used music to symbolize a society that has lapsed into refined and sophisticated triviality, and he put it into a context of selfish indulgence that is always one of the dangers of leisure. Amos pictures people who "stretch themselves upon their couches" (the original couch potatoes?), who "sing idle songs to the sound of the harp," who "drink wine in bowls," and who "anoint themselves with the finest oils" (Amos 6:4–6). Here are the leisure pursuits of idleness, the pursuit of luxury, entertainment, drinking, and the pursuit of physical attractiveness. The picture is as up-to-date as what we glimpse in the latest magazines. Amos himself denounces the leisure lifestyle of his day as morally degenerate and deserving of God's imminent judgment.

The pursuit of leisure is part of the human quest for pleasure, and the Bible makes it clear that pleasure became susceptible to perversion after the Fall. Although (as we will see in chapter 19) the Bible endorses pleasure in principle, it contains many more negative references to pleasure-seeking than positive ones. In the New Testament, for example, we read about "lovers of pleasure rather than lovers of God" (2 Timothy 3:4), about foolish and disobedient people who are "slaves to various passions and pleasures" (Titus 3:3), and about how Moses by faith preferred to "share ill-treatment with the people of God than to enjoy the fleeting pleasures of sin" (Hebrews 11:25).

The perversions of leisure in our time have expanded the repertoire of abuses. Boredom continues to be a problem for many, especially the retired and unemployed. The search for distraction afflicts the young, at video arcades and on the street. Many people are lonely in their leisure time, while others long for time away from the crowd. People in the electronic age are subject to mindless and mind-numbing leisure pursuits, and the excursions into immoral leisure pursuits such as illicit sex, pornography, and drugs have never been more prevalent.

Leisure is not exempt from moral judgment, though a secular culture tends to treat it as exempt. Faced with the enormity of moral problems posed by leisure pursuits in a secular society, the church has tended to act as though leisure itself is ignoble and something with which Christians should not dirty their hands. This is tragic. The voice of conscience in leisure matters has frequently been lost in society at large, while Christians, pretending they are too spiritually-minded to engage in leisure, have actually gravitated to a low level in their own leisure by default.

Summary

It is inaccurate to claim that "we must not expect to derive from the Bible any explicit guidance upon the right use of leisure."[6] In addition to the positive rationale for leisure, accompanied by guidelines for both its quantity and quality, the Bible raises our awareness of the perversions of leisure that resulted from the Fall. The Fall made possible the abuse of leisure in such forms as immorality, self-centered indulgence, and triviality. The quest to find satisfaction in leisure is as likely to result in emptiness as is our life of work, as the writer of Ecclesiastes reminds us.

Further Reading

I did not find modern sources on the subject of this chapter and I think I know why: people who explore what the Bible says about work and leisure are so oriented toward finding a biblical endorsement of these activities that they overlook what the Bible says negatively about them. The best source I can recommend therefore is a Puritan classic, Richard Baxter's *A Christian Directory*, available in a modern reprint by Soli Deo Gloria.

On the subject of work, even though Baxter is primarily interested in espousing the Puritan work ethic, he has a good grip on such abuses as laziness, idleness, greed, the encroachment of work on the spiritual life, working for the wrong reasons, and choosing a vocation for inadequate reasons. Although I do not share Baxter's low view of leisure and entertainment, his constant barrage of negative statements on these matters does an excellent job of raising one's consciousness about what can go wrong with leisure in a fallen world.

6. Alan Richardson, *The Biblical Doctrine of Work* (London: SCM, 1952), 51.

15

The Heart of the Matter

Work and Play as a Christian Calling

The idea of calling is an immense topic, difficult to delineate but essential to a biblical understanding of work and leisure. The Reformers and Puritans are our best guide to the subject, which is at the very heart of what this book is about.

Work as Vocation: God's Initiative in Human Work

The Reformers and Puritans spoke regularly of a double calling that God imposes on every person. They called these the general calling and the particular calling, and it is a helpful starting point for reaching an understanding of the concept of vocation.

The Call to Salvation, Godliness, and Discipleship

God first of all calls his people to a godly life. This general calling takes precedence over everything else, including our work. The Bible speaks frequently of the call to the godly life. For example, God called Abraham to leave a settled life and follow his leading "to the land that I will show you" (Genesis 12:1). In his book *Christian Vocation*, W. R. Forrester claims that "Abraham was the first man with a definite, explicit sense of vocation. 'Faith' ever afterwards was a response to a 'call' from God."[1]

---

1. Forrester, *Christian Vocation*, 23.

The call to Abraham subsequently became a general call to the Old Testament nation of Israel to follow God, and again it was primarily a spiritual call. It was, moreover, a corporate call, as Paul Minear explains:

> This establishment of God's covenant with Israel made the corporate vocation the primary basis for each person's vocation. Wherever an individual was given a specific mission, he was in one way or another carrying forward the mission of the whole community. Wherever the community was assigned a task, implicit in it was a vocation for every person within the community.[2]

The call to accept God's salvation and to follow him in a life of service permeates the New Testament. It no longer applies to an entire nation but to the individuals who make up the body of Christ.

Examples of calling abound. Paul wrote to Timothy about "the eternal life to which you were called when you made the good confession" (1 Timothy 6:12). He wrote to the Corinthians about being "called into the fellowship of [God's] Son, Jesus Christ our Lord" (1 Corinthians 1:9), and to the Thessalonians about being "called . . . through our gospel" to "be saved" (2 Thessalonians 2:13–14). Christians are "called . . . out of darkness into [God's] marvelous light" (1 Peter 2:9). They are also "called in the one body" of believers (Colossians 3:15) and are "called to be saints" (1 Corinthians 1:2).

The call to be followers of God in the life of salvation and sanctification may seem a long way from the subject of work, but it is not. It reminds us of the primacy of the spiritual in all of life. It puts work in its place. Work is not the most important thing in life. Being faithful to God is.

The Puritans were very clear on this point. They elevated the general call to the Christian life over the specific call to tasks and occupations. William Perkins wrote, for example, that "the particular calling of any man is inferior to the general calling of a Christian: and when they cannot both stand together, the particular calling must give place; because we are bound unto God in the first place."[3]

The Call to Religious Service

A second category of calling that the Bible describes is the call to specific spiritual tasks or offices. As I say that, I am already aware of a certain ambiguity about what constitutes "spiritual" tasks. I will use the

---

2. Minear, "Work and Vocation in Scripture," in *Work and Vocation,* 48–49.
3. Perkins, *Vocations or Callings of Men,* in *Works,* 1:758.

term to mean such tasks as prophesying in God's name, preaching the gospel, or filling an office in the church.

The Old Testament prophets were called by God to proclaim messages from God. Isaiah, for example, received a vision from God and heard "the voice of him who called" (Isaiah 6:1–10). God "took" Amos "from following the flock, and . . . said . . .'Go, prophesy to my people Israel'" (Amos 7:15). God also set apart the Levites to perform the priestly duties of temple worship (Numbers 18:1–7).

A similar pattern exists in the New Testament, although the offices themselves have changed. The Gospels record how Jesus called his disciples to the office of apostle. In a similar way, Paul begins most of his epistles by asserting that he was "appointed a preacher and apostle and teacher" (2 Timothy 1:11). Within these offices, he was called to the specific task of preaching, as indicated by his statement in Acts 16:10 that "God had called us to preach the gospel."

In the New Testament we also read about specific church offices to which God calls people. In Ephesians 4:11 we read that God's "gifts were that some should be apostles, some prophets, some evangelists, some pastors and teachers." A parallel passage mentions apostles, prophets, teachers, workers of miracles, healers, helpers, administrators, and speakers in tongues (1 Corinthians 12:28). From such references we may conclude that God calls some people to specific ministries within the church. These ministries can be either offices (careers) or tasks. Applied to the subject of work, this means that in God's design some people are called to tasks and occupations that are specifically religious or church-related. This still leaves most occupations and tasks unaccounted for.

Are Ordinary Work and Occupations Also a Calling?

The important question thus becomes: What about other work and occupations? Can they also be regarded as a calling from God?

This question has been a point of immense disagreement through the centuries. A study of the history of the word *vocation* reveals that in the early Christian centuries, only those who renounced ordinary occupations and entered "the church" (broadly defined to include monasteries) were considered to have a calling from God.[4] Only with the advance of the Reformation was the concept of vocation extended beyond church offices and specific acts to general occupations and their related activities in the world. The history of the word "thus shows a complete reversal of its meaning. At first it meant the monk alone has a calling; Luther says just the reverse, it is exactly monasticism which has no

4. Karl Holl, "The History of the Word Vocation," *Review and Expositor* 55 (1958): 126–154.

calling; the genuine calling of God realizes itself within the world and its work."[5]

Was the Reformation right in its claim? I believe that the Bible supports the idea that ordinary occupations and tasks are something to which God calls people, even though the phraseology is not always specifically that of calling.

For example, God called Moses to lead the nation of Israel (Exodus 3–4). What kind of office was this? It was certainly more than a religious office. It was also a political office of national leadership. God similarly "chose" David and "took him from the sheepfolds" to be the king of Israel (Psalm 78:70–71). When Samuel confronted King Saul at Gilgal, he reminded him that "the Lord anointed you king over Israel" (1 Samuel 15:17). In the Old Testament, national leadership was a calling from God.

The same sense of calling by God extended to the artists who created the art work for the tabernacle. The terminology could not be clearer than in the following account:

> The Lord said to Moses, "See, I have called by name Bezalel . . . and I have filled him with the Spirit of God, with ability and intelligence, with knowledge and all craftsmanship, to devise artistic designs, to work in gold, silver, and bronze, in cutting stones for setting, and in carving wood, for work in every craft. And behold, I have appointed with him Oholiab . . . and I have given to all able men ability, that they may make all that I have commanded you" (Exodus 31:1–6).

Here the concept of calling is applied to a range of occupations, including art and teaching.

There is also a more general line of evidence in the Bible. It is simply that God's providence led his people to have occupations in the world. God called Abraham to follow him, but this did not mean that Abraham ceased to give his daily attention to tending his flocks and herds. Although Paul was called to be an apostle he continued to be a tentmaker as a way of earning his living (1 Corinthians 9:12–15). He did not speak of tentmaking as a calling, but there is no evidence that it was any less pleasing to God than his preaching. In fact, Paul goes out of his way to defend its importance and to offer it as a model of work for others to imitate (2 Thessalonians 3:7–9).

An office or task does not have to be termed a calling in order to be regarded as such. The picture that emerges from the Bible is that God arranged society in such a way that there are farmers, housewives, hunters, soldiers, kings, chariot drivers, and dye makers. God's providence and endowment of people with aptitudes, moreover, leads people

5. Holl, "History," 153.

into one or another of these. If they are not callings from God, what are they? How do people come into them, if not by God's design? If they are unworthy of people, why did God arrange things in such a way that people have to do them?

The key biblical text in this regard has unfortunately produced competing interpretations. It is found in 1 Corinthians 7:

> Let every one lead the life which the Lord has assigned to him, and in which God has called him. . . . Every one should remain in the state [KJV, calling] in which he was called (vv. 17, 20).

Some interpreters believe that the calling in which Christians are to remain is the Christian life and that it has nothing to do with occupation. I disagree. The context makes it clear that Paul is raising the issue of how conversion should affect one's everyday life. His answer: it does not affect one's ability to stay in an external role or station in life at all. Christians should remain married (1 Corinthians 7:10–16), circumcised or uncircumcised (vv. 18–19), slaves until given the opportunity to gain their freedom (vv. 21–23).

By *calling* Paul means our external situation, not the inner spiritual life. Paul has no reason to command new Christians to remain Christian. That is not even open to question. The context makes it clear that Paul is speaking about whether new Christians should abandon their family situations or occupations.

Fortunately we have a parallel passage in the Gospels to confirm this interpretation. When converts asked John the Baptist what they should do in regard to their occupation, he implied that they should remain in it, provided they could be honest in such a vocation:

> Tax collectors also came to be baptized, and said to him, "Teacher, what shall we do?" And he said to them, "Collect no more than is appointed you." Soldiers also asked him, "And we, what shall we do?" And he said to them, "Rob no one by violence or by false accusation, and be content with your wages" (Luke 3:12–14).

The point is clear: the Christian life infuses moral and spiritual values into earthly occupations, but the occupations themselves retain their integrity.

Paul's command to remain in the calling in which one was found is key to understanding the biblical teaching about ordinary occupations. The Reformers were right in stressing it. In its New Testament context, it was a revolutionary idea for the Greek world. Kenneth Kirk claims that Paul was forced to use the word *calling* in an entirely new sense from its customary use in order to express the idea that one's work in the world is just as much a calling from God as the call to the

Christian life. He writes, "Quite deliberately he places these secular conditions and circumstances . . . on the same spiritual level as . . . conversion itself."[6]

Wade Boggs agrees with this interpretation and cites others who are of the same mind.[7] Boggs notes that when Paul speaks of the new convert's remaining in "the calling wherein he was called" (KJV), he

> uses the same Greek stem in two different senses. The second is the usual New Testament meaning and refers to the summons by which Christians are "called" into God's Kingdom. The first is defined by the context as meaning one's station or status in life as married or unmarried (vv. 25–29), circumcised or uncircumcised (vv. 18–19), bond or free (vv. 21–23), buyer or seller (vv. 30–31).

Furthermore, notes Boggs, this understanding of ordinary work and occupations as a calling from God accords with such broad biblical doctrines as the sovereignty of God that directs a person's life, the Lordship of Christ over every aspect of a Christian's life, work as something delegated to the human race by God at the time of creation, and a person's stewardship of what God has given to him or her.

Work as Vocation: The Human Response

Unless we place work into the context of Christian calling we have little to say about a Christian view of occupations. If, however, we agree that work in general and occupations in particular can be viewed in terms of Christian vocation, we can explore what this means in practical terms.

As I proceed with such an exploration, I want to accentuate the fact that work involves much more than one's job. It encompasses the whole range of tasks and duties that attach themselves to the roles God has given us, all the way from putting in our time on the job to driving children to music lessons. Calvin said that God "has assigned distinct duties to each in the different modes of life."[8] The Puritan William Perkins spoke in similar terms when he described a calling as "a certain manner of leading our lives in this world."[9]

6. Kenneth E. Kirk, *The Vision of God* (New York: Harper and Row, 1932), 81.
7. Wade H. Boggs, *All Ye Who Labor* (Richmond: John Knox, 1962), 41–45.
8. Calvin, *Institutes*, 3.10.6, trans. Henry Beveridge (Grand Rapids: Eerdmans, 1972), 2:34.
9. Perkins, *Vocations or Callings*, 1:250.

Acknowledging Who Does the Calling

The doctrine of calling implies that someone does the calling. That "someone" is of course God. Calvin said a person's calling "is connected with God, who actually calls us."[10] Perkins elaborated the concept:

God is the general, appointing to every man his particular calling and as it were his standing. . . . God himself is the author and beginning of callings. This overthroweth the heathenish opinion of men, which think that the particular condition and state of man in this life comes by chance, or by the bare will and pleasure of man himself.[11]

Since God is the one who calls people to their tasks, it follows that God wants people to work. In an earlier chapter I noted that work is a creation ordinance, a command from God. This has important consequences. Can a person who is underemployed or trapped in unfulfilling work regard such work as a calling? The answer is yes. If God wants people to work—if this is the minimal condition for a calling—then work, as opposed to idleness, is a calling. Of course we have reason to wish for more than the minimum.

Work as a Response to God

Viewing work as a calling makes it something personal. If God calls us to work, then to do the work is to obey God. That is why the Reformers made so much of the attitude of the worker. Work becomes a calling only if we recognize God's hand in it and view it as part of our relationship with God. Here is a specimen statement by Luther:

If you ask an insignificant maidservant why she scours a dish or milks the cow she can say: I know that the thing I do pleases God, *for I have God's work and commandment.* . . . God does not look at the insignificance of the acts *but at the heart that serves Him* in such little things [italics added].[12]

As the italicized phrases show, it makes all the difference in the world if we regard work as a call from God. Viewing it that way provides a spiritual context of faith and obedience within which to do our work.

Ideally, then, work becomes a service, a means of glorifying God. The American Puritan John Cotton described it thus:

10. Calvin, commentary on 1 Corinthians 7:20, in *The First Epistle of Paul the Apostle to the Corinthians*, trans. John W. Fraser (Grand Rapids: Eerdmans, 1960), 153.

11. Perkins, *Vocations or Callings*, 1:750

12. Martin Luther, exposition of 1 Peter 2:18–20, as excerpted in *What Luther Says*, 1500–1501.

We live by faith in our vocations. . . . A man therefore . . . doth his work sincerely as in God's presence, and as one that hath a heavenly business in hand, and therefore comfortably knowing God approves of his way and work.[13]

Divine Providence as the Context for Work

An important part of the idea of calling that is usually overlooked is that reliance on God's providence takes the place of the self-reliance that underlies the prevailing modern work ethic. Again the original Protestants can put us on the right track, since the theme of providence is woven throughout their discussions of vocation.

Since God is the one who has "appointed to every man his proper post," and since we "are working for God, who will reward you,"[14] it is logical to conclude that workers find their work and succeed in it by God's provision. Thus John Cotton spoke of how a person "may see God's providence leading him to" his or her calling, of how a worker "depends upon God for the quickening and sharpening of his gifts in that calling," and of how, when faced with "care about the success" of one's calling, a worker in "faith casts its care upon God."[15] The natural result of resting in God's providence is a life of prayer and dependence, not self-reliance. In the words of George Swinnock, "If thou wouldst exercise thyself to godliness in thy particular calling, look up to God for a blessing upon thy labours therein. . . . The way to thrive in thy trade is not to trust to thy own head or hands, but to trust in the Lord for a blessing on thy endeavours."[16]

The Significance of All Legitimate Work

Viewing work as a calling also puts all work on the same plane of spiritual significance. The doctrine of vocation is a great equalizer, and there is something radically democratic about it. In analyzing the biblical concept of vocation, Minear notes,

> One effect of this was to give workers in all trades a genuine equality before God and genuine importance in the life of the community. . . . Equality was thus posited not on the basis of an immediate appeal to inherited rights or social utility but by reference to the horizons of God's call. . . . No menial work was in itself beneath the dignity of prophet, priest, or king. In fact, God chose an obscure shepherd boy as king and an unheralded carpenter as Messiah.[17]

13. Cotton, *Way of Life*, 443.
14. Steele, *Tradesman's Calling*, 4, 92.
15. Cotton, *Way of Life*, 440–445.
16. George Swinnock, *The Christian Man's Calling*, in *Works* (Edinburgh: James Nichol, 1868), 1:311, 313.
17. Minear, "Work and Vocation," 49.

If every legitimate task or job is a calling from God, its value is independent of the prestige games the human race is always busy playing. The Christian concept of calling liberates us from bondage to human value systems and rebukes people who use those systems to feed their pride or stigmatize others.

Contentment with One's Work

Yet another practical result of viewing work as a calling from God is the potential it carries for inducing contentment and patience in work. This too is part of the redemption that Christian vocation brings to the curse and drudgery of work. Tasks such as preparing surfaces for painting or typing all day or washing dishes do not carry their own reward, but if God calls us to such work we have a reason to accept it with a degree of contentment.

The original Protestants made much of this encouragement. John Cotton's statement is typical:

> Faith . . . encourageth a man in his calling to the most homely and difficult . . . things. . . . If faith apprehend this or that to be the way of my calling, it encourages me to it, though it be never so homely and difficult. . . . Such homely employments a carnal heart knows not how to submit unto; but now faith having put us into a calling, if it require some homely employment, it encourageth us to it.[18]

Cotton Mather agreed: "Is your business here clogged with any difficulties and inconveniences? Contentment under those difficulties is no little part of your homage to that God who hath placed you where you are."[19]

Loyalty to a Vocation

The original Protestants saw something else in the idea of calling that may not sit well with a society that conceives of work mainly in economic terms and that lives with images of upward mobility involving job changes. Even though social and economic conditions have changed, we should give the Reformers a hearing in the matter. Calvin, for example, wrote this about 1 Corinthians 7:20:

> Each should be content with his calling and persist in it, and not be eager to change to something else. . . . [Paul] wishes to correct the thoughtless eagerness which impels some to change their situation without any prop-

18. Cotton, *Way of Life*, 443.
19. Mather, *A Christian at His Calling*, in *Puritanism*, 127.

er reason. . . . He condemns the restlessness which prevents individuals from remaining contentedly as they are.[20]

In a similar vein, Luther spoke slightingly of "fickle, unstable spirits" who "gape after that which has been committed and given to someone else" and therefore "cannot continue in their calling."[21] And Mather, while not questioning that a person could change occupations, nevertheless observed that "many a man, merely from covetousness and from discontent throws up his business."[22]

What is at stake here? Certainly much more than an overly conservative social theory. That part of it we can discard as excess baggage. But if we are going to take the idea of a calling from God seriously, modern notions of a job become deficient.

The doctrine of vocation removes the element of arbitrariness from one's choice of work. For one thing, God's providence is seen as the force that arranged circumstances in such a way that a person has a particular work. God also equips a person with the necessary talents and abilities to perform the work. In fact, the original Protestants made this one of the tests to know whether one was in the right calling. God ordinarily blesses a person's calling with signs of approval and achievement.

Given this framework of God's sovereign activity in one's calling, how can people lightly turn their back on their vocation? If God has called us, how can we be anything other than faithful to that calling? A calling should be something with great dignity and stature in our thinking. It is not a mere job. If it becomes a mere job, this may be a sign that God is calling that person to other work, but if so, the change should be validated as a calling from God, not an arbitrary choice or a choice made from selfish motives.

Calvin stated one other aspect of loyalty in one's calling that I have found personally useful. He compared a calling to a watchman or sentry that keeps a person from being distracted from his or her main business in life.[23] Thus conceived, a sense of calling can keep us on the path of our greatest service to God and society. Above all, it can allow us to say "no" to opportunities with a clear conscience.

Much of the overwork and sloppy work that we sometimes find in Christian circles could be curbed if people stuck to their main calling or the task for which they are best suited and if they did not feel pressured to say "yes" to every request for their services. Dorothy Sayers said, "When you find a man who is a Christian praising God by the ex-

20. Calvin, *Corinthians*, 153.
21. Luther, sermon on 1 Peter 4:8–11, in *What Luther Says*, 1497.
22. Mather, in *Puritanism and the American Experience*, 127.
23. Calvin, *Institutes*, 3.10.6.

cellence of his work—do not distract him and take him away from his proper vocation to address religious meetings and open church bazaars. Let him serve God in the way to which God has called him."[24]

The Practical Effect of Viewing Work as a Calling

The Christian doctrine of vocation comes as good news to all who work, especially those who do not have a church-related occupation. It opens the way to regard work not simply as the arena *within which* one serves God but *through which* one serves him.

There is a crucial difference between these two conceptions. Most American Christians believe they can be a Christian at work. To do so involves being a diligent worker, being honest in one's dealings with an employer, and evangelizing fellow workers. But this still leaves the work itself untouched by one's Christian faith. The original Protestants were right in going beyond this and claiming that the work itself is a spiritual issue and a means of glorifying God. We can be Christian not only in our work but through our work if we view our work as an obedient response to God's calling.

A sense of calling not only relates the worker to God; it also changes the way in which she or he relates to work itself. As Russell Barta notes, "There is a certain intimacy in the way the concept of vocation links us to our work. When we say that teaching is a vocation, we convey a sense of personal dedication that is absent if we use, instead, the word 'career.'"[25]

How Do We Discover Our Vocation?

The Bible offers no explicit teaching on the question of how we can discover our vocation. The suggestions that I offer are my own thinking, as influenced by the research I have conducted on the subject and my own experience, and are in keeping with the general tenor of the Bible.

At the most rudimentary level, our calling is the job that currently provides our livelihood (even if the job is temporary) or represents our contribution to family or home life. As we will see in chapter 18, the Bible makes it plain that God expects people to provide for their needs through diligent work. God is honored by excellence in work. The job by which God is currently providing for our needs is our calling and as such is worthy of our best effort. This is the minimal requirement a job or task must meet to rank as a proper vocation, assuming that the job is itself morally legitimate.

24. Sayers, "Why Work?" in *Creed or Chaos?*, 59.
25. Russell Barta, "Work: In Search of New Meanings," *Chicago Studies* 23 (1984):166.

But of course when we raise the question of how we know what our calling is, we usually presuppose that we can choose our vocation. When such is the case, our choice should be guided by the principles of effective service to God and society, maximum use of our abilities and talents, and the providence or guidance of God as it is worked out through the circumstances of life. In none of these instances should we unduly mysticize the process by which God calls us. To discover our calling requires our best reason, research, analysis, and prayer.

First, to the extent to which we are free to choose our vocation we should do so on the basis of the opportunities that the job provides for service to God and people. No doubt we can have a Christian witness and meet people's needs in a wide range of vocations, but some jobs provide more opportunity for such service than others. Christians should make career choices as citizens of God's kingdom first of all.

Second, we also know that God has made us as unique persons with our individual talents, interests, and temperaments. God is glorified, and his purpose for our lives is fulfilled, when we pursue a vocation that meets our aptitudes. Within such a context of Christian stewardship (using the abilities God has given us), I believe that the conventional criterion of self-fulfillment in our vocation is one legitimate test of whether we are in the right place; lack of self-fulfillment or well-being is reason to reconsider our current occupation. Such an assessment must of course take into account the other criteria by which we choose a vocation (such as the ideal of serviceableness to God and society).

Discovering the vocation for which we are best suited may require aptitude tests and career counseling. These can be God's appointed means of guiding us into the right vocation, made all the more necessary by the myriad occupations in our complex society. The advice of trustworthy acquaintances including family and friends is likewise an indispensable source of counsel about where our talents lie.

Third, we choose our vocation by following God's providence and arrangement of circumstances in our lives. It is obvious that many of the "choices" that lead to our vocation are made for us by God, through the agency of people and circumstances. The journey by which we arrive at any job is a series of opened and closed doors. Here we need to pray for God to lead us into the vocation and specific job that will be serviceable and fulfilling.

Once we are in a vocation or job, how do we know whether we should stay in it? By the same criteria I have urged for choosing a career. If we are of service to God and people, if our talents are being used, if we are fulfilled in our work, and if God through circumstances blesses our work with positive results, then we have every reason to believe we are in the right vocation. Conversely, if these things are lacking, we should question whether we are in the right place.

In proposing these criteria for discovering a vocation, I have avoided mysticizing the process. Personally I am skeptical when I hear people say with an aura of piety that they came to their current occupation because they "felt called by God," with the implication that it was not a reasoned or deliberate choice. Upon further questioning I usually find that either these people took the position without careful planning, or they followed the very human process of reasoning that I have outlined. As with the other major decisions in our lives, God does not relieve us of the burden of human responsibility and choice. When asked how we came to our current occupation, I think we should have an explanation of exactly *how* God called us to that position, not simply a pious statement *that* he called us.

In considering the question of our occupation, we must not lose sight of the big picture. As the Puritans insisted, our primary calling is to live a godly life. Our occupation is not the most important thing in life, though our own society would have us believe that it is. No job that hinders our spiritual development can be the right one. And if the degree of personal satisfaction we find in our job leaves a lot to be desired, we must remember that it is, after all, a secondary consideration to the life of faith and holiness.

In discussing vocation, I have mainly focused on occupation or career, but the early Protestants rightly conceived of our callings as being much broader than our job. All of our roles in life are callings. Being a spouse, a parent, a church member, a neighbor, and a Christian are all callings. So is our leisure, as I am about to argue. These callings, too, are part of the big picture into which we must place our occupation. We should not make career choices without considering their impact on our other callings.

I have said nothing thus far about the level of pay as a criterion by which to choose an occupation. Economic considerations have been given an unduly high place by our secular society. According to surveys in recent years, the prospect of high salaries is a leading factor in the choices today's college students make regarding academic majors and careers. Salary considerations often take precedence over a student's aptitude and interests, and not infrequently parents pressure their children in this direction. One observer of the current scene writes that by the seventies "students had become careerists" whose "life decisions were determined not out of a sense of vocation, but in terms of career."[26]

There is no justification for Christians to elevate salary over the considerations of service to God and society and maximum use of their God-given talents. I am not opposed to Christians making a lot of

26. Michael Maccoby, *The Gamesman: The New Corporate Leaders* (New York: Simon and Schuster, 1976), 192.

money; if used properly, money can be a great blessing, while constant financial anxiety is detrimental to family happiness and one's spiritual life. But I continue to believe that it is better to choose a vocation on the criteria of serviceableness and aptitude than on the basis of a large income.

In concluding these remarks about viewing our work as a vocation, we might note that to view work in this light is to run counter to the prevailing viewpoint of our society, where careerism is a common outlook. Russell Barta has written,

> What if, instead of using career as our organizing model of work life we used vocation? A vocation demands that we search out our unique gifts, it demands self-knowledge and, at the same time, calls for an effort to convert our gifts into a service for others, for the community.[27]

Summary

To think Christianly about work requires a thoroughgoing concept of vocation. Such a concept includes the ideas that God calls people to work and to specific tasks and roles. To believe this opens the way for the worker to regard his or her work as an act of stewardship to God and to be content and thankful in one's work. Within a context of vocation, work is more than work—it is a way of life.

Leisure as a Calling: What God Expects

Is leisure also a Christian calling? This might appear to be a hard case to make, but upon closer analysis the case can be made on much the same basis as that for work being a calling. That basis includes the activity of God himself, the provision that God made for human life at the creation of the world, and the commands that God gives for human life. If God's command for people to work is regarded as a calling, his command that they rest is no less a calling, in the ordinary sense of something that God calls us to do.

In the Beginning

Since believers are called to be like God, they are called to rest from their work, for the story of creation makes it clear that God himself ceases from work. After six days of creation, God "rested from all his work" (Genesis 2:3) and "was refreshed" by that rest (Exodus 31:17). Human life is incomplete if it does not follow the lead of God in bal-

27. Barta, "Work," 166.

ancing work with leisure. In the words of Pope John Paul, "Man ought to imitate God both in working and also in resting, since God Himself wished to present His own creative activity under the form of work and rest."[28]

While the account of life in Paradise does not explicitly state that Adam and Eve enjoyed leisure as well as work, it is fair to infer that they did so. After all, Paradise is synonymous with pleasure and retired leisure. Even the garden setting embodies the feeling of leisure. God deliberately "planted a garden in Eden . . . ; and there he put the man whom he had formed" (Genesis 2:8). Why did he place Adam in this delightful setting? Partly for pleasure, because we read that God "made to grow every tree that is pleasant to the sight and good for food" (2:9). It is instructive to note that the perfect human environment as created by God served a dual purpose—artistry and usefulness, leisure and necessity.

It is symptomatic of the original Protestant ethic that its adherents made constant reference to the detail in Genesis 2 that Adam was given work to do in Paradise, while remaining silent about the leisure that was also part of the paradisal life. Luther's wording as he comments on work as a creation ordinance that prevailed in Paradise before the Fall speaks for a whole movement: "Man was created not for leisure but for work, even in the state of innocence."[29] But wait a minute: why must it be one or the other? Why could it not have been both? The original Protestants were so intent on sanctifying work that it apparently did not occur to them that Adam and Eve also enjoyed rest from work as part of God's perfect provision for them in the Garden.

God's Prescription for Rest in the Old Testament

In addition to God's pattern for human life as we find it in early Genesis, we have specific Old Testament prescriptions to rest from labor. One prescription is the fourth commandment of the Decalogue:

> Six days you shall labor, and do all your work; but the seventh day is a sabbath to the Lord your God: in it you shall not do any work (Exodus 20:9–10).

Since God commands rest, his people are called to obey that command. Jewish scholar Abraham Heschel has written that "the love of the Sabbath is the love of man for what he and God have in common. Our keeping the Sabbath day is a paraphrase of His sanctification of the seventh day."[30]

28. Pope John Paul II, *On Human Work*, 58.
29. Luther, commentary on Genesis 2:14, in *What Luther Says*, 1494.
30. Heschel, *The Sabbath*, 16.

The days on which God called his people to cease from work included much more than Sabbath observance. Leviticus 23, for example, outlines six annual religious festivals that the Israelites were instructed to keep. They were called "holy convocations" and "appointed feasts," and they were accompanied by a prohibition of labor. No doubt they resembled the American Thanksgiving Day when it is kept as a day of thanks to God.

When Moses later recapitulated the Sinai laws, three of the festivals were expanded to include annual pilgrimages to worship God in the temple in Jerusalem (Deuteronomy 16:16). Here we have something resembling our annual camp or retreat experiences. Group travel was part of the picture. So was camping out in remote places.

We might note in passing that the fifteen psalms that bear the heading "A Song of Ascents" (Psalms 120–134) provide an interesting index to what went through the worshiper's mind on these occasions. These songs were sung or recited as pilgrims "went up" to Jerusalem on their annual pilgrimages. These psalms celebrated such things as God's providence, national security, agricultural prosperity, everyday work, family, and communal fellowship. Here, in short, is good confirmation of Josef Pieper's theory that in leisure "human values are saved and preserved."[31] The sense of exuberance and group celebration that characterized these religious pilgrimages is also hinted at in the Old Testament pictures of shouting and musical performances in temple worship.

For an account of what Jewish religious festivals were really like, we can turn to Nehemiah 8. When the law was read to the remnant living in Jerusalem, "they found it written in the law that the Lord had commanded by Moses that the people of Israel should dwell in booths during the feast of the seventh month," and that they should "go out to the hills and bring branches of olive, wild olive, myrtle, palm, and other leafy trees to make booths" (vv. 14–15). The people did just that, and the result was "very great rejoicing" as the people "kept the feast seven days" (vv. 17–18).

This was a form of leisure—leisure of a specifically religious kind, but leisure nonetheless. The people camped out. They did it with other families. Social interaction ran high. Jewish tradition claims that during the feast of booths the leafy roofs should be left with cracks so the people could look up at night and see the stars in the sky. With this as a context, we might note Ezra's prayer: "Thou art the Lord, thou alone; thou hast made heaven, the heaven of heavens, with all their host . . . and the host of heaven worships thee" (Nehemiah 9:6).

---

31. Pieper, *Leisure the Basis of Culture*, 2.

These are not simply pictures of leisure showing that God's people took time for leisure. They belong to a category of activities that God actually commanded his people to follow. In short, they have the force of a calling.

Two Commands from Jesus

The New Testament confirms that God not only allows leisure but requires it. Jesus commanded his disciples, when they were so beset by people that "they had no leisure even to eat," to "come away by yourselves to a lonely place, and rest a while" (Mark 6:31). The other key passage is Jesus' discourse against anxiety (Matthew 6:25–34), in which he commanded his followers to take time to "consider the lilies of the field" (v. 28). The specific lesson that we must learn from the lilies is trust in God's providence, but the very act of contemplating the lilies engages us in leisure.

Summary

Leisure is not a vocation in the sense that our life's work is, but it is a provision of God that we are not simply invited to accept but commanded to observe. It is in the true sense a calling from God.

Leisure as a Calling: The Human Responsibility

God created people with the capacity and need for rest and leisure. He gave commands that obligate people to set a boundary to their work and the other responsibilities of life. In short, if God calls people to rest, they have an obligation to respond to that calling, just as much as they respond to their calling to work.

Leisure as a Personal Responsibility

In view of what I have said about leisure as a calling, it would appear that the title of Wayne Oates's book *Your Right to Rest* understates the responsibility we all face in regard to leisure.[32] Rest is not only something to which we have a right, but also something to which we have an obligation.

For one thing, our mental, physical, and emotional well-being requires us to rest. One of the common problems in the work force today is burnout, which in its lesser form is simply fatigue and stress. One study of employees in eighteen organizations found that nearly half of

32. Wayne Oates, *Your Right to Rest* (Philadelphia: Westminster, 1984).

the workers suffered from psychological burnout.[33] Burnout and unrelieved stress are not God's goal for human life. Leisure is one of the protections that God has given to the human race against ceaseless work, whether physical, mental, or religious.

Living responsibly includes living in accordance with the kind of creatures God made us to be. Not only the Bible but also the human social sciences tell us that we are leisure-seeking creatures. Human nature craves more than work and more than utilitarianism. Indulging this capacity is not selfish. In fact, it can be unselfishness, letting go of one's urge to acquire and be successful, relinquishing one's status that in our society is too closely bound up in one's work. Leisure certainly can assume the quality of selfish indulgence, but it just as often has the opposite quality of allowing people to get beyond themselves. Leonard Doohan notes that "people who refuse to rest on the sabbath or reject genuine sabbatical living are those who trust in their own strength rather than God's grace. . . . It is only in the sabbatical pause that we can truly open ourselves to appreciate and acknowledge what God has done."[34]

Wayne Oates speaks of the self-deception of trying to live as if we do not have a body.[35] When people deceive themselves in this way they operate on the premise that their spiritual energy and service to God have nothing to do with their bodies. This, too, is a self-defeating way of life. It also happens to be a heresy, since the Bible is very clear that God made us physical creatures and that our bodies are important; the doctrines of creation and the resurrection of the body leave no doubt about the matter. Even the Sabbath implies a unity of body and soul. Abraham Heschel comments regarding the Sabbath that

> it is a day of the soul as well as of the body; comfort and pleasure are an integral part of the Sabbath observance. Man in his entirety, all his faculties must share its blessing. . . . The soul cannot celebrate alone, so the body must be invited to partake in the rejoicing of the Sabbath.[36]

The Bible also speaks clearly about the importance of serving God in our physical activities. First Corinthians 10:31 states, "So, whether you eat or drink, or whatever you do, do all to the glory of God." Romans 12:1 is equally important: "I appeal to you therefore . . . to present your bodies as a living sacrifice, holy and acceptable to God, which is your spiritual worship." Because we are physical creatures subject to physi-

33. Muriel Dobbin, "Is the Daily Grind Wearing You Down?" *U.S. News and World Report*, 24 March 1986, 76.
34. Leonard Doohan, *Leisure: A Spiritual Need* (Notre Dame: Ave Maria, 1990), 46.
35. Oates, *Your Right to Rest*, 25.
36. Heschel, *Sabbath*, 19.

cal and psychological laws, to have regular times of leisure is to live in accord with the Creator's plan for us.

In addition to making us physical creatures who need rest, God made us time-bound creatures. To take time for leisure pursuits is to submit to our status as time-bound people. Robert Lee is right to stress time as an important element in a Christian view of leisure.[37]

Leisure as a Reward for Toil

Another feature of our make-up that leisure helps to fulfill is our need for rewards. We do not have to accept untenable theories of behavioralism to agree that people function best when they receive rewards for their effort. The Bible takes a similar approach. It is filled with talk about the rewards of the righteous and the diligent. Ecclesiastes 4:9 speaks of those who "have a good reward for their toil." Or consider Paul's well-known comment that "the labourer is worthy of his reward" (1 Timothy 5:18 KJV). In context, the primary meaning of these statements is that a worker's reward is the wage he or she receives, but the principle of reward for labor reaches beyond that.

Leisure can be one of the rewards that come from labor. It is something that God wants the worker to have. A work ethic based solely on the premise that we work in order to make leisure possible is of course deficient, since it robs work of its character as a calling from God. But in a more modest sense there is nothing objectionable about saying that we work partly to make leisure possible. To work in order to have time to fulfill and develop ourselves and enrich our relationships in leisure pursuits is a more worthy motivation for work than the urge to acquire more and more things. Jesus' comment that a person's "life does not consist in the abundance of his possessions" (Luke 12:15) is a foundational principle in thinking Christianly about both work and leisure. It asserts that a rich life requires more than ceaseless acquisition. Leisure is one of these nonacquisitive ingredients of the good life.

We might also listen to the wisdom of the utopian tradition. Writers of utopias tend to have naive attitudes toward work, acting as if the drudgery of work does not even exist. But on the subject of leisure this same utopian tradition contains accurate insights into the deep-seated human longing for fulfilling leisure. Thomas More, who wrote the first self-conscious utopia, describes a country where people work only six hours a day. More's utopians do not dislike work; they have simplified their lifestyle in order "to give all citizens as much time as public needs permit for freeing and developing their minds." They rest two hours after dinner. They read and attend public lectures. They love gardening.

---

37. Robert Lee, *Religion and Leisure in America* (Nashville: Abingdon, 1964), 199–263.

After supper they "spend an hour in some recreation, in summer gardening, in winter diverting themselves in their dining halls with music or talk."

There is, of course, an element of wishful thinking in any utopia. But that is exactly the point. The utopian tradition clarifies human values and envisions a better world than the one we inhabit. When writers of utopias treat enlightened leisure as a major reward of work and an essential ingredient of the good life they are telling us something we need to know—and that we do know when we look within our own hearts.

Be Still and Know

If leisure testifies to the human responsibility to accept our need for physical and emotional rest and to accept legitimate reward for our effort, it also meets the human need for self-fulfillment. Leisure provides opportunities to discover and develop ourselves as individuals. Freed from obligations, we are free to be ourselves. There is a sense in which leisure provides the time for us to get in touch with ourselves. Introspection is a necessary ingredient (though not the only ingredient) of a full leisure life.

So is solitude. Perhaps we have heard too much in recent years about the social dimension of leisure and about the importance of community in Christian living. We have even been made to feel guilty about time spent by ourselves. To spend leisure time by oneself, we are told, is narcissistic and antisocial.

I cannot agree. We should remember that Jesus spent time in solitude and told his disciples to do likewise. One of the great deficiencies in our fast-paced society is that many people have lost the values that come from spending time alone. The French philosopher Blaise Pascal found even in his day that "all the unhappiness of men arises from one single fact, that they cannot stay quietly in their own chamber."[38] When we do not find time for solitude in leisure we cut ourselves off from one of the richest sources of personal discovery and renewal. We learn things about ourselves and develop ourselves in solitude in ways that we do not when we are with others.[39]

Summary

Because God calls us to leisure we have a responsibility to heed that call. To do so is only to live in accord with the kind of people we are—people whose physical and emotional make-up require them to rest,

38. Blaise Pascal, *Pensées*, II, 139.
39. A comprehensive treatment of solitude from a psychological perspective is Anthony Storr, *Solitude: A Return to the Self* (New York: Free Press, 1988).

whose desire is to enjoy the rewards of toil, and who are fully human only when they fulfill themselves in leisure and solitude. God would not have called us to leisure without equipping us to benefit from it.

Further Reading

Josef Pieper, *Leisure the Basis of Culture* (1952).

W. R. Forrester, *Christian Vocation* (1953).

Paul S. Minear, "Work and Vocation in Scripture," in *Work and Vocation: A Christian Discussion*, ed. John Oliver Nelson (1954).

Gustaf Wingren, *Luther on Vocation* (1957).

Donald R. Heiges, *The Christian's Calling* (1958).

Wade H. Boggs, *All Ye Who Labor* (1962).

Carl F. H. Henry, *Aspects of Christian Social Ethics* (1964), Chapter 2.

Martin E. Clark, *Choosing Your Career* (1981).

Robert K. Johnston, *The Christian at Play* (1983).

Leonard Doohan, *Leisure: A Spiritual Need* (1990).

16

"Whatever You Do"

All of Life Is God's

Thinking Christianly about work and leisure presupposes the Lordship of God over all of life. If one accepts that presupposition, implications follow for one's work and play that would otherwise be absent.

The Earth Is the Lord's

The territory that I wish to cover in this chapter is rooted in one of the broadest of all theological concepts—that all of life is God's. This cornerstone of Protestant thought has a biblical basis that we should take time to note.

The Psalms are a good starting point. "The earth is the Lord's and the fullness thereof," writes the Psalmist, "the world and those who dwell therein" (Psalm 24:1). And again, "May his glory fill the whole earth" (Psalm 72:19). If God is Lord of the earth and its creatures, he is also Lord of work and leisure. All human actions within a world owned by God become the arena of creaturely stewardship. If the desire of the believing heart is to fill the whole earth with God's glory, that impulse will extend to work and leisure as well as to other areas of life.

Some key New Testament passages express the same vision. Paul stated it as a command: "So, whether you eat or drink, or whatever you do, do all to the glory of God" (1 Corinthians 10:31). Eating and drinking are thoroughly physical and earthly activities. In terms of the topic of this book, they might be ascribed with equal plausibility to the life of work and the life of leisure. In either case, they can be the sphere in which we glorify God. Colossians 3:17 commands, "Whatever you do, in word or deed, do everything in the name of the Lord Jesus." First Peter 4:10–11 encourages Christians to live "as good stewards of God's varied grace," so that "in everything God may be glorified through Jesus Christ." This is the general backdrop for us to consider the need to make our work and leisure a conscious part of our spiritual lives.

Elton Trueblood provides a good preview to this chapter when he writes, "The exciting idea behind the New Testament use of 'calling' is that ours is God's world, in all its parts. The way in which we grow potatoes is as much a matter of God's will as is the way in which we pray or sing."[1] The view that all of life is God's was the cornerstone of Calvinistic and Puritan thought, and I will allow Richard Sibbes to be its spokesman:

> The whole life of a Christian . . . is a service to God. There is nothing that we do but it may be a "service to God." No. Not our particular recreations, if we use them as we should. . . . We would not thrust religion into a corner, into a narrow room, and limit it to some days, and times, and actions, and places. . . . To "serve" God is to carry ourselves as the children of God wheresoever we are: so that our whole life is a service of God.[2]

Work in the Spirit: Rejecting the Sacred-Secular Dichotomy

The reclamation of work in a fallen world begins where the Protestant ethic began—by declaring the sanctity of all legitimate work in the world, no matter how common. This means that no vocation, including church work, is regarded as more "spiritual" or more pleasing to God than other types of work. We must remember, too, that work is much broader than simply one's job. If work in this broader sense is to be redeemed in our thinking and doing, we obviously need a view of the goodness of mundane work.

To believe that all of life is God's opens the door for all types of work to be glorifying to God. This is how the Bible portrays work. Paul urged Titus to remind Christians "to be ready for any honest work" (Titus 3:1). He also practiced what he preached. Paul was called to be an apostle, yet even in that calling he remained a tentmaker as a way of earning his livelihood. One could not ask for a better justification for the Protestant re-

---

1. Elton Trueblood, *Your Other Vocation* (New York: Harper and Brothers, 1952), 63–64.
2. Richard Sibbes, *King David's Epitaph*, in *The Complete Works of Richard Sibbes* (Edinburgh: James Nichol, 1863), 6:507.

jection of the sacred-secular dichotomy. Paul could have become a professional cleric but he refused to do so (cf. 1 Corinthians 9:3–18; 2
Thessalonians 3:7–9). Furthermore, as Alan Richardson notes, "It is assumed throughout the New Testament that daily work, so far from being
a hindrance to Christian living, is a necessary ingredient of it."[3]

Common Work in the Bible

The dignity of common work is established in the Bible not so much
by specific proof texts as by the general picture of life that emerges. As
we read the Bible we find a veritable gallery of people engaged in the ordinary work of life. Many biblical characters are known to us by their
occupations. There are soldiers, chariot drivers, garment makers, farmers, merchants, and judges. We see King Saul not only as a king but also
as a farmer plowing with his oxen in the field (1 Samuel 11:5). His suc-
cessor David was a shepherd:

> [God] chose David his servant,
>   and took him from the sheepfolds;
> from tending the ewes that had young he brought him
>   to be the shepherd of Jacob his people,
>   of Israel his inheritance.
> With upright heart he tended them,
>   and guided them with skillful hand (Psalm 78:70–72).

Here we find no hierarchy of occupations in the sight of God; tending
sheep or a nation both have the same validity.

The list of God-ordained occupations keeps expanding as we read the
Bible. God called Abraham to be a wandering pilgrim, which at the
same time entailed being a nomadic shepherd. God called Bezalel to be
an artist (Exodus 31:1–5) and Moses to be a national leader (Exodus 3:1–
10). We find lists of people who mixed the spices and made the flat
cakes for worship in the temple (1 Chronicles 9). Ruth was a farmer's
wife and mother, greatly blessed by God in her common work. Richardson summarizes the picture thus:

> The Hebrews looked upon daily work as a normal part of the divine or-
> dering of the world, and no man was exempt from it. . . . No stigma is at-
> tached to being a "worker" in the Old Testament; on the contrary, it is
> expected that every man will have his proper work to do.[4]

Paul Minear's analysis of Psalm 127:1 confirms this assessment:

3. Alan Richardson, *The Biblical Doctrine of Work* (London: SCM, 1952), 36–37.
4. Ibid., 20–21.

The Psalmist . . . does not draw up a list of preferred occupations which God approves. . . . He does not discuss the merits of masonry as over against those of army life. He focuses attention upon the persons who work. . . . The teaching [that the Psalmist states in this verse] is relevant to all types of work, and to every worker in his own employment. . . . His work is endowed with a significance that goes far beyond the visible results of that work. . . . By placing the accent on the person who labors, the Psalmist gives to every kind of work a genuine . . . significance.[5]

The Example of Jesus

The same regard for the sanctity of the common can be seen in the life of Jesus. His vocation during most of his adult life was that of a carpenter. The early Puritan Hugh Latimer commented,

Our Saviour Christ before he began his preaching . . . was a carpenter, and got his living with great labor. Therefore let no man disdain . . . to follow him in a . . . common calling and occupation. For as he blessed our nature with taking upon him the shape of man, so in his doing he blessed all occupations and arts.[6]

In his discourses and parables Jesus repeatedly showed his familiarity with the common world, talking about breadbaking, sowing, harvesting, fishing, tending sheep, and caring for a vineyard. Here, as elsewhere in the Bible, we find no cleavage of life into sacred and secular. It is assumed rather that the commonplace is sacred. The prophet Zechariah's vision of the millennium included this picture:

On that day there shall be inscribed on the bells of the horses, "Holy to the Lord." And the pots in the house of the Lord shall be as the bowls before the altar; and every pot in Jerusalem and Judah shall be sacred to the Lord of hosts (Zechariah 14:20–21).

Literary scholar Erich Auerbach's analysis of the stories of the Bible concluded that "the sublime influence of God here reaches so deeply into the everyday that the two realms of the sublime and the everyday are not only actually unseparated but basically inseparable."[7]

Protestant Glorification of Earthly Work

In view of the biblical data, it is clear that the Reformers and Puritans were right to reject the two-world mentality that made work in the

---

5. Minear, "Work and Vocation in Scripture," in *Work and Vocation*, 40–41.

6. Hugh Latimer; quoted in H. M. Robertson, *Aspects of the Rise of Economic Individualism* (New York: Kelley and Millman, 1959), 10.

7. Erich Auerbach, *Mimesis: The Representation of Reality in Western Literature*, trans. Willard R. Trask (Princeton: Princeton University Press, 1953), 22–23.

world (as opposed to church work or activities like prayer and Bible reading) second-best. Whereas the Catholic tradition tended to make acts of spiritual contemplation and devotion the sphere in which a person can find God, the goal of the Reformation was to find God in everyday life. It is in the shop, wrote the Puritan Richard Steele, "where you may most confidently expect the presence and blessing of God," adding that if one pursues his or her calling in a godly manner "every step and stroke in your trade is sanctified."[8]

The two-world mentality tends to make life in the world exempt from Christian spirituality. But the Protestant tradition, in keeping with what we find in the Bible, exempts no part of life from Christian awareness and sanction. The American Puritan John Cotton claimed, "Not only my spiritual life but even my civil life in this world, all the life I live, is by the faith of the Son of God: He exempts no life from the agency of His faith."[9]

A final conclusion that follows from this rejection of the two-world model is that the earthly arena takes on a sense of ultimacy. As in Jesus' parables and the Bible generally, early Protestantism made it clear that the spiritual issues of life are determined in the here and now, not in some "other" spiritual world. Gustaf Wingren has noted that Luther often used the imagery of "below" or "down here" when talking about vocation.[10] Christian service to God does not occur only in a "sacred" place such as a church, but in the everyday routine as well. As Luther put it, if we viewed the matter aright, "the entire world would be full of service to God, not only the churches but also the home, the kitchen, the cellar, the workshop, and the field of the townsfolk and farmers."[11]

The Bible provides a model for this attitude. Biblical scholar Amos Wilder, in commenting on the realism of Jesus' parables, concluded that a byproduct of this realism is that we are led to understand that the great spiritual issues are resolved in the here and now, not in a transcendent world:

> Jesus, without saying so, by his very way of presenting man, shows that for him man's destiny is at stake in his ordinary creaturely existence, domestic, economic and social. This is the way God made him. The world is real. Time is real. Man is a toiler. . . . The parables give us this kind of humanness and actuality.[12]

8. Steele, *Tradesman's Calling*, 83, 92.
9. Cotton, *Way of Life*, 437.
10. Gustaf Wingren, *Luther on Vocation*, trans. Carl C. Rasmussen (Philadelphia: Muhlenberg Press, 1957), 125.
11. Martin Luther, sermon on Matthew 6:24–34, as excerpted in *What Luther Says*, 560.
12. Amos N. Wilder, *Early Christian Rhetoric: The Language of the Gospel* (Cambridge, Mass: Harvard University Press, 1971), 74.

Sallie McFague Te Selle similarly concluded that "the parables again and again indicate that it is in the seemingly insignificant events [of life] that the ultimate questions of life are decided."[13]

The Practical Result

This doctrine of the sanctity of common labor has immense implications for our daily work, beginning with our jobs. Anxiety among Christians about their job does not affect only people with menial jobs, though it certainly includes them. I have known wealthy, successful Christians with financially prestigious jobs who felt guilty because their work seemed far removed from "kingdom service." There are, of course, jobs about which one should feel guilty (such as those that provide immoral services or involve immoral actions), but any job that serves humanity and in which one can glorify God is a kingdom job.

The Christian glorification of common labor also obliterates the social distinctions that society puts on occupations. In general, occupations that pay well or involve power are high on the ladder of prestige; menial or poor paying jobs are stigmatized. This hierarchy of value with regard to work has an insidious way of infiltrating churches and boards of Christian organizations. Some church boards consist wholly of successful professional people whose professional accomplishments are flaunted at election time. The biblical view of the worthiness of all legitimate occupations shows that such an attitude is wrong. In God's sight, a banker or businessperson is not engaged in more important work than a carpenter or homemaker.

Finally, the Christian attitude toward common work comes as good news regarding the work we do off the job. Here, in fact, is where we tend to have particularly negative attitudes toward work because it is unpaid and usually unglamorous work. God is interested in our washing of the clothes and painting of the house. In the words of Luther, "What you do in your house is worth as much as if you did it up in heaven for our Lord God."[14]

Work as Stewardship to God

The Christian doctrines that all of life is God's and that God calls people to their work are two mighty assaults against the curse of work. A third follows naturally from these two: the worker is a steward who serves God.

13. Sallie McFague TeSelle, *Speaking in Parables: A Study in Metaphor and Theology* (Philadelphia: Fortress, 1975), 76–77.
14. Luther; quoted in Forrester, *Christian Vocation*, 147.

A steward is one who is entrusted with a master's property. When applied to work this means that the work we perform in the world is given to us by God. To accomplish our work is to serve God with what he has entrusted, including strength, time, and ability.

The Parable of the Stewards

The key biblical text is Jesus' parable of the talents (Matthew 25:14–30). The story revolves around a master who entrusted his talents (weights of money) to three stewards before going on a long journey. Two of the stewards invested the money wisely and doubled its amount during their master's absence. The third servant, called "the wicked and slothful servant," hid his entrusted money in the ground. Upon the master's return, the industrious servants were rewarded, while the slothful servant was cast into "outer darkness."

This allegorical story is clearly about stewardship in general. The importance of what it says about work cannot be overemphasized. At least five principles emerge.[15] First, the parable underscores the doctrine of vocation. God is the sovereign provider of all opportunities, abilities, and time for work. He provides the very materials for work, as represented in the parable by the entrusted money. Having provided the things that make work possible, he calls people to work for him. The implication is clear: everything that makes up the activity we call work is a gift from God. Work is owned by God and lent to his creatures.

Second, the expectations of God are clear: he expects service. Workers are servants, actively working to produce something for their master. Work is thus a duty imposed by God on his creatures. Laziness and inactivity are judged harshly. We might say that the goal is work at full capacity.

Third, work becomes the arena of creaturely choice. Once stewards have been entrusted with their master's wealth, it is up to their choice and initiative to do something with it. Moral responsibility is a necessary part of work, once we grant the premise that workers are stewards.

Fourth, God judges his creatures on the basis of their service. Good servants are rewarded, though not with conventional standards or reward. By contrast, the unprofitable servant is banished from God's sight and the joyful community. What matters most is obviously what the master thinks about the service and work of his servants. The world's

---

15. Lester De Koster, *Work: The Meaning of Your Life* (Grand Rapids: Christian's Library Press, 1983), 39–43, has good commentary on the parable as it relates to the subject of work.

assessment of the servants' work is not even mentioned. What matters is the workers' faithfulness to opportunity.[16]

Finally, the parable of the talents reverses the customary view of the rewards of work. In the parable, the reward of the faithful stewards is the approval of their master. Financial rewards do not even enter the picture. Instead the master promises that because the workers "have been faithful over a little, I will set you over much," and he invites them to "enter into the joy of your master." This is a picture of heavenly reward for those who have served God by their stewardship. In the short term, faithful workers are rewarded with increased responsibility and opportunity for service.

Some Practical Results of Viewing Work as Stewardship

Several important ideas emerge from the principle that work is essentially a form of stewardship in which the worker serves God. One is that work is a gift. God gives the materials for the worker and the very ability of the worker to perform the work. Gratitude for work is the natural response. To complain about a gift we have received has always been near the top of the list of ignominious behavior. Complaining about the gift of work is no exception.

The perspective of stewardship also affects our attitude toward the "ownership" of work. When work began to be viewed in primarily economic terms with the arrival of the industrial revolution, it became customary to look upon work as something the worker owns and sells to the highest bidder. Alternatively, capitalism often operates on the premise that the employer owns the work of people (since work is a means of production), while socialism operates on the premise that society owns work. The Christian view of the worker as steward suggests something truly revolutionary: God is the rightful owner of human work. There is a sense in which workers offer their work back to God.

Leisure as Stewardship to God

Just as the conviction that all of life is God's extends a spiritual and moral dimension to work, so also with leisure. Leisure is not beyond the bounds of what God is interested in and what we should therefore regard as part of our relationship to him. Leisure, like work, money, and time, is a sphere in which we express stewardship (either good or bad) over something that God has given to us.

16. I am indebted for this insight to an anonymous pamphlet entitled *Reward: God's Criteria*, in the *Ministry in the Marketplace* series (Knoxville, Tenn: Vision Foundation, 1991).

Leisure as a Steward's Response to God

Earlier chapters presented evidence that God is the ultimate source of human leisure. He placed Adam and Eve in an environment that made leisure an inevitable part of daily life—a garden that included not only food but also "every tree that is pleasant to the sight" (Genesis 2:9). He commanded the human race to rest. He created people as beings who seek pleasure and leisure.

Because God is the source of leisure, the proper response is obviously gratitude to the Giver. It is no wonder that we find it natural to thank God for our enjoyable leisure experiences. The enjoyment is incomplete and somehow seems stolen until it expresses itself in gratitude to God. We are often most conscious of God during leisure occasions, from encountering beauty in nature to celebrating a birthday to observing a holiday to enjoying music. Any activity with this potential for joining people to their God deserves to be protected and nurtured.

Perhaps the presence or absence of a Godward orientation is measure by which to judge the relative worthiness of leisure pursuits. In any case, to view leisure as a form of stewardship influences the types of leisure activities a person chooses.

On the one hand, it rules out leisure activities that are immoral. For example, some leisure activities involve violence: boxing, professional wrestling, and professional hockey (where spectators are as much a part of the problem as the players). Violence is also a staple in many movies and television dramas. To expose oneself to the spectacle of violence cannot possibly be good stewardship of leisure time. Pornography, from the subtle to the blatant, has infiltrated the world of reading, viewing, and listening. In more general terms, leisure activities always presuppose certain values. What we do in our leisure time supports some values and undermines others. What goes on at a typical rock concert undermines Christian moral values. So do many movies and television programs. As stewards of our leisure time, we have a moral obligation to reject leisure activities that are hostile to Christian values. The sheer triviality and shallowness of much entertainment is an issue of stewardship.

On the other hand, treating leisure as a sphere of stewardship in which we respond to a gracious Giver encourages good leisure pursuits. A profitable way to explore this is to consider the types of stewardship we exercise in our leisure.

Types of Stewardship in Leisure

In leisure we exercise stewardship of time. Time has value because it is the gift of God and the arena within which we live out our lives before God. To be a good steward of time means to use it well, with gratitude to God who gave it. This applies equally to our work and our play. To use time well begins with a concern not simply for the quantity of time we have at our disposal but also the quality of it. The content of our time, including our leisure time, is what counts. Good leisure is thus more than mere distraction. It is the infusion of positive experience into our life.

Another way of saying this is that we are called to *be* as well as *do*. Our attitude toward time determines our attitude toward leisure. "Time is money," says the utilitarian ethic. But such a narrow view of the possibilities of time fails to do justice to the kind of people God made us to be.

In addition to exercising stewardship of time in our leisure, we are called to exercise stewardship of God's world. The creation mandate in which God commanded the human race to "have dominion over" the world (Genesis 1:26, 28) is usually interpreted as a summons to work, but this is an arbitrary limitation. We are also called to exercise dominion over the earth in our leisure activities. Dominion over creation involves reverencing and protecting the natural creation. We can exercise reverence when we admire a sunset or go for a hike in the woods or look at the morning mist. We do so when we simply let nature be what it is instead of turning it to our own acquisitive uses.

In addition to valuing God's creation in this way, we exercise dominion over it by protecting it from destruction. The advent of the machine as an ingredient in leisure frequently undermines human dominion over the world as God intended it and in many cases ends up destroying the very materials provided for our enjoyment. Quiet lakes are now overrun with gas-guzzling, noisy motor boats that use up the earth's nonreplaceable fuel and erode the shoreline. We drive our cars endlessly, polluting the environment, upsetting the ecosystem, and destroying the beauty of nature with roads and parking lots. We turn walkways into motorbike paths until erosion sets in.

A third type of stewardship we can exercise in leisure is stewardship of beauty, including both natural beauty and the beauty we find in culture and the arts. A duty is attached to every capacity we possess, including our God-given capacity for beauty. The purpose of beauty in human life is simply enjoyment and pleasure, both for their own sake and the glory of God.

The way to exercise stewardship of beauty is to enjoy it as a gift from God and to resist the utilitarian impulse to despise beauty as an extraneous luxury in life. That impulse is always present in a culture oriented toward what is useful. The case of Charles Darwin is particularly instructive. In his *Recollections*, written for his children, Darwin recalled that up to the age of thirty, music, painting, and poetry gave him "intense pleasure" and "very great delight."[17] But immersion in sci-

17. Charles Darwin, *Recollections;* quoted in Walter Kerr, *The Decline of Pleasure* (New York: Simon and Schuster, 1962), 67–68.

ence destroyed his aesthetic sense. Darwin reached the point where he could not "endure to read a line of poetry" and where he "almost lost [his] taste for pictures and music." Darwin lamented that "my mind seems to have become a kind of machine for grinding general laws out of large collections of facts," while his "higher aesthetic tastes" atrophied. His final conclusion is instructive:

> If I had to live my life again, I would have made a rule to read some poetry and listen to some music at least once every week; for perhaps the parts of my brain now atrophied would thus have been kept active through use. The loss of these tastes is a loss of happiness, and . . . injurious . . . to the moral character, by enfeebling the emotional part of our nature.

If God did not consider beauty important, he would not have put it into his world, nor the capacity for its enjoyment into his human creatures.

In leisure we also exercise stewardship (good or bad) over our bodies and emotions. Here, too, we can appeal to the kind of person God created each of us to be. He created us physical and emotional creatures. To be good stewards of our bodies and emotions means maintaining their health. There is both a positive and negative side to such maintenance, encouraging us to some pursuits and restraining us from others.

Positively, we can use our leisure to foster physical and emotional well-being. Taking time for leisure is the starting point. The kind of physical activity that is best for us depends on what our daily work is like. For those involved in active physical labor, active recreation is not essential, though some may choose it for its intrinsic pleasures. People who sit behind a desk all day need physical exercise to maintain a healthy body.

Much the same pattern prevails in our emotional needs. Most people need some type of repose in their leisure in order to balance the emotional strain of daily living. But there are also people and occasions where what is most needed is emotional stimulation.

The criterion of physical and emotional health also sets boundaries for legitimate leisure pursuits. Some physical recreations simply have a bad track record for injuries. Boxing, professional wrestling, football, and perhaps skiing fall into this category. Devotees of such sports will not like my negative comments, but the relative likelihood of injury in such sports is a moral issue. Of course many other recreations produce injuries when they are pursued too aggressively and in an overly competitive way. No physical sport is totally safe. Still, avoiding physical harm in what we choose as recreation and in how we pursue it remains an issue of stewardship.

The criterion of emotional well-being should also influence our choice of leisure activities. The sheer strain of getting to a leisure activity can make it self-defeating. We should also avoid extending our nonleisure problems into our leisure life, (e.g., someone suffering from family discord probably will not benefit emotionally from watching a movie or television drama dealing with family problems). A salesperson whose life is hemmed with competitiveness is unlikely to be emotionally soothed by a competitive leisure activity. The therapeutic value of leisure lies partly in its being a break from everyday life.

Yet another type of stewardship that we can exercise in our leisure life is stewardship of the mind and imagination. God did not give us minds and imaginations so that we could spend our leisure in mindless and unimaginative activities. Here, in fact, is a large part of the Christian case against mass leisure (leisure shared by most people in a society), which tends to be mindless and intellectually impoverished.

To develop ourselves intellectually is not necessarily to turn leisure into something utilitarian. It all depends on how we approach it. When we learn because we want to and because it gives us pleasure, our learning is a leisure pursuit. Once we leave school, the quality of our intellectual life depends largely on what we do in our leisure time. The intellectual decline evident in our culture in recent decades is due in large measure to the loss of reading as a leisure activity, accompanied by the rise of the electronic media.

When I speak of stewardship of the imagination, I have in mind especially the arts, which have fallen upon hard times in a sports- and media-oriented society. Schools struggle to maintain their music programs as students inundate the athletic program. To be well-rounded people in God's world means finding time in leisure for art, music, and literature as well as sports.

Stewardship as Concern for the Quality of Our Leisure

Underlying all the types of stewardship I have noted is a concern for the quality of our leisure life. If excellence in work is a moral virtue, so is excellence in leisure. Here, too, God wants us to be all we can be. God created us as multifaceted people with a range of capacities. Leisure presents us with an immense range of opportunities. We obviously cannot participate in every available leisure activity, but we can insure that we are complete people.

One theory of leisure is that it is the place in life where we are free to seek our ideal identity.[18] Freed from the constraints that determine much of our daily lives, in leisure we can more fully choose to become what we aspire toward. It is a mark of good stewardship to aspire toward the best rather than the mediocre.

18. Glasser, "Leisure Policy, Identity and Work," in *Work and Leisure,* ed. J. T. Haworth and M. A. Smith (Princeton: Princeton Book Company, 1976), 36–52.

To do so is to resist the common pattern of our society. One of the foremost authorities on leisure, Sebastian de Grazia, has rightly observed that leisure is not simply free time but "a state of being . . . which few desire and fewer achieve."[19] Commitment to excellence in leisure means to aspire to be among those who achieve the ideal of enlightened leisure. To do so has virtually nothing to do with our level of income. It has everything to do with our attitude. Laziness in exerting ourselves toward excellence is the greatest obstacle; fatigue is also a factor.

Excellence in leisure also depends on our education. This includes but is not limited to the education we receive in school. One of the best tests of whether people are well educated is what they do in their leisure time. One of the foremost obligations of education is to educate people for leisure, not simply in the sense of introducing them to recreational opportunities but in fostering well-rounded people who can enjoy excellence in a wide range of cultural activities.

Of course all education is ultimately self-education. We are responsible for the quality of our leisure life regardless of the nature of our formal education. It is possible to learn how to have a rich cultural and recreational life on one's own initiative. Simply exposing oneself to excellence in these areas develops the capacity and taste for them. Furthermore, no one can rest on what he or she has learned in school because our leisure patterns keep changing throughout the life cycle.

The quest for excellence in leisure extends also to the church. Here, too, it is glorifying to God when we achieve excellence. Since leisure is God's gift to the human race we should foster an appetite for the best in leisure in the church, including such activities as music, reading, viewing, and attending events. Nor would I exempt the church from the educational aspect of leisure. It would be highly desirable if people developed an interest in excellent leisure pursuits under the auspices of the church.

Summary

Because all of life is God's, leisure is his as well as our work and worship. Leisure matters to God and is therefore an arena in which we are called to exercise good stewardship rather than mediocre stewardship. In our leisure lives we can pursue excellence in our stewardship of time, our experiences of beauty, our physical and emotional health, our minds and imaginations, and care of the earth.

19. de Grazia, *Of Time, Work, and Leisure*, 8.

Elevating the Laity

Something remains to be said about the link between the idea that all of life is God's and the lay movement of the past two decades. While there may be no necessary link between a biblical view of work and the elevation of the laity, the two have gone hand in hand in recent moves to bring faith to the workplace.

Robert Banks has given the movement theological visibility. In his book *Redeeming the Routines* he notes that "in recent times we have seen a recapturing of the vision not only of the role of ordinary Christians but more generally of the connection between faith and daily life. Those involved in this arise in different settings and approach it in different ways."[20] To confirm that assessment, Banks includes a ten-page appendix that lists the names and addresses of organizations in North America that are actively promoting the application of the Christian faith to all of life.

This lay movement is ecumenical in nature in a double sense. While some of the organizations are denominational, they cover such a range of denominations that the overall effect is ecumenical. Beyond that, many of the organizations are themselves ecumenical in makeup.

The movement reaches into the Catholic church in America, where the promotion of tenets that were at the heart of the Reformation is being vigorously pursued. The doctrinal basis for the movement was hammered out in "A Chicago Declaration of Christian Concern," issued in 1977. The practical outworking of this concern to make Christian principles active in people's lives in the world is admirably implemented by the National Center for the Laity [205 West Monroe Street #300, Chicago, IL 60606], an organization that serves as a clearinghouse for workshops, support groups, retreats, and publications (especially a newsletter *Initiatives* and a series of books relating the Christian faith to specific vocations).[21]

Also noteworthy is the thriving movement that has sprung up among businesspeople to relate the Christian faith specifically to the problems of the business world. An organization called Vision Foundation typifies the movement. It publishes a series of pamphlets bearing the series title *Ministry in the Marketplace*.[22] Starting with the premise that ministry is everyone's calling, it relates that conviction to such is-

20. Robert Banks, *Redeeming the Routines: Bringing Theology to Life* (Wheaton, Ill.: Victor, 1993), 31.

21. A good index to Catholic thought and publications on lay involvement can be found in William L. Droel and Gregory F. Augustine Pierce, *Confident and Competent: A Challenge for the Lay Church* (Chicago: ACTA, 1991).

22. Vision Foundation, Inc., 8901 Strafford Circle, Knoxville, Tenn 37923.

sues as work, money, motivation, and how to build a devotional life into a working person's routine.

The growing impatience with the clerical and theological establishment has itself received a theological foundation. Richard Mouw's book *Called to Holy Worldliness* could be a weathervane signaling the direction the winds are blowing across the Christian world today.[23] The book is part of a series bearing the title *Laity Exchange Books,* whose goal is to clarify "the calling and responsibilities of the laity today." The agenda includes developing a theology not only *for* the laity but *by* the laity. While the traditional topics of theology as formulated by the clergy need not necessarily be abandoned, they need to be applied to the context in which people actually live their daily lives. For theology to matter it must speak to where people live. When it does, it will necessarily address issues that have been slighted in the church for a long time.

This movement toward lay theology encompasses a great deal more than work and leisure, but its relevance to this book is obvious. If all of life is God's, we need to explore exactly how God's presence can be discerned and his will obeyed in such areas of life as our work and play.

Further Reading

H. Richard Niebuhr, *Christ and Culture* (1951).
Elton Trueblood, *Your Other Vocation* (1952).
Larry Peabody, *Secular Work Is Full-Time Service* (1974).
Douglas Sherman and William Hendricks, *Your Work Matters to God* (1987).
Robert Banks, *Redeeming the Routines: Bringing Theology to Life* (1993).

23. Richard J. Mouw, *Called to Holy Worldliness* (Philadelphia: Fortress, 1980).

17

Why Work and Play?

Motives and Goals for Work and Leisure

This chapter is preliminary to the next two chapters, which discuss the morality of work and leisure, or *how* God directs us to work and play. A question that exists logically prior to that question is *why* God wishes us to work and play.

The Purposes of Work

Why work? Earlier chapters have provided one very clear answer: we must work because God wants and expects us to work. But why does God want us to work?

In practical human terms, the primary purpose of work is to provide for human needs, both our own and those of others.[1] This is the context within which biblical writers praise work and denounce laziness.

On the positive side we have comments such as these from Old Testament wisdom literature:

---

1. Here I follow Arthur F. Holmes, *Contours of a World View* (Grand Rapids: Eerdmans, 1983), 219. Pope John Paul II's encyclical *On Human Work* likewise makes much of work as the means for meeting human needs.

He who tills his land will have plenty of bread,
   but he who follows worthless pursuits will have plenty of poverty
(Proverbs 28:19).

A worker's appetite works for him;
   his mouth urges him on (Proverbs 16:26).

Work is rooted in the necessity to provide for basic human needs. In the New Testament, Paul laid down the command for Christians to "work in quietness and to earn their own living" (2 Thessalonians 3:12).

This same view of work as the means of provision can be found in biblical passages that criticize idleness for its failure to provide for human needs. Thus "an idle person will suffer hunger" (Proverbs 19:15), and "the sluggard . . . will seek at harvest and have nothing" (Proverbs 20:4). Again, "Love not sleep, lest you come to poverty; open your eyes, and you will have plenty" (Proverbs 20:13).

At this level, work quite obviously rests on a utilitarian ethic. Work is commendable because it is useful to oneself and society in providing for the basic needs of life. Such a work ethic does not foster work done to feed extravagance or ostentatious consumption. It also brings into question a leading feature of our own consumer-oriented economy— the manufacture and consumption of goods and services that people do not really need. In fact, most of our advertising is based on the premise of inducing people to buy things they do not need and in many cases do not have the time to use after they buy them.

I am reminded of comments made by two well-known British Christians of this century. In a discussion of Christian ethics, C. S. Lewis gives a brief glimpse into what the Christian society outlined in the New Testament would look like if put into practice. Part of the picture is this:

> There are to be no passengers or parasites: if man does not work, he ought not to eat. Every one is to work with his own hands, and what is more, every one's work is to produce something good: there will be no manufacture of silly luxuries, and then of sillier advertisements to persuade us to buy them.[2]

Dorothy Sayers paints a much grimmer picture of the consumer society into which Western civilization has fallen in the twentieth century.[3] "The gluttonous consumption of manufactured goods," she writes, has become "the prime civic virtue." It has resulted in a "vicious circle of production and consumption." Accompanying ills in-

2. C. S. Lewis, *Mere Christianity* (New York: Macmillan, 1960), 80.
3. Sayers, *Creed or Chaos?*, 69–70.

clude a "furious barrage of advertisement by which people are flattered
into a greedy hankering after goods which they do not really need," a
decline in the quality of goods ("you must not buy goods that last too
long, for production cannot be kept going unless the goods wear out, or
fall out of fashion, and so can be thrown away and replaced with others"), and designing work in such a way that it does not engage the interest of the worker, lest the worker "desire to make a thing as well as
it can be made, and that would not pay." Sayers' final conclusion has a
prophetic ring: "The sin of Gluttony, of Greed, of overmuch stuffing of
ourselves, is the sin that has delivered us over into the power of the machine."

Both Lewis and Sayers alert us to the fact that there is a vast difference between work based on a utilitarian ethic and work based on a
consumer ethic. At a personal level, it would seem that Christian workers should ask the question of the usefulness of the work they do.
Harold Lehman has written that "any work in which a contribution can
be made somewhere to the total needs of man must be regarded as a
good and natural way for a Christian to live in his calling."[4] The reverse
of this principle is that if a person's work does not contribute to the
needs of society, it might not be fulfilling a God-intended purpose.

A second purpose of work is to provide meaning and self-fulfillment
for human life. The Bible does not state this directly, but it follows logically from the fact that God, who himself is a creative worker, made
people in his image and gave them work to do. God gave Adam and Eve
dominion over the world (Genesis 1:26, 28). Work was originally creative, declaring both the creature's humanity and link with deity (inas-
much as people were created in the image of God who works).

This ideal remains the goal of work, even though work in a fallen
world often falls short of that purpose. Judged according to this purpose,
work is good when it leads to human fulfillment and bad when it dehu-
manizes a worker, since such work does not meet God's intention for
work. As John Stott has written,

> Our potential for creative work is an essential part of our Godlike human-
> ness, and without work we are not fully human. If we are idle (instead of
> busy) or destructive (instead of creative) we deny our humanity and so
> forfeit our self-fulfillment.[5]

In our consumer-oriented society, the tendency is overwhelming to
act on the premise that work is acceptable if it produces what society
wants. The result, as we know, is an abundance of jobs that are uncre-

---

4. Lehman, *In Praise of Leisure*, 117.
5. John Stott, "Reclaiming the Biblical Doctrine of Work," *Christianity Today*, 4
May 1979, 36.

ative and dehumanizing. If we gave priority to the principle that work should be as fulfilling as possible, instead of giving priority to the human appetite for goods, we would eliminate many jobs and the goods or services they produce. From the viewpoint of Christian ethics, this would be a step in the right direction.

In addition to providing for human needs and human fulfillment, work has as its purpose the glory of God. God's own work glorifies him as creator. Furthermore, God is the one who calls people to their tasks. To accept those tasks is to obey God and thus bring glory to him. Of course perversion of work remains a possibility. People can carry out their work with no thought of God as the one who calls them to it, and they can perform their work in an immoral way.

It goes without saying that work done in an immoral way or in the service of immoral activities does not glorify God. The Bible cites examples of trade based on idolatry (Acts 19:19–27), exploitation (numerous prophetic passages), and dishonesty (Luke 3:12–14). In our day, the moral decline in society at large has greatly amplified the incidence of work based in immorality. Examples include the practice of deceiving people into paying for unnecessary work, cheating either management or the consumer, dishonest business practices, and work related to such immoral practices as pornography or drunkenness.

Summary

Work serves three main purposes in the world. It exists to provide for human needs, to fulfill our humanity, and to glorify God. These goals, in turn, are standards by which we can weigh the worthiness of work.

Motivations for Work

The motivations for work correspond to the purposes of work. Employers are perpetually preoccupied with the psychological motivations of work. Basically they fall into the categories of appealing to workers' self-interest and meeting workers' needs. While these are legitimate concerns, the Bible has nothing directly to add to the discussion.

When, however, we move to the notion that one purpose of work is to glorify God a whole new area of motivation opens up. Our society encourages us to think of our work as something we do for ourselves, our employer, or the public we serve. In addition to asking "what's in it for us," modern notions of accountability and job performance have also made us obsessed with pleasing the boss or the public. But where do we hear about pleasing God as the primary motivation in our work?

When we turn to the New Testament, we find an emphasis that sounds strange to modern ears:

> Whatever your task, work heartily, as serving the Lord and not men, knowing that from the Lord you will receive the inheritance as your reward; you are serving the Lord Christ (Colossians 3:23–24).

> Be obedient to those who are your earthly masters . . . as to Christ; not in the way of eyeservice, as men-pleasers, but as servants of Christ, doing the will of God from the heart, rendering service with a good will as to the Lord and not to men (Ephesians 6:5–7).

Our secular society lacks the antennae by which to understand such a view of work, and I fear that Christians today find it just as foreign to their thinking.

It did not seem foreign to the original Protestants. Luther said that "the life of all Christians is intended for the eyes of God alone. . . . It is enough that our action is intended to satisfy and to glorify the One who sees it."[6] The same view is expressed in a poem written by a young Puritan on the occasion of his twenty-third birthday. John Milton's seventh sonnet opens with self-rebuke at his lack of achievement to date. But the consolation expressed in the famous ending of the poem is based on the idea of work as stewardship to God: "All is, if I have grace to use it so, / As ever in my great task-master's eye."

The most plausible interpretation of the lines is this: "All that matters is that I have the grace to use my time in such a way that I am always conscious of living in my great taskmaster's presence." The evocative phrase "my great task-master" sums up the Puritan consciousness of working for God. The identity of the worker, in this view, comes from his or her relationship to God, not from the prestige or financial rating of the job or task. The motivation likewise comes from a desire to please a heavenly master more than an earthly master.

This fits well with Calvin's distinctive contribution to the history of work. Calvin made the glory of God the goal of work:

> Calvin's contention was that a person's body . . . is not his own but is God's. Thus any talents he has in the performing of his work came not from himself but from God and should therefore be used for God's enhancement and not his own. All should be done to the glory of God. Work, then, should be discharged in this spirit of glorification, of duty, and of service to Him through service to fellow men.[7]

---

6. Martin Luther, sermon on Matthew 6:16–18, in *Luther's Works*, 21:164.

7. Robert S. Michaelson, "Changes in the Puritan Concept of Calling or Vocation," *New England Quarterly* 26 (1953):317.

Here, in fact, is one of the antidotes to the syndrome of overwork that characterizes the contemporary work scene. We cannot imagine God being glorified by the type of strain that some people bring upon themselves as they pursue the advancement of their career or a lifestyle that requires overwork.

Summary

The motivation for work—pleasing God—is also a pattern for *how* to work, namely, in an awareness of serving God through work. The best summary I can provide for this discussion of the motivations and goals of work is a poem by the seventeenth-century British poet and Anglican priest George Herbert. The poem is entitled "The Elixir," an allusion to the search by medieval alchemists to find the magical element that would turn all other elements to gold:

> Teach me, my God and King,
> In all things thee to see,
> And what I do in any thing,
> To do it as for thee. . . .
>
> All may of thee partake:
> Nothing can be so mean [mundane],
> Which with his tincture (for thy sake)
> Will not grow bright and clean.
>
> A servant with this clause
> Makes drudgery divine:
> Who sweeps a room as for thy laws,
> Makes that and th' action fine.
>
> This is the famous stone
> That turneth all to gold:
> For that which God doth touch and own
> Cannot for less be told.

The Personal Functions of Leisure

Leisure theorists and psychologists alert us to the broad range of functions served by leisure. They include repose from work, relaxation, diversion, personal development, and participation in common humanity. What does the Bible encourage us to think about these functions of leisure? We can profitably divide the material into the personal functions of leisure and the social functions.

Is Self-Pleasure a Reason for Leisure?

Both secular and Christian thinkers have taken aim in recent years at the self-absorption and individualistic spirit of our own moment in history. It is of course a caution that we need to hear. The biblical view of the person is that people never find complete fulfillment and meaning in isolation from relationships with other people, their community, and God. But in some circles we have heard so much about the dangers of self-centeredness that we are in danger of losing the balance that ought to prevail. What *does* the Bible say about indulging our desire for self-pleasure?

We can start with the example of Jesus, who sometimes drew a boundary around his obligations to serve others. On one occasion, with a throng of inquirers looking on, Jesus sent his disciples out on a boat, dismissed the crowd, and took off to spend time in solitude (Mark 6:45–47). On another occasion he told the disciples to "come away by yourselves to a lonely place, and rest a while" (Mark 6:31). I am reminded of an anecdote recounting an orthopedic surgeon's heading out with his wife on a bike ride while his beeper goes off.[8] We cannot fight against the way in which God created us. One of our needs is for rest and renewal. There is a time for self-sacrifice and a time for self-satisfaction.

To this we can add the repeated statements in the Bible commanding us to delight ourselves and offering us the promise of reward for our labors. Looking at these patterns C. S. Lewis noted that although the New Testament says a lot about denying ourselves, "nearly every description of what we shall ultimately find if we do so contains an appeal to desire."[9] Furthermore, wrote Lewis,

> If there lurks in most modern minds the notion that to desire our own good and earnestly to hope for the enjoyment of it is a bad thing, I submit that this . . . is no part of the Christian faith. Indeed, if we consider the unblushing promises of reward and the staggering nature of the rewards promised in the Gospels, it would seem that Our Lord finds our desires not too strong, but too weak.[10]

The general principle is simply that the Bible does not discredit our desire to seek our own joy and fulfillment. Jesus even "endured the cross" for "the joy that was set before him" (Hebrews 12:2). Leisure is one of the desires that we seek for ourselves.

8. James C. Dekker, "Playing Squash While People Starve," *The Banner*, 11 March 1991, 16.
9. C. S. Lewis, *The Weight of Glory and Other Addresses* (Grand Rapids: Eerdmans, 1965), 1.
10. Ibid., 1–2.

The golden rule itself points in the direction of a legitimate self-love. It commands us to desire for others what we desire for ourselves, thereby setting up an equation between ourselves and others. If we desire the pleasures and rewards of leisure for others we may desire them for ourselves.

Psalm 23 is an evocative meditation on the provisions of God for us. As it chronicles the events in a typical day in the life of a shepherd, the psalm notes the steps a shepherd takes to provide for the needs of his sheep. One of the provisions is leading the sheep to green pastures and still waters where the sheep can have their vitality restored by noontime rest in a lush, shady oasis. The psalm is a metaphoric picture of the provisions that God provides for his human creatures. One of those provisions is leisure—an oasis in the world of work and duty. Personal refreshment is not extraneous to life or a selfish indulgence, but a gift from God to the individual.

Leisure as Part of the Redemption of Life

At the heart of the Christian faith is the experience of redemption—the return to a state that was lost. Leisure is part of this redemptive principle. Its purpose is to bring us back to physical, mental, and emotional strength and wholeness. We can perhaps regain the fullness of meaning in a word that has become somewhat trivialized in current usage by inserting an unexpected hyphen in *re-creation*. The purpose of leisure is to re-create a person, to restore him or her to an earlier condition.

Ralph Glasser, writing from a social scientific perspective, believes that in leisure people pursue an ideal identity that they have created for themselves.[11] But as Glasser notes, in a secular society that has lost its spiritual roots, the ideal identity that people hold is confused and emaciated. In the words of a sociologist of leisure, "Separated from [a] spiritual view, the idea of recreation has the aimless circularity of simply restoring us to a state in which we can best continue our work."[12]

The Christian faith supplies depth to the very idea of leisure as personal fulfillment. The person in Christ has an identity toward which to aspire. Leisure, because it is "the growing time of the human spirit" and a time "for rest and restoration, for rediscovering life in its entirety,"[13] provides space for a Christian to re-establish that identity.

Within this context we can see a kinship between worship and leisure. Both worship and leisure require that we call a temporary halt

11. Ralph Glasser, "Leisure Policy, Identity and Work," in *Work and Leisure,* ed. J. T. Haworth and M. A. Smith (Princeton: Princeton Book Company, 1976), 36–52.
12. Parker, *Sociology of Leisure,* 107.
13. Lee, *Religion and Leisure in America,* 35.

to our work and duties. Both equip us for life by temporarily removing us from it. They also share the goals of re-creation and refreshment and recalling us to our true selves. Worship and prayer raise leisure to a spiritual plane, but in function they share the place of leisure in our lives. That is why Josef Pieper, who has a high view of leisure as "a condition of the soul," believes that the basis of leisure is divine worship. "Cut off from the worship of the divine," Pieper writes, "leisure becomes laziness and work inhuman."[14] One of the personal functions of leisure is to restore people to the highest inner wholeness of which they are capable.

The Social Functions of Leisure

Leisure provides for personal satisfaction, but its function does not stop there. Leisure is inherently (though not exclusively) social. Many leisure activities occur in group settings. Leisure is considered a responsibility of society and government, all the way from providing park land and building recreational facilities to running city recreational programs and sponsoring cultural events.

The social dimension of leisure is itself sufficient to make it a concern for Christians. The Bible portrays people as relational beings intended to live with other people. Such a view of the person makes leisure a key ingredient in the Christian life. Freed from the obligations of daily living, in leisure we can enjoy people and activities for their own sakes.

Leisure and the Family

The family is perhaps the most important social arena within which leisure occurs. We have not been accustomed to regard leisure as a responsibility of the Christian family, but we should begin to look upon it in this light. Families have the potential to spend more time together in leisure activities than in working together. But it is only a potential.

The first step toward accepting the responsibility to cultivate family relationships in leisure is to curb the tendency for family members to separate from each other and join people of their own age group. We live in a highly specialized society, and our leisure patterns tend to reflect this. In giving in to this pattern Christian families have lost many opportunities to build family unity through shared leisure experiences, and this at a time when the family is losing its force as an institution in our society.

14. Pieper, *Leisure the Basis of Culture*, 48.

The responsibility of a Christian family in regard to leisure extends beyond simply doing leisure activities together. Education for leisure is also a family responsibility, especially for parents. I say this because leisure always reflects the values of people, and Christian parents are responsible to instill the best possible values in their children. Of course children can also be excellent educators of leisure in a family, but for the most part, children learn their leisure patterns from their parents. If parents provide no clear guidelines, children will learn their leisure patterns elsewhere. Leisure is a learned behavior. People do in their leisure time what they have learned to do. To ignore the importance of inculcating leisure values in children is a serious abdication of parental duty.

In fact, I will not shrink from saying that family leisure is a moral responsibility, with particular application to people who like to work all the time. While workaholics tend to be happy with their lifestyle,[15] when placed into a framework of responsibility to family we should conclude that people are obligated to participate in leisure activities with their families.

Leisure and Friendships

Another social function of leisure is the fostering of friendships. Without shared leisure pursuits, most of our friendships would be anemic and eventually die. Friendships require the nurturing power of leisure.

Many things make up the leisure that is available to friends. One is conversation over shared meals. The Bible portrays hospitality as a duty or obligation (as, indeed, it often is), but the festivity of extending or receiving hospitality is just as much a part of this virtue. Participating in leisure activities together is another dimension of leisure in friendship. Of course it takes additional planning to go to an event with another family or other people, but the rewards are high. I think of occasions when my wife and I have attended concerts, films, and picnics with another couple or family as leisure time well spent because it enhanced both a friendship and our enjoyment of the event.

In talking about the role of leisure in family living and friendships I am impressed again by the way in which leisure helps restore distinctly human values. In leisure we put ourselves in touch with what is truly valuable in our lives.

Leisure and Romance

The Song of Solomon is a good reminder of the role that leisure plays in the rituals of courtship and romantic love. For most people, court-

---

15. Machlowitz, *Workaholics*.

ship and romance provide the occasion for some of the most memorable leisure experiences in a person's lifetime. People in love want to be together, and their customary way of being together is in leisure pursuits.

Part of the appeal of the courtship that we recreate as we read the Song of Solomon is its leisureliness. What one literary critic says of the romance of Adam and Eve in Milton's *Paradise Lost* also applies to the couple in the Song of Solomon: "Their love is not urgent because they are perpetually in love. They process through the Garden with a dignity immune to the pressure of lapsarian time."[16] The main activity of the lovers in the Song of Solomon is simply being together, enjoying the delights of each other and nature. Their goal is a retreat from the worries ("the little foxes") of the workaday world. A holiday spirit breathes through this idealized collection of love lyrics.

Although we might not ordinarily look upon the Song of Solomon as a repository of biblical teaching about play and leisure, it is such. It shows us that one of the functions of leisure is to allow love to flourish, including love between man and woman. Without leisure, romance would hardly have a chance. Courtship and romance (including married romance) are a great impetus to leisure by prompting people to take time for it.

Leisure and the Church

Leisure reaches beyond the family and our circle of friends to include the church as well. Several things make up the function of leisure in the church.

One obligation of the church in regard to leisure is to assert a Christian view of leisure from the pulpit and in the classroom. Many churchgoers would be surprised to learn that one can think Christianly about leisure. We should not assume that the average person in the pew believes that leisure is good. Commitment to work, to achievement, and to Christian service runs strong in most churches.

Of course the opposite situation also exists; some church people are so busy pursuing leisure activities that they are seldom or never available to serve within the church. Television and sports have made the Sunday evening service obsolete in many churches. In such cases the church needs to preach a message of moderation in leisure and the need for balance in the Christian life.

In general, the church in our century has ignored the issue of leisure. It would be easy to get the impression that Christians should be above indulging in leisure. The truth is, of course, that no one in our society gets by without spending some time in leisure activities. By pretending

16. J. B. Broadbent, *Some Graver Subject: An Essay on Paradise Lost* (London: Chatto and Windus, 1967), 190.

that they are exempt from leisure, many Christians drift by default into a relatively low-quality leisure life.

In addition to providing direction to people's thinking about leisure, the church would do well to provide occasions for leisure among its members. Writing this book has given me a new appreciation for the legitimacy of church-sponsored leisure activities. Youth programs require them, but so do adult programs. If sociologists are right about the function of leisure in relating people to each other and to groups, we must conclude that much of what the New Testament Epistles say about the unity of believers can be fostered and expressed by shared leisure activities, from visiting in each other's homes to attending events together.

We should not make too sharp a distinction between the spiritual and social functions of the church. The church is first of all a spiritual fellowship, to be sure, but it is also an institution made up of people with normal human needs. These needs include sociability, relaxation, and enjoyment. In our efforts to avoid the liberals' error of turning the church into a social club we must not ignore the need for human fellowship and shared enjoyment.

Leisure and Worship

Spiritual exercises such as worship services, Bible studies, and prayer groups share some of the same qualities as leisure. They remove us from the world of work and daily obligation and then send us back to that world refreshed. They clear a space for important values to reassert themselves. If I am right in these observations, church life contains within it at least a partial counter-balance to its tendency to rob people of leisure with its duties and work.

Something needs to be said, too, about the relationship between Sunday observance and leisure. The principle of sabbath rest can be traced back to God's rest after his work of creation, which suggests that leisure has important connections to Sunday observance. I am not recommending desecration of the Lord's Day but a renewed awareness that what happens in church on Sunday has an element of leisure to it, and that the free time on Sunday afternoon can be an occasion for godly leisure.

Summary

Why play? The Bible supports the findings of the social and psychological sciences that leisure serves important functions in the human economy. It allows for renewal and fulfillment of the individual, and it provides opportunity for people to relate to their family, friends, and church.

Leisure as Celebration and Festivity

One of the functions of leisure is to provide celebration and festivity in our lives and in society. Its very status as a parenthesis in the duties of life makes it seem festive. Furthermore, many of our leisure pursuits consist of celebrating such things as God's achievement in nature and human achievement in culture.

Much of our leisure is organized by society. I have in mind religious holy days such as Easter and Christmas, national holidays such as the Fourth of July and Labor Day, and seasonal celebrations such as Thanksgiving and New Year. On such days we celebrate an event or occasion. The same is true of such private commemorations as the celebration of weddings, anniversaries, and birthdays.

In view of the large place such celebration and festivity plays in our leisure lives, it is appropriate to note how they played an equally important role in the life of God's people in the Bible.

Religious Festivals in the Old Testament

In chapter 15 I noted how Hebrew life was structured around the annual calendar of holy days. The effect of that calendar was to insure a regular diet of communal festivals.

In addition to the prescribed religious festivals, at least one additional festival evolved during the exile, the feast of Purim whose origin is recounted in the book of Esther. The festival commemorates Esther's heroism that delivered the Jews from the plot of Haman. On the day after the Jews had defended themselves against their enemies, "they rested and made that a day of feasting and gladness" (Esther 9:17). In later Jewish history it became "a day for gladness and feasting and holiday-making, and a day on which they send choice portions to one another" (Esther 9:19).

While we no longer celebrate such Old Testament festivals, they provide a model for how leisure can fulfill the human need for communal ritual and festivity. The Bible does not sanction the specific communal celebrations that we observe in our nations today, but it confirms the important functions that these can serve.

Even the modern institution of the weekend shares something with a festival like the Feast of Purim. Witold Rybczynski speaks of the weekend as sharing "this sense of reenactment with sacred time," an interval characterized, like the rituals of older cultures, by ritual, by making ordinary time stand still, by calling a halt to ordinary work, by the presence of conventions like raking leaves, grilling steaks, going for rides, and visiting.[17] Granted, this is a thoroughly secularized version

17. Rybczynski, *Waiting for the Weekend*, 230–31.

of "sacred space," but thinking about the weekend in this way opens up some legitimate avenues for Christians to value the weekend.

Private Feasting and Hospitality in the Bible

In addition to the officially prescribed holy days of biblical times, we read about private feasting and hospitality. These accounts, too, give us pictures of the function of leisure in meeting the human need for celebration and festivity.

The "classic" among these stories is the meal that Abraham and Sarah prepared for three angelic visitors (Genesis 18:1–8). The event meets all the criteria of a leisure occasion. It is set apart from ordinary daily life. The three visitors rest under a tree while Abraham and Sarah, as ideal hosts, prepare a meal. A lavish meal it is, replete with cakes, curds, milk, and roast beef. Having provided the materials for leisure, Abraham stands under a tree while his guests eat and then enters into conversation with them after the meal. It was in every way an occasion of festive entertainment and leisure.

Play in the Coming Kingdom

If we shift the historical focus from the Hebrew past to the Bible's eschatological pictures of the coming kingdom we find that there, too, people will join in playful celebration and festivity. The brief pictures of the future life that the Bible gives us provide no hint of work but only an abundance of feasting and celebration. In addition to the rest that remains for the people of God (Hebrews 4:9–10), there is play and festivity. Here are three specimen descriptions from the Bible:

> The streets of the city shall be full of boys and girls playing in its streets (Zechariah 8:5).

> The city shall be rebuilt upon its mound,
>   and the palace shall stand where it used to be.
> Out of them shall come songs of thanksgiving,
>   and the voices of those who make merry (Jeremiah 30:18–19).

> Again you shall adorn yourself with timbrels,
>   and shall go forth in the dance of the merrymakers. . . .
> Then shall the maidens rejoice in the dance,
>   and the young men and the old shall be merry.
> I will turn their mourning into joy,
>   I will comfort them, and give them gladness for sorrow,
> I will feast the soul of the priests with abundance,
>   and my people shall be satisfied with my goodness (Jeremiah 31:4, 13–14).

Celebration and festivity will make life full in the coming kingdom, and they serve the same function now.

Eating and Drinking with Jesus

The human need for celebration and festivity is equally endorsed in the New Testament, where the chief example is Jesus. The wedding party that Jesus attended at Cana in Galilee (John 2:1–11) was simultaneously a social and religious occasion. It was a wedding celebration carried out according to the best ceremonial rules, as evidenced by the large water jars for purification rituals that figure prominently in the story. Not only did Jesus' presence at such a party lend sanction to it— he actually turned water into wine to keep the party going. C. S. Lewis interpreted the event thus: "The miracle at Cana in Galilee by sanctifying an innocent, sensuous pleasure could be taken to sanctify . . . a recreational use of culture—mere 'entertainment.'"[18]

We see here in microcosm something that pervades the Gospels. If we arranged Jesus' life during his public years into a few composite portraits, one of these would be a picture of Jesus attending dinners or parties. It was rightly said of him that "the Son of man has come eating and drinking"—so much so that Jesus' critics were offended by his behavior, saying, "Behold, a glutton and drunkard, a friend of tax collectors and sinners!" (Luke 7:34).

What the Biblical Endorsement of Celebration Means

The biblical information about religious festivals, the entertainment of guests, and the convivial lifestyle of Jesus tell us something important about the celebratory function of leisure. Two writers on leisure have elaborated this point.

Josef Pieper makes celebration and the feast the center of leisure.[19] He writes that "the soul of leisure . . . lies in 'celebration.'" The meaning of celebration, moreover, "is man's affirmation of the universe and his experiencing the world in an aspect other than its everyday one." Because Pieper writes as a Christian he believes that the basis of true celebration is divine worship. There can be no festival or marriage without God, writes Pieper, and nothing shows this more clearly than the emptiness that accompanies celebrations devoid of a sense of Christian worship. He speaks of the difference between "a living and deeply traditional feast day, with its roots in divine worship, and one of those rootless celebrations, carefully and unspontaneously prepared beforehand, and as artificial as a maypole."

18. C. S. Lewis, *Christian Reflections* (Grand Rapids: Eerdmans, 1967), 15.
19. Pieper, *Leisure the Basis of Culture*, 44–46.

Harvey Cox has written at much greater length about the intersections between leisure and festivity.[20] Festivity, says Cox, is a form of play, "the special time when ordinary chores are set aside while man celebrates some event, affirms the sheer goodness of what is, or observes the memory of a god or hero." It is a distinctly human activity. In Cox's view, "Man is *homo festivus*," but forces in modern culture have conspired to the point where "man's celebrative . . . faculties have atrophied." Christianity has failed to preserve the elements of festive leisure that it once supplied to Western culture.

Summary

Life without festivity is less than human. While the private and public celebrations of modern society are decidedly secular, Christians can resist that trend by making them Christian. To do so, they need to self-consciously bring thoughts of God into their merrymaking and rituals.

Further Reading

Dorothy L. Sayers, "Why Work?" in *Creed or Chaos?* (1949), 46–62.
Josef Pieper, *Leisure the Basis of Culture* (1952).
Harold D. Lehman, *In Praise of Leisure* (1974).
Lewis B. Smedes, "Theology and the Playful Life," in *God and the Good*, ed. Clifton Orlebeke and Lewis Smedes, (1975), 46–62.
Robert K. Johnston, *The Christian at Play* (1983).
Leonard Doohan, *Leisure: A Spiritual Need* (1990).

20. Harvey Cox, *The Feast of Fools: A Theological Essay on Festivity and Fantasy* (New York: Harper and Row, 1969).

18

Work in the Spirit

A Christian Work Ethic

The Bible is a rich source of practical advice about work. Paul Minear has rightly observed that

> the Bible has . . . far more to say about daily chores than most of its readers realize. Indeed, we may think of it as an album of casual photographs of laborers. . . . A book by workers, about workers, for workers—that is the Bible.[1]

From the Bible we can assemble an ever-expanding picture of how God intends us to work.

Work as a Moral Duty

The common denominator among people who have what we call "a strong work ethic" is not that these people enjoy their work (which they may or may not) but that they accept it as their duty. The Bible approves of this attitude.

The Moral Virtue of Performing Work

The Bible views work as a moral duty laid upon the human race. God expected Adam and Eve to work both before and after the Fall. "Six days

1. Minear, "Work and Vocation in Scripture," in *Work and Vocation*, 33.

you shall labor, and do all your work," says God's fourth commandment (Exodus 20:9). Psalm 104 places human work in the cycle of nature, describing work as being as natural as the rising of the sun:

When the sun rises . . .
Man goes forth to his work
    and to his labor until the evening (vv. 22–23).

Other parts of the Bible likewise treat work as a duty and industriousness as a virtue. Paul enjoined Christians "to be ready for any honest work" (Titus 3:1). To the Thessalonians Paul commanded, "We exhort you . . . to work with your hands" (1 Thessalonians 4:10–11). In the Old Testament, Nehemiah recalled that the wall of Jerusalem was rebuilt with dispatch because "the people had a mind to work" (Nehemiah 4:6).

Industriousness is one of the chief traits of the virtuous wife described in Proverbs 31. She "does not eat the bread of idleness" (v. 27), but instead "works with willing hands" (v. 13) and "rises while it is yet night" (v. 15). She also "plants a vineyard" (v. 16) and "puts her hands to the distaff" (v. 19). Proverbs is full of praise for diligence in labor, such as the observation that "he who tends a fig tree will eat its fruit" (Proverbs 27:18).

Whereas leisure is based rather thoroughly on a hedonistic ethic of pleasure-seeking, a work ethic is based on a degree of self-denial and asceticism. In a fallen world we perform much of our work from a sense of duty rather than for its inherent pleasure. Another way of saying this is that people who cannot move beyond self-indulgence are likely to have an emaciated work ethic.

Idleness as a Vice

The most customary biblical way of asserting the moral duty of work is to denounce idleness or sloth. The Book of Proverbs can hardly stay away from the subject, as the following specimens suggest:

Go to the ant, O sluggard;
    consider her ways and be wise.
Without having any chief,
    officer or ruler,
she prepares her food in summer,
    and gathers her sustenance in harvest.
How long will you lie there, O sluggard?
    When will you arise from your sleep?
A little sleep, a little slumber,
    a little folding of the hands to rest,
and poverty will come upon you like a vagabond,
    and want like an armed man (6:6–11).

The soul of the sluggard craves, and gets nothing (13:4).

Slothfulness casts into a deep sleep,
   and an idle person will suffer hunger (19:15).

The desire of the sluggard kills him
   for his hands refuse to labor (21:25).

The common denominator of proverbs such as these is that to refuse to work conscientiously is to abdicate one's responsibility to oneself and to the human race.

Other parts of the Bible also condemn laziness or sloppiness in work. We read, for example, that "through sloth the roof sinks in, and through indolence the house leaks" (Ecclesiastes 10:18). Paul disparaged those who lived "in idleness, mere busybodies, not doing any work" (2 Thessalonians 3:11).

Such denunciation of idleness implies a positive and liberating attitude toward work. David Herreshoff says that Proverbs' view of work presents "disciplined work as a means to liberation from want and oppression" and celebrates "work as a liberating activity." The most obvious example is the vignette of the industrious ant in Proverbs 6, who "works rationally, with foresight rather than under the goad of immediate need," reaping as a reward "a life without taskmasters, without a slave-driving state or the whip of the market."[2]

It has become common for writers in our day to debunk the original Protestants for praising the virtue of hard work. From a biblical perspective, it is the modern attitude, not the original Protestant ethic, that needs correcting. As one Puritan wrote, "Religion does not seal warrants to idleness. . . . God sets all his children to work. . . . God will bless our diligence, not our laziness."[3]

At its simplest, then, an adequate work ethic requires the acceptance of the duty of work. Within this framework, diligence in work is a virtue, while sloth or laziness is a vice.

Work and the Self

The morality of work is especially concerned with the worker's relationships. The logical starting place is to consider work in relation to the worker.

2. David S. Herreshoff, *Labor into Art: The Theme of Work in Nineteenth-Century American Literature* (Detroit: Wayne State University Press, 1991), 151.
3. Thomas Watson, *The Beatitudes* (Edinburgh: Banner of Truth, 1971), 257.

Several factors have conspired to make us feel guilty when we think that work exists for the fulfillment and pleasure of the worker. We know that work is often a curse. Christians, moreover, operate on the premise that the ultimate purpose of their work is not something selfish but something at least potentially sacrificial in the service of God and humanity.

Christians, however, do not need to apologize for finding enjoyment and fulfillment in work. Jesus commanded people to love their neighbor *as they love themselves* (Matthew 22:39, italics added). God does not call workers to be masochists. In fact, the Bible has plenty to say about the rewards that should come to workers. God intends work to be a joy, not a pain that we inflict on ourselves.

There is a legitimate satisfaction that workers can take in the provision they earn by their work. Psalm 128 begins with this pronouncement of blessing:

> Blessed is every one who fears the Lord,
>   who walks in his ways!
> You shall eat the fruit of the labor of your hands;
>   you shall be happy, and it shall be well with you.

The poet's wish for the virtuous wife is, "Give her of the fruit of her hands" (Proverbs 31:31). Enjoying the benefits of what one has worked for is one of the moral pleasures of life.

The Bible also does not frown on the idea of working in order to be prosperous and successful. Without that hope, in fact, one's work ethic tends to wither. Here are some variations on the theme from the Book of Proverbs:

A slack hand causes poverty,
    but the hand of the diligent makes rich (10:4).

The hand of the diligent will rule,
    while the slothful will be put to forced labor (12:24).

The soul of the sluggard craves and gets nothing, while the soul of the diligent is richly supplied (13:4).

The plans of the diligent lead surely to abundance but everyone who is hasty comes only to want (21:5).

Do you see a man skillful [KJV, diligent] in his work?
    he will stand before kings;
    he will not stand before obscure men (22:29).

The Bible is hostile to the success ethic in which people worship success, but it does not disparage the legitimate satisfaction that workers take in being successful in their work or in the material prosperity that might come from such success. There is nothing immoral about working to have a successful career, though such a career must, of course, not be gained at the expense of other moral concerns. Biblical heroes such as Joseph and Daniel had astoundingly successful careers, to the glory of God and the benefit of society. Paul was a successful missionary.

In addition to satisfaction in the rewards of work, the Bible encourages a spirit of joy in one's work. The God-centered passages in the Book of Ecclesiastes are filled with exuberance over the worker's delight in his or her work:

> There is nothing better for a man than that he should eat and drink and find enjoyment in his toil. This also, I saw, is from the hand of God (2:24).

> It is God's gift to man that every one should eat and drink and take pleasure in all his toil (3:13).

> Sweet is the sleep of a laborer (5:12).

> Behold what I have seen to be good and to be fitting is to eat and drink and find enjoyment in all the toil with which one toils. . . . Every man also to whom God has given wealth and possessions and power to enjoy them, and to accept his lot and find enjoyment in his toil—this is the gift of God (5:18–19).

Work, at its best, is personally fulfilling. Not all of our tasks, of course, measure up to this ideal, but when they do, we should accept the joy they bring with gratitude. Dorothy Sayers has written that

> work is not, primarily, a thing one does to live, but the thing one lives to do. It is, or it should be, the full expression of the worker's faculties, the thing in which he finds spiritual, mental, and bodily satisfaction, and the medium in which he offers himself to God.[4]

This is the goal of a Christian work ethic as related to the life of the worker.

Work and Society

A work ethic also involves the relationship between worker and society. After all, work occurs in a social context. The work we do nearly always brings us into contact with other people. Work "joins us to the

---

4. Sayers, *Creed or Chaos?*, 53.

community of fellow workers. . . . Work remains . . . the expression of a unique human connectedness—a gift each human gives to every other human and each generation gives to the next."[5]

Work as a Means of Providing for Human Needs

The work we do to provide for our own needs is something we owe to society. The Bible takes a very negative view toward social parasites who refuse to support themselves. The best-known passage on the subject is 2 Thessalonians 3:10–12:

> Even when we were with you, we gave you this command: If any one will not work, let him not eat. For we hear that some of you are living in idleness, mere busybodies, not doing any work. Now such persons we command and exhort in the Lord Jesus Christ to do their work in quietness and to earn their own living.

Paul declined to accept payment for his work as a missionary, choosing instead to work "night and day, that we might not burden any of you" (1 Thessalonians 2:9).

The duty people have to work for their livelihood extends to their families as well as themselves. Paul wrote to Timothy that "if anyone does not provide for his relatives, and especially for his own family, he has disowned the faith and is worse than an unbeliever" (1 Timothy 5:8).

As 1 Timothy 5:8 suggests, for Christians there is an element of witness in the work they perform. After all, unbelievers look on as we work or fail to work, whether on the job or around the house. This, too, is part of the communal dimension of work. Again Paul is the leading biblical source:

> We exhort you . . . to work with your hands, as we charged you; so that you may command the respect of outsiders, and be dependent on nobody (1 Thessalonians 4:10–12).

Elsewhere Paul claims that the Christian's work itself serves as a model for others to follow:

> For you yourselves know how you ought to imitate us; we were not idle when we were with you, we did not eat anyone's bread without paying, but with toil and labor we worked night and day, that we might not burden any of you. It was not because we have not that right, but to give you in our conduct an example to imitate (2 Thessalonians 3:7–9).

---

5. Raines and Day-Lower, *Modern Work and Human Meaning*, 16–17.

Yet another way in which our work relates us to society is that the profits we reap from our work enable us to help people in need. This is the picture that emerges, for example, from the hyperbolic portrait of the industrious wife in Proverbs 31. This human dynamo works almost nonstop not only for herself and her family; she also "opens her hand to the poor, and reaches out her hands to the needy" (Proverbs 31:20). The apostle Paul put it into the form of a command: "Let the thief no longer steal, but rather let him labor, doing honest work with his hands, so that he may be able to give to those in need" (Ephesians 4:28).

The social dimension of work keeps expanding, reaching out to include not being a burden to society, providing a witness to society, and extending compassion to society. Work is a way to serve humanity. Support for this ideal comes mainly from the Puritans, but the principle appears in the Bible as well.

Work as a Service to Others

At the heart of the Christian faith is the idea that we are called to be servants. "Whoever would be great among you," Jesus told his disciples, "must be your servant, and whoever would be first among you must be your slave; even as the Son of man came not to be served but to serve" (Matthew 20:26–28). On the basis of the example of Christ, Paul wrote,

> Let each of you look not only to his own interests, but also to the interests of others. Have this mind among yourselves, which is yours in Christ Jesus, who . . . [took] the form of a servant (Philippians 2:4–5, 7).

Service is the heart of Christian morality. Applied to work, it means that an element of self-sacrifice and service to others is a necessary part of a healthy work ethic.

Viewing work as a form of service to humanity redeems almost any task that is in itself unrewarding. It is the redeeming factor in work that does not carry its own reward and that we do not find inherently satisfying. This encompasses much of our work. We conduct our work between the poles of self-fulfillment and service toward others. To view ourselves as serving others can give unsatisfying work a moral purpose and a reason for us to be satisfied in doing it. If we are involved in work that we cannot defend as being a genuine service to others we should look for other work. John Stott once received a letter from the chief health inspector of the Port of London. Although working for his own ends did not satisfy him, he went on to say, "I like to think that I am responsible for a part of the greater field pattern whereby all serve human welfare and obey the will of our wonderful Creator."[6]

6. Stott, "Reclaiming the Biblical Doctrine of Work," 37.

The people who said the most on the subject were the original Protestants. It should be noted that one looks in vain for their affirmation of personal prosperity as the goal of work, the attitude with which "the Protestant ethic" is often charged. The Reformation view of calling was rooted in the idea of service. "All stations," wrote Luther, "are so oriented that they serve others."[7] Luther denounced people who "do not use their talents in their calling or in the service of their neighbor; they use them only for their own glory and advantage."[8]

The theme of service to humanity was a virtual obsession with the Puritans. "God hath made man a sociable creature," wrote Cotton Mather; "we are beneficial to human society by the works of that special occupation in which we are to be employed, according to the order of God."[9] One of the reasons the Protestants denied that Catholic monks had a legitimate calling is that their life did not serve society.

To view work as service to others should, said the Puritans, govern one's choice of a vocation. Richard Baxter wrote, "Choose not that [calling] in which you may be most rich or honorable in the world; but that in which you may do most good."[10] The same ethical outlook affects how one pursues his or her work after entering a vocation. Baxter, for example, enjoined lawyers to be more interested in promoting justice than making money, and physicians to "be sure that the saving of men's lives and health be first and chiefly your intention before any gain or honor of your own."[11]

The most complete Puritan discussion of this matter is by William Perkins. "The main end of our lives," said Perkins, "is to serve God in the serving of men in the works of our callings."[12] God could have chosen to preserve people "without the help of man, but his pleasure is that men should be his instruments, for the good of one another."[13] "By this we learn," added Perkins,

> how men of mean [humble] place and calling may comfort themselves. Let them consider that in serving of men ... they serve God. ... And though their reward from men may be little, yet the reward at God's hand shall not be wanting. ... And thus may we reap marvelous [contentment] in any kind of calling, though it be but to sweep the house or keep sheep.[14]

7. Martin Luther, in Wingren, *Luther on Vocation*, 5.
8. Luther, sermon on 1 Peter 4:8–11, as excerpted in *What Luther Says*, 1497.
9. Mather, *A Christian at His Calling*, in *Puritanism*, 122.
10. Baxter, *Christian Directory*, in *Works*, 1:114.
11. Ibid., 1:770–73.
12. Perkins, *Vocations or Callings of Men*, in *Works*, 1:756.
13. Ibid., 757.
14. Ibid.

There can be little doubt that one of the problems with work today is an overly individualistic work ethic. People overwhelmingly accept the duty of work, if they accept it at all, in a spirit of asking, What's in it for me? To view work as service to society introduces a moral perspective that is at odds with the prevailing ethic of our society.

To stress work as service to others does not cancel what was said earlier about working to meet our own needs. We can follow the Puritans in being realistic and balanced on this score. A worker must be diligent in his or her calling, claimed Mather, "so he may glorify God, by doing of good for others and getting of good for himself."[15] The same balance is present in the formulation of Perkins:

> Some man will say perchance: What, must we not labor in our callings to maintain our families? I answer: this must be done, but this is not the scope and end of our lives. The true end of our lives is to do service to God in serving of man.[16]

Work in Relation to God

An adequate work ethic relates work not only to the worker and society but also to God. This relationship is rooted in God's calling of people to their tasks and occupations. When we work with this sense of vocation, we do our work in a spirit of faith and obedience.

Viewing work as something God entrusts to us as stewards carries with it a set of moral attitudes. Because finding enjoyment in our work "is from the hand of God" (Ecclesiastes 2:24), we can pray that God would help us find that enjoyment. The same doctrine of stewardship offers a new motivation for doing work, which is done ultimately "as to the Lord and not to men" (Ephesians 6:7).

The same Godward view of work affects how we enter a vocation or decide what tasks to undertake. If work is something to which God calls us, we have every reason to listen to his call. This, in turn, prompts us to other considerations than the common criterion of financial reward. The topic of choosing a career is beyond the scope of this book.[17] Let me simply note that if we believe our work is something that relates us to God as stewards we will choose careers and tasks on

---

15. Cotton Mather, *Two Brief Discourses*, in Ralph Barton Perry, *Puritanism and Democracy* (New York: Vanguard, 1944), 312.

16. Perkins, *Vocations or Callings of Men*, 757.

17. Good discussions on choosing a career include: Jerry White and Mary White, *Your Job: Survival or Satisfaction?* (Grand Rapids: Zondervan, 1977); Martin E. Clark, *Choosing Your Career* (Phillipsburg, N.J.: Presbyterian Reformed, 1981); Pamela Moran, *The Christian Job Hunter* (Ann Arbor: Servant, 1984).

the basis of such considerations as the degree to which those careers utilize the talents and abilities that God has given us, allow for maximum achievement (and therefore represent a good stewardship of our time as well as our abilities), and provide the greatest potential for witness (on the job, through our work, and as an outgrowth of our work).

The Worker's Relationship to Work Itself

A final relationship comprising a work ethic is the worker in relation to work. Commitment to excellence in work is one of the prime moral virtues that the Bible prescribes for workers. Excellence is a Christian ideal for all of life. Christians are called to excellence because the God they serve is excellent.[18] It is an ideal that is bigger than work but includes work.

The work of God himself is "very good" (Genesis 1:31). The work of his image bearers should aspire to the same quality. Paul's command to Timothy about the work of preaching states a principle that applies to work more generally: "Do your best to present yourself to God as one approved, a workman who has no need to be ashamed" (2 Timothy 2:15).

In our century Dorothy Sayers has written the best material on the subject of the Christian's commitment to excellence in work.[19] She begins by rejecting the commonly accepted notion that a person's life "is divided into the time he spends on his work and the time he spends in serving God." The ideal is for a Christian "to serve God in his work, and the work itself must be accepted and respected as the medium of divine creation." This requires a belief that work has inherent integrity. No degree of piety in the worker, writes Sayers, "will compensate for work that is not true to itself; for any work that is untrue to its own technique is a living lie." Sayers believes that the church in our century "has forgotten that the secular vocation is sacred. Forgotten that a building must be good architecture before it can be a good church; that a painting must be well painted before it can be a good sacred picture; that work must be good work before it can call itself God's work."

Sayers concludes that "The only Christian work is good work well done. . . . The worker's first duty is to *serve the work.*"

18. See Frank E. Gaebelein's essay "The Idea of Excellence and Our Obligation to It," in *The Christian, the Arts, and Truth,* ed. D. Bruce Lockerbie (Portland, Ore.: Multnomah, 1985), 141–49.

19. Sayers, *Creed or Chaos?* 56–60.

A second moral stance of a worker toward his or her work is that work should be done with zest. A memorable proverb on that topic is this: "Whatever your hand finds to do, do it with your might" (Ecclesiastes 9:10). Colossians 3:23 urges a similar attitude: "Whatever your task, work heartily, as serving the Lord and not men." The implied vice is half-heartedness in one's work.

A third attitude that we should bring to our work is to avoid making an idol of it. An idol is anything that people elevate to the place of supremacy that only God should have. Everyone elevates something to a position of supremacy. Claus Westermann, in his book *Praise and Lament in the Psalms*, concludes, "Exalting is part of existence. It is so much a part of it, that when one has ceased to exalt God, something else must be exalted. . . . Exalting remains a function of existence."[20] Chad Walsh, in a book on utopian literature, voices a similar viewpoint.

> Man is incurably religious. . . . If one thinks of religion as the ultimate concern, most men have it. The American who does not worship an authentic God is almost certain to have a substitute deity: The American Way of Life, Free Enterprise, the Standard of Living, the arts—or sex—at least something. Whatever his deity, he offers sacrifices to it, whether he is the young executive conforming to the expectations of his superiors or the young artist half starving in the service of his Muse. . . . The Bible devotes remarkably little time to the menace of atheism. The biblical viewpoint seems to be that atheism is a rare and puny adversary compared to idolatry.[21]

The workaholics discussed in chapter 4 have made work their religion. Richard Phillips called them "the new Calvinists."[22] "Work is the religion of the young and ambitious," notes Phillips, who writes about people who forego personal relationships to work seventy hours per week. "You shall have no other gods before me" says the first commandment (Exodus 20:3). Excessive devotion to work is one of the forbidden gods.

This leads naturally to a final strand in a worker's moral stance toward his or her work—the principle of moderation. The moral ideal of a golden mean between extremes belongs to the wisdom of the human race, having been first imprinted on Western consciousness by Aristotle. It is also a biblical standard. Proverbs 30:8 applies the principle to

20. Claus Westermann, *Praise and Lament in the Psalms,* trans. Keith R. Crim (Atlanta: John Knox, 1981), 160.

21. Chad Walsh, *From Utopia to Nightmare* (New York: Harper and Row, 1962), 143–44.

22. Richard Phillips, "The New Calvinists," *Chicago Tribune,* 5 November 1986, section 7, pp. 5–7.

the realm of work and economics: "give me neither poverty nor riches; feed me with the food that is needful for me." Moderation in work means avoiding the extremes of laziness and overwork. We have already noted the biblical and Puritan prohibition against slothfulness in work. The more likely abuse in our society is overwork.

The original Protestants warned against it, and their cautions remain valid. The Scottish divine Robert Woodrow commented, "The sin of our too great fondness for trade, to the neglecting of our more valuable interests, I humbly think will be written upon our judgment."[23] Puritan Phillip Stubbes claimed that workers should not allow "immoderate care" to "surpass the bounds of . . . true godliness."[24] In a society that worships economic and vocational success, the danger of immoderate work is a constant moral temptation. Ecclesiastes 4 paints a memorable picture of the golden mean between the compulsive money-maker and the dropout: "Better is a handful of quietness than two hands full of toil and a striving after wind" (v. 6). On the opposite sides of this picture of contentment are people who wear themselves out keeping up with the Joneses (v. 4) and the fool who "folds his hands" and withers away (v. 5).

Summary: Working to the Glory of God

A Christian work ethic states: the worker is more important than the work. The Bible says a great deal more about the *attitudes* of the worker than about either work or its institutional and societal structures. Minear concluded,

> Throughout the Bible it is the person who works to whom most attention is given, rather than the form or conditions of his work. . . . Biblical writers [emphasize] the agent more than the act, the motive of the laborer more than the mode of his labor.[25]

It is therefore not so much work that is moral or immoral but the worker.

What, then, characterizes the moral worker? The moral worker accepts the duty of work as a means of providing for human needs, of finding purpose in life, and of glorifying God. The moral worker attempts to find legitimate self-fulfillment and satisfaction in work, to serve so-

23. Robert Woodrow: quoted in R. H. Tawney, *Religion and the Rise of Capitalism* (New York: Harcourt, Brace, 1926), 238.

24. Phillip Stubbes, *Anatomy of the Abuses in England*, quoted in Tawney, *Religion*, 216.

25. Minear, "Work and Vocation," 40–41.

ciety through his or her work, and to view work as a medium for living a life of faith before God. In regard to work itself, the moral worker is committed to excellence and moderation.

The traditional theological triad of faith, hope, and love also provides a good summary for how we can work in a moral manner. We work in faith that God has called us to our work and will supply what we need to perform it. We work in hope that God will prosper our work and make it productive. We work in love as we view our work in terms of service to society. In all of these endeavors Christian workers pray that God will lead them to meaningful work, grant prosperity through it, and use their work as a service to humanity.

The importance of the worker's attitude toward work is aptly summarized by an interchange in a medieval stone mason's yard. "What are you doing?" a visitor asked the first stone mason. "I'm cutting a stone," the mason replied. A second stone mason replied, "I'm earning my living." A third responded, "I'm building a cathedral."

Further Reading

Dorothy L. Sayers, "Why Work?" in *Creed or Chaos?* (1949).

Paul S. Minear, "Work and Vocation in Scripture," in *Work and Vocation: A Christian Discussion,* ed. John Oliver Nelson, (1954) 32–81 .

Arthur F. Holmes, *Contours of a World View* (1983), chapter 14 .

Lee Hardy, *The Fabric of This World* (1990).

David L. McKenna, *Love Your Work!* (1990).

19

"Richly All Things to Enjoy"
A Christian Play Ethic

$\mathbf{I}$n common parlance the phrases "work ethic" and "play ethic" are broadly construed to mean any aspect of a philosophy of work and leisure. In this chapter and the previous one I am interested specifically in the moral or ethical dimensions of work and leisure. Because the domain of ethics is human behavior, especially as seen in relationships, morality has much to say about the virtues and vices of a given activity.

Leisure as the Arena of Moral Choice

A leisure ethic begins with an awareness that leisure presents us with unavoidable choices. The first choice is whether to accept the responsibility to make time for leisure. Once we have made time for leisure, further choices confront us—in fact, many more choices than we usually face in regard to work.

Frank Gaebelein notes that "the very word *leisure* implies responsibility. . . . We are accountable for the stewardship of our leisure as well as of our working time."[1] Harold Lehman agrees:

---

1. Frank Gaebelein, "The Christian Use of Leisure," in *The Christian, the Arts, and Truth*, ed. D. Bruce Lockerbie (Portland, Ore.: Multnomah, 1985), 228.

> Leisure time is the arena of choice. Here we must make decisions every
> day about how to use free time. We cannot evade leisure-time choices,
> even a non-choice amounts to a choice by default.[2]

Choice by default is exactly what often prevails. The leisure patterns of
most Christians are much the same as those of a secular society. We
have not been encouraged by pastors and teachers to become self-conscious about our leisure choices, nor have we given adequate attention
to educating ourselves to enhance the quality of our leisure.

Because God calls us to be good stewards of our leisure time, the
choices that we make are necessarily moral choices. C. S. Lewis expressed this, as he did so many things, in memorable and incisive form:

> Our leisure, even our play, is a matter of serious concern. There is no neu-
> tral ground in the universe; every square inch, every split second, is
> claimed by God and counterclaimed by Satan. . . . It is a serious matter to
> choose wholesome recreations.[3]

If we realized the urgency of the matter we would not so aimlessly plop
down in front of the television to watch whatever happens to be on, nor
would our young people thoughtlessly listen to the music and view the
movies that they do. To be truly moral about our leisure will require us
to attach the value to it that it deserves and to realize what is at stake
in our choices and non-choices.

To say that leisure is the arena of moral choice implies that the usual
moral standards that apply to our play also apply to the rest of life.
When serving on a panel of Christians on the subject of leisure I was
taken aback to hear a fellow panelist argue that once we commit ourselves to a leisure activity we must abandon ourselves to it and refrain
from moral judgments. I suggest on the contrary that Christian morality does not take a holiday when we engage in play and leisure. This
means that sexual immorality, violence, destructiveness to people and
the environment, drunkenness, and similar vices are as immoral in our
leisure lives as they are elsewhere.

Allowing Leisure to Be Leisure

It is a principle of ethics that things should be allowed to have the integrity of what they are inherently in their created properties. God created the world purposefully. Creatures in God's world have a *telos*, an inherent end for which they were created and toward which they tend.

2. Lehman, *In Praise of Leisure*, 147.
3. Lewis, *Christian Reflections*, 33–34.

The most common violation of this principle in regard to leisure is to turn leisure, which is inherently nonutilitarian, into something utilitarian. Leisure should carry its own reward and be fulfilling in itself, but the human race has found ways to twist that purpose.

One way to do so is to treat leisure as an appendage to work. In such a climate people value leisure only as it contributes to their ability to work. The results are detrimental to leisure. People who are preoccupied with work in this way give little time to leisure, and the quality of the little leisure these people have is often low. People who have studied workaholics find that their leisure often degenerates into idleness or passivity and sometimes consists wholly of sleeping.

Other people fall into the trap of working at their play. They try to get work time results from something intended to be nonwork. They read for improvement, so that reading becomes *homework*. Physical exercise becomes *working out*. Witold Rybczynski (who, you will recall, longed for the good old days of genuine amateurism in such leisure pursuits as skiing) notes that "people used to 'play' tennis; now they 'work' on their backhand."[4] By the time leisure has been filtered through the work mentality it has frequently ceased to be leisure and is instead a form of work.

Another feature of leisure that can easily get violated is its status as a break from the obligations of life. Leisure is, in the best sense of the word, an escape. Pleasurable work does not meet this test. People who enjoy their work and therefore work pretty much all the time have not found a place for leisure in their lives, although they have achieved an ideal of leisure-in-work.

In order for leisure to be an escape we must also leave behind the competitive spirit that often characterizes the workplace. Relaxation is one of the inherent qualities of leisure. Compulsively competitive people often fail to draw a boundary around the competitive impulse and thereby twist leisure from its intended purpose. When they play games, they drive themselves to win and spoil the occasion for everyone with their unhappiness when they lose.

Note also how quickly the act of using something (the utilitarian ethic) destroys our ability to enjoy it. In subdividing a field we lose the beauty of the landscape. In building a house we lose what was pleasing about the trees used for lumber. When we eat an apple we forfeit our ability to enjoy its sensory attractiveness.

There is something analogous to these physical examples in the realm of leisure. Leisure activities should be self-rewarding. In the sense of not using them but simply enjoying them, we should (paradoxical as it may sound) come away from them empty-handed, "with noth-

---

4. Rybczynski, *Waiting for the Weekend*, 18.

ing left to us but a memory of delight, an increase in well-being so deep and so central and so invisibly distributed throughout the psyche that it cannot even be located."[5] Gordon Dahl has said perceptively that "the work ethic has inspired a morality of use; the leisure ethic will inspire a morality of enjoyment."[6]

The Legitimacy of Pleasure and Enjoyment

The rise and fall of leisure throughout history have been closely bound up with prevailing attitudes toward pleasure and enjoyment. If pleasure is regarded as bad, then obviously leisure and play are also bad. By definition, leisure is something we do because we want to, not because we have to. A healthy play ethic is rooted in some form of hedonism.

The spirit of self-denial and asceticism (rejecting earthly pleasure as evil) has run strong in the Christian tradition. So has the sense of duty. Surely self-denial and duty are necessary parts of the Christian life, but they are not the whole of it. When carried beyond their legitimate place, they end up robbing the Christian life of the joy that should accompany it.

It is good to be reminded, therefore, that the Christian life is intended to be a life of God-directed enjoyment. A decade ago John Piper wrote a book entitled *Desiring God: Meditations of a Christian Hedonist.*[7] Some people criticized the author for using the word *hedonism* to describe the Christian life, but the author gave a good explanation for his choice of the term (pp. 259–62). To buttress his argument Piper wrote a sequel on an even more daring thesis—God as hedonist, or, in the words of the title, *The Pleasures of God: Meditations on God's Delight in Being God.*[8]

Piper's main thesis is closely related to a Christian play ethic. Regarding his first book he explains, "This is a serious book about being happy in God. It's about happiness because that is what our Creator commands: 'Delight yourself in the Lord' (Psalm 37:4)." Because God wants us to enjoy ourselves we should spend part of our time in leisure, since that it is the very point of leisure.

---

5. Kerr, *Decline of Pleasure*, 241.
6. Gordon Dahl, *Work, Play, and Worship in a Leisure-Oriented Society* (Minneapolis: Augsburg, 1972), 98.
7. Piper, *Desiring God.*
8. John Piper, *The Pleasures of God: Meditations on God's Delight in Being God* (Portland, Ore.: Multnomah, 1991).

Pleasure: God's Gift

Exactly what does the Bible say about the pleasure principle? For starters, it claims God as the source of good pleasures. God "made to grow every tree that is pleasant to the sight" in the paradisal garden that he created for Adam and Eve (Genesis 2:9).

Pleasure is one of the recurrent themes and moods in the Psalms, a book where, as John Piper notes, we can find "the language of hedonism everywhere."[9] The writer of Psalm 16 rejoices in the fact that "the lines have fallen for me in pleasant places" (v. 6), and he asserts that at God's "right hand are pleasures for evermore" (v. 11). Equally evocative is the image that we find in Psalm 36:8: God's people "feast on the abundance of thy house, and thou givest them drink from the river of thy delights." Elsewhere we read that the "harp with the psaltery is pleasant" (Psalm 81:2, KJV).

Once alerted to the biblical pattern, we find an ever-expanding vision of legitimate pleasures that God has given to the human race. Spiritual fellowship among worshipers of God is "good and pleasant" (Psalm 133:1). The raptures of romantic love are a "great delight," and the beloved is "fair and pleasant" (Song of Solomon 2:3; 7:6). Married sex is designed to "fill you at all times with delight" (Proverbs 5:19). In fact, all of life is potentially pleasurable: knowledge is "pleasant to your soul" (Proverbs 2:10), the words of the wise "will be pleasant if you keep them within you" (Proverbs 22:18), a righteous land is "a land of delight" (Malachi 3:12), and on and on.

God-centered Hedonism in the Book of Ecclesiastes

The most extended biblical affirmation of pleasure comes from the much misunderstood Book of Ecclesiastes.[10] Ecclesiastes is structured on a dialectical principle of opposites. There are "under the sun" passages in which the author describes the futility of trying to find meaning and happiness in a purely earthly scale of values, and there are "above the sun" passages in which the author celebrates the God-centered life as an antidote to life "under the sun." Significantly, the affirmations of pleasure and enjoyment come from the God-centered passages. In fact, enjoyment is exactly what the writer finds denied when he limits his quest to the earthly sphere. Here are three endorsements of enjoyment that come from passages describing the God-centered life:

9. Piper, *Desiring God*, 17.

10. For an extended discussion of Ecclesiastes along the lines suggested here, see my book *Words of Delight: A Literary Introduction to the Bible* (Grand Rapids: Baker, 1992), 319–28.

There is nothing better for a man than that he should eat and drink and find enjoyment in his toil. This also, I saw, is from the hand of God; for apart from him who can eat or who can have enjoyment? For to the man who pleases him God gives wisdom and knowledge and joy (2:24–26).

[God] has made everything beautiful in its time. . . . I know that there is nothing better for them than to be happy and enjoy themselves as long as they live; also that it is God's gift to man that every one should eat and drink and take pleasure in all his toil (3:11–13).

Behold, what I have seen to be good and to be fitting is to eat and drink and find enjoyment in all the toil with which one toils. . . . Every man also to whom God has given wealth and possessions and power to enjoy them, and to accept his lot and find enjoyment in his toil—this is the gift of God (5:18–19).

I would note in passing that, although I have chosen to discuss the pleasure principle as part of a Christian play ethic, these passages from Ecclesiastes are a reminder that enjoyment is equally a goal of any good work ethic.

Elsewhere the writer of Ecclesiastes sounds the variations on the theme of God-given pleasure. We are commanded, for example, "Go, eat your bread with enjoyment, and drink your wine with a merry heart; for God has already approved what you do" (9:7). Again, "Enjoy life with the wife whom you love" (9:9). The simplest commonplaces of life are cause for pleasure to the godly person: "Light is sweet, and it is pleasant for the eyes to behold the sun" (11:7).

Here is the ideal of godly hedonism. It is not escapist. It does not reject everyday life in favor of some spiritual world. In fact, it is in the routine of life and work that the ancient Preacher urges us to find enjoyment. John Calvin's comment about enjoying food is very much in keeping with the spirit of Ecclesiastes: "If we ponder to what end God created food," wrote Calvin, "we shall find that he meant not only to provide for necessity but also for delight and good cheer."[11]

New Testament Confirmations

This positive attitude toward enjoyment of God's good gifts continues in the New Testament. The classic passage is Paul's instruction to Timothy concerning the wealthy: "As for the rich in this world, charge them not to be haughty, nor to set their hopes on uncertain riches but on God who richly furnishes us with everything to enjoy" (1 Timothy 6:17). The King James Version is even more evocative, claiming that God "giveth us richly all things to enjoy." Here we learn three important principles

11. Calvin, *Institutes*, 1:720.

about enjoyment: (1) God is the giver of all good things; (2) God gives them so people can enjoy them; (3) the misuse of them consists not in the enjoyment of them but in trusting them and making idols of them.

We should also note that the biblical doctrine of heaven exalts pleasure. Because heaven is the place where there is no more pain (Revelation 21:4), C. S. Lewis correctly asserted that "all pleasure is in itself a good and pain in itself an evil; if not, then the whole Christian tradition about heaven and hell and the passion of our Lord seems to have no meaning."[12] The seventeenth-century Anglican Jeremy Taylor's twist on this was that "God threatens terrible things if we will not be happy."[13]

The desire to enjoy life and seek happiness is a God-implanted impulse. It can, of course, be perverted to wrong ends. It can also be killed, producing a psychological aberration that goes by the clinical name *anhedonia* ("without pleasure"). Between these extremes stands the biblical ideal: legitimate pleasure and enjoyment as God's gifts to the human race. The way to show gratitude for the gift of enjoyment is to accept it and experience it.

What is at stake in our view of pleasure is our view of God. Does God want people to enjoy themselves or to be miserable? The question is as simple as that. To assume that God does not want people to enjoy themselves is to charge him with being sadistic toward his creatures. In his article entitled "The Christian As Pleasure-Seeker," Norman Geisler wrote, "God is not a celestial Scrooge who hates to see his children enjoy themselves."[14]

Summary

The fact that the Bible contains more negative references than positive references to pleasure does not negate the fact that pleasure is good in principle. Enjoyment, in turn, provides a context in which play and leisure can flourish. A Christian play ethic rests partly on an adequate view of the goodness of pleasure.

Moderation and Balance in Leisure

Two of the time-honored moral guidelines of the human race are moderation and balance. Their relevance to a Christian play ethic is obvious.

Moderation in leisure means steering a middle course between too much and too little. These of course are relative, and there is no objec-

12. Lewis, *Christian Reflections*, 21.
13. Cited by Piper, *Desiring God*, 9.
14. Norman Geisler, "The Christian As Pleasure-Seeker," *Christianity Today*, 25 September 1975, 11.

tive measurement by which to tell whether we have met the criteria. They vary with our situation and age, but some broad principles will prove helpful.

One measure of whether we are getting enough leisure is the degree to which the purposes of leisure are adequately achieved in our lives. Those purposes include providing a break from work and obligation, relaxation, entertainment, celebration, self-fulfillment, and the nurturing of family and social bonds. If we are notably deficient in these things we obviously need either more or different leisure in our lives.

On the other side of the ledger there are several tests of whether we are excessive in our leisure. The chief test is whether our leisure renders us incapable of meeting our moral and Christian obligations. These obligations involve time, money, and work. Our obligations in these areas reach out to embrace our devotional life, our willingness to help in church work, our meeting of family responsibilities, and our availability to help people in need.

These obligations cannot absorb all of our lives. When they do we collapse physically and emotionally. Yet the sense of duty that lies at the heart of Christian morality means that a major portion of our lives is taken up with them. My own reflection suggests that the time we spend on leisure should not exceed the time we spend in service to family, acquaintances, church, and community. In other words, there should be a balance between the nonworking time that we spend on ourselves and that we give to others.

Moderation in leisure also means avoiding idolatry in leisure. Many people in our society value their leisure (broadly defined to include things they buy for their enjoyment) above everything else. Of special mention is the status of sports as a folk religion in the contemporary world.[15] This is to say that it has the qualities and loyalties that characterize a religion, including the embodiment of a set of values and beliefs held by a culture, the presence of collective cult observances, and a history that is passed on from generation to generation. To these I would add hero worship, intensity of devotion, ability to elicit financial commitment and sacrifice, domination of people's Sundays, and becoming the central life interest of people.

Of course other leisure pursuits are capable of becoming a religion as well. Whenever people do not put God in the center of their lives they put another interest there. Many of these interests fall into the category of leisure. We can find devotees of cars, culture, physical fitness, clothes, physical appearance, eating, and shopping. By Christian standards, a leisure pursuit becomes an idol whenever it absorbs the time,

15. James A. Mathisen, "From Civil Religion to Folk Religion: The Case of American Sport," in *Sport and Religion*, ed. Shirl J. Hoffman (Champaign, Ill.: Human Kinetics, 1992), 17–33.

devotion, and financial commitment that God requires of those who follow him.

In addition to moderation, the principle of balance can help us in our leisure choices. One element of balance is the cultivation of solitary and social leisure pursuits. Both are necessary ingredients in a full leisure life. Our social leisure, moreover, should include family, friends, and church.

We can also achieve balance among the broad categories of leisure activities. These extend in three general directions. One is sports, games, and recreation, where the emphasis is often on the physical or competitive. A second is culture, where the emphasis is on the mind and imagination. A third is festivity, celebration, and ritual, such as commemorating a holiday or celebrating a birthday. A full leisure life embraces all three categories.

Summary: Playing to the Glory of God

Our pursuit of leisure turns out to be a variation on the most basic of all moral issues—the quest for the good life. From a Christian perspective, that quest is a noble one. God wants people to live a life that is good in every way.

A good leisure life meets several moral standards. It contributes to one's personal well-being in constructive ways by opening up possibilities not present in the routine of work and obligation. It also fosters one's relationships with people and God. In all these spheres leisure is a form of stewardship in which we are called to make the most of what God has given us.

Leisure is part of the search for enjoyment and pleasure. It is moral if the pleasures that it gives meet the usual criteria of Christian morality. Moderation in the amount of leisure we pursue and balance among the types of leisure are also worthy moral goals for our leisure lives.

To achieve high quality in our leisure requires us to choose the excellent rather than the inferior. The goals and moral criteria for our leisure choices can be stated in Paul's words to the Philippians:

> Whatever is true, whatever is honorable, whatever is just, whatever is pure, whatever is lovely, whatever is gracious, if there is any excellence, if there is anything worthy of praise, think about these things (Philippians 4:8).

To paraphrase the final command, pursue these qualities in your leisure life.

Further Reading

Rudolph F. Norden, *The Christian Encounters the New Leisure* (1965).
Harold D. Lehman, *In Praise of Leisure* (1974).
Arthur F. Holmes, *Contours of a World View* (1983), chapter 15.
Robert K. Johnston, *The Christian at Play* (1983).
Paul Heintzman, Glen Van Andel, Thomas Visker, eds., *Christianity and Leisure: Issues in a Pluralistic Society* (1994).

20

Redeeming the Time

How the Bible Encourages Us to View Time

W e will not solve our problems of work and leisure without also solving our problem of time. It is appropriate, therefore, to conclude this section on what the Bible says about work and leisure by considering what it also says about time.

I do not intend to make a full scale philosophic inquiry into time. In fact, my primary source will be the Old Testament book of Ecclesiastes. My presupposition is that the only people who have enough time to do what they want to do are retired people, who often feel as though they have too much time. Therefore, our starting point is acknowledging that until we retire we will never feel that we have enough time to accomplish all our goals in work and leisure. The problem then is how to find satisfaction in both work and leisure within a daily and weekly schedule that provides less time than we need. I will argue that we fare best when we view time as a quality rather than a quantity.

Contemporary Views of Time

The backdrop against which we can best appreciate a biblical view of time is the range of attitudes that make up most people's view of time today. Even people who do not philosophize about time live by a philosophy of time—and are often tyrannized by it.

Clock Time

It is impossible to overemphasize the difference that the advent of the clock brought into Western life. Prior to the mechanical measurement of time, life was lived according to the natural rhythm of the day. Sunrise and sunset determined one's daily schedule. With time measured in such large blocks, and with work ceasing at nightfall, life was generally felt to be less pressured than it is today.

Today we measure time in increasingly smaller units, and we typically slice the entire twenty-four-hour period into time units. A decade ago a national magazine ran a cover article on time in which the cover carried a sketch of a person's head with a clock inside. This is, in fact, how most adults live their lives, constantly conscious of the passing of time and of where they are on a time schedule. Above all, time has become a quantity, and this situation has produced a schedule-dominated life.

The Quest for Efficiency

The clock became popular as a means to efficiency. It made time more manageable. Going by the sun had been inefficient. I recall an occasion from my childhood when my father neglected to take his watch with him on a morning when we were mowing hay far from the farm house. Using the time honored shadow method of calculating time, we arrived home for the noon meal half an hour early and sat around idly. We experienced that extra time as an ignominious bit of inefficiency.

By contrast, the clock measures time precisely, day and night. Its effect has been to make life regimented. It makes work more efficient, but also more harried. And it has created a mindset in which we find it hard not to measure and limit our leisure by the clock.

Time as Money

Another common attitude toward time is expressed in the cliché that "time is money." The underlying premise here is that time is primarily an economic entity. It exists to allow us to work and to make money, usually as a way of financing an acquisitive lifestyle.

We should not deceive ourselves about the degree to which our lives are determined by economic factors. It simply takes a lot of work to finance our lifestyles, or even to make ends meet. Marx was doubtless wrong when he conceived of people as primarily economic creatures, but I think Christians sometimes underestimate the degree to which all people, including Christians, are economically driven.

The chief effect of this economic view of time is that leisure gets shortchanged. Leisure does not put money in our pockets or food on the table. It is a "dependent" and therefore an economic liability. When we regard time as money we conceive of it in economic terms as being *valuable, scarce, at our disposal, to be saved,* and *useful.* Once again leisure is the loser.

Time as Personal

All of these attitudes conspire to make us feel that time is at a premium. The natural response is to hoard it for oneself. One feature of contemporary life is therefore a prevailingly personal attitude toward time; with time felt to be so hurried, people are almost forced to protect their time as their own possession. This is especially true of time apart from one's job, since on-the-job time is pretty much coerced and not felt to be our own.

The result of personalized time is a loss of shared time. People feel less obligation to give their time to others than they once did, and so the social dimension of time is in jeopardy today. While influential social critics ascribe this to individualism and self-absorption, I am inclined to attribute it to current attitudes toward time. It is partly our time famine that leads people to think that they have no time to share.

Time as Present

A variety of factors has conspired to make people look upon time in terms of the present moment only. A fictional character named Meursault in the novel *The Stranger* by the French writer Albert Camus says at one point, "I've always been far too much absorbed in the present moment, or the immediate future, to think back." This loss of a historical sense of the past is one of the most salient features of contemporary life.

Equally absent from the current scene is the eschatological sense of the future that once undergirded Christian societies. Gone is the daily awareness that time will some day end and eternity begin.

The modern view of time lacks depth of field. Captive to the present moment, people do not have anything transcendent or timeless to serve as a ballast against the vicissitudes and distractions of the present moment.

Contemporary Fallacies Regarding Time

All of the foregoing attitudes have produced several fallacies regarding time. Foremost is the illusion that if we only managed time properly we would have enough time for everything. After all, it is in the nature of quantities that they can be controlled and manipulated. If time is a series of discreet units, then it can be managed in such a way as to produce what we want. The whole time management movement, while no doubt helping some people get a handle on their lives, has also been the cause of a great deal of heartache because it misleads people into thinking that they can find enough time for everything.

We have also been led to think that we ought to be able to do more than we actually can. The clock greatly expanded the number of units with which we measure time. With so many minutes in a day comes the corresponding idea that we *should* have lots of time to do an infinite number of things. The clock has created unrealistic expectations regarding the amount of time people actually have.

A third fallacy is that the present moment is all there is. The modern view of time was both the cause and the effect of a loss of awareness of the transcendent in daily living. This modern view of time is, however, part of the total social package in which Christians must struggle to live with one foot in a transcendent heavenly reality as they go about their daily lives.

The Result of Contemporary Attitudes toward Time

The main result of contemporary views of time is an overstimulated and frenzied lifestyle. Beset with a desperate feeling that they should be accomplishing more than they are, people try to cram more and more into their lives. They are like vehicles gaining speed as they barrel down a mountain. If time is a quantity, then the natural human impulse is to want more and more of it and the experiences that it offers.

Carried to its logical conclusion, a frenzied life leads to paralysis and despair. After all, people can take only a limited amount of stress and hurry in their lives. Author-artist Ralph Barton, illustrator of *Gentlemen Prefer Blondes*, left a suicide note that epitomizes an important side of modern life: "I have run from wife to wife and from home to home in a ridiculous effort to escape from time. I'm fed up with the effort of living twenty-four hours a day."[1]

Life under the Sun

The problem of time is not a new arrival. It has haunted Western humanity throughout its history. The Book of Ecclesiastes, the most modern in spirit of all biblical books, gives us a veritable anatomy of modern attitudes toward time. In a book that traverses the whole range of human experiences, including work and leisure, the narrator begins with a prolonged meditation on time. In doing so he is only being realistic.

Time is the arena within which all human quests run their course. It is within time that the issues of life are contested and sometimes resolved. Without making one's peace with time, a person will not solve the question of how to find the good life.

Central to Ecclesiastes is the notion that people live "under the sun." This phrase, which occurs more than thirty times in twelve chap-

1. Cited in Lee, *Religion and Leisure in America*, 228.

ters, denotes life lived by purely human and earthly values. We might think of it as life at ground level. This is, in fact, where most people today live their lives.

As he pursues the perennial quest to find the good life under the sun, the ancient writer experiences time much as people today do. He finds time to be an enemy. Time is an endless cycle of repeated daily happenings that never progress in a meaningful direction (1:4–11). Any quest for permanent achievement is wiped out by death: "How the wise man dies just like the fool! So I hated life" (2:16). Time takes away a person's fortune (5:13–14) and makes people subject to sudden calamity (9:12).

Most of all, the ancient quester turns life into a whirl of activities, including work and leisure, in an attempt to outrun time and make it yield satisfaction. He throws himself into the pursuit of knowledge (1:12–18), the pleasures of acquisition, entertainment, and sex (2:1–11), and work (2:18–23). The more he chases these things, the more satisfaction eludes him. The frantic quest for knowledge ends in disillusionment: "He who increases knowledge increases sorrow" (1:18). The mad pursuit of pleasure ends in emptiness: "Behold, all was vanity and a striving after wind" (2:11). And his career as a workaholic produced only "toil and strain" (2:22), days spent in "darkness and grief, in much vexation and sickness and resentment" (5:17), days "full of pain" and nights in which one's "mind does not rest" (2:23). The lessons that the ancient preacher learned from his futile quest are ones that we can learn by looking at our own society's misguided attitudes toward time.

Summary

Contemporary attitudes toward time indicate the underlying cause of much of the difficulty we have in regard to work and leisure. Viewing time as a quantity that seems to offer us infinite possibilities, we overschedule our lives and lose the feeling of leisureliness. Viewing time in terms of money and the acquisition of goods, Western society has been devoting more and more of its weekly allotment of time to work and less and less to leisure. Here is the backdrop against which we can see how a biblical view of time can help us out of our dilemma.

Time: God's Gift and the Arena of Human Life

Biblical writers show a sophisticated and complex awareness of many different types of time. Although we hear a great deal in the Bible about sacred space, including the idea that the whole earth is filled with the glory of God, it is possible that biblical religion is even more oriented toward sacred time than sacred space. Abraham Heschel writes that in contrast to mythical religions, where the gods above all create a holy place, in the Bible "it is *holiness in time* . . . which comes first." Biblical religion, Heschel argues, "is a *religion of time* aiming at *the sanctification of time.*"[2]

On the opening page of the Bible we encounter *created time*—time as something created by God as he divides reality into day and night. References to *natural time* (e.g., day and night, the seasons, seedtime and harvest) abound throughout the Bible. Also common are references to *life time*—the life cycle from birth through death. *Historical time* is a virtual obsession with some biblical writers, especially in the Old Testament, as characters and events are repeatedly placed in a framework of historical dates and genealogies.

But to these ordinary understandings of time the biblical writers add a barrage of more transcendent concepts. They think in terms of *prophetic time*—a future in which prophecies will be fulfilled and present conditions reversed. *Eschatological time*—events at the end of history—is prominent. *Kingdom time*, consisting of messianic history or salvation history, provides the overarching organizing pattern for biblical events. Within this framework, Old Testament writers look forward to *the fullness of time*, while New Testament writers speak of *times past* and also of the *latter days* that have prevailed since the Incarnation of Christ. Individual lives, too, are plotted on a pattern of "before" and "after" conversion in what we might call *the time of salvation*. Finally, biblical writers are continuously aware of *eternity* above and beyond time.

Being alert to these concepts liberates us from the confined concept of time that our secular age accepts and that we tend to absorb by cultural osmosis. Time encompasses a great deal more than the physical reality of the present moment. Once alerted to this, options arise that we might not otherwise consider. With the general biblical orientation thus established, I turn to the Book of Ecclesiastes.

Time as God's Possession and Gift

Ecclesiastes presupposes a two-tiered cosmos. While the main focus of the book is life under the sun, the book consistently gives us glimpses of a reality that exists above the sun. In the writer's words, "God is in heaven, and you upon earth" (5:2).

The third chapter of Ecclesiastes begins with a famous poem that gives us a human perspective on time and ends with God's view. The most conspicuous truth that emerges on the latter subject (3:10–22) is that time belongs to God. Human endeavor in time is something "that God has given to the sons of men to be busy with" (3:10). God is the one

2. Heschel, *The Sabbath*, 8–9.

who "has appointed a time for every matter, and for every work" (3:17). God also tests people in time (3:18), showing again that he is in control. Time, in other words, is the arena within which God has placed people. It is also his gift to people.

There are practical implications that flow from regarding time as God's possession. One is the lesson of creaturely humility before God. I suggest the possibility that God placed us under the limitations of time partly as a continuous reminder that he is the Creator and we the creatures. Furthermore, if God is the one who allots us our time, we have a reason to conclude that we have sufficient time to do what *God* wants us to do. If our agendas are loaded beyond what we have time for, we are probably trying to do more than God expects or allows us to accomplish.

As a follow-up to the earlier poem about "a time for every matter," the writer asserts that "God has made everything beautiful in its time" (3:11a). Whereas the human urge through the ages has been to freeze time—to hold the golden moments of life and stop the inevitable process of aging—the writer here locates beauty *in* time. Derek Kidner comments, "Instead of changelessness, there is something better: a dynamic, divine purpose, with its *beginning* and *end*. Instead of frozen perfection there is the kaleidoscopic movement of innumerable processes, each with its own character and . . . contributing to the overall masterpiece which is the work of one Creator."[3]

Beyond even that affirmation is one of the truly important statements in the book of Ecclesiastes: "also [God] has put eternity in man's mind" (3:11b). In other words, we have been created with a capacity for transcendence, an ability to aspire toward something beyond the earthly and to bring its reality into the everyday routine. Work and leisure within time do not have to yield their full meaning within a closed earthly system.

The Practical Result

The practical implications of viewing time as God's gift are far-reaching. An obvious response is for people to accept time as God's gift with gratitude. Time is not a curse but a gift. Applied to work and leisure, we have a reason to accept every moment of them as something sent from God. They may be wearisome or delightful, but in either case they are something that God has designed for us. As a later directive puts it, "In the day of prosperity be joyful, and in the day of adversity consider; God has made the one as well as the other" (7:14).

If time is the arena of human endeavor, moreover, we also can view it as fraught with meaning. It is a place of testing in which what we do matters.

3. Kidner, *A Time to Mourn*, 39.

Such a view redeems work and leisure from the apparent triviality that so often characterizes them when they are experienced as self-contained. If time is the arena within which God expects us to find meaning and satisfaction it becomes a sphere of continuous stewardship and opportunity.

The repeated focus of the passage I have been exploring is what God does with time: *God has given, he has made, he has put, it is God's gift, whatever God does, God has made it so, God seeks, God will judge, he has appointed a time.* An obvious human response is to join God's program. According to Kidner, the believer can accept life "as an assignment. It is a *gift* from God (13), an allotted portion in life, whose purpose is known to the Giver and is part of His everlasting work."[4]

While all of this does not yet address the specific syndrome of not having enough time it does provide a perspective on how to view the work and leisure that we perform within time. I repeat my earlier point that we will never have enough time to do everything until we reach retirement. Our real quest, therefore, is not to find *enough* time but to find the *quality* of time that will make our work and leisure satisfying. Not surprisingly, it is right in the middle of this section of Ecclesiastes, in which the author gives us a God's-eye view of time, that he offers the possibility of finding enjoyment in work and leisure:

> I know that there is nothing better for [people] than to be happy and enjoy themselves as long as they live; also that it is God's gift to man that every one should eat and drink and take pleasure in all his toil (3:12–13).

It is the God-centered perspective on time, work, and leisure that enables us to enjoy them. In the "under the sun" passages of Ecclesiastes the author pictures a humanistic quest in which he tried to secure happiness by his own efforts. The "above the sun" passages find the path to enjoyment by accepting life as God's gift:

> There is nothing better for a person than that he should eat and drink and find enjoyment in his toil. This also, I saw, is from the hand of God; for apart from him who can eat or who can have enjoyment? For to the person who pleases him God gives wisdom and knowledge and joy (2:24–26).

Freed from the panic of Western materialism we can enjoy life after all.

Summary

Solving the problem of time begins by acknowledging that time is not our possession. It is a gift from God. We are simply allowed to use it as stewards to whom it has been entrusted. While this acknowledg-

4. Ibid.

ment does not solve the problems surrounding the *quantity* of time at our disposal, it instills an attitude toward time that can make us value the *quality* of the time that God has given us as a gift. If time is holy, then the work and leisure with which we fill it are also holy.

A Time for Every Matter: A Human View of Time

We come, finally, to the world's most famous poem on the subject of time. The word *time* appears twenty-nine times in eight verses:

> For everything there is a season,
> and a time for every matter under heaven:
> a time to be born, and a time to die;
> a time to plant, and a time to pluck up what is planted;
> a time to kill, and a time to heal;
> a time to break down, and a time to build up;
> a time to weep, and a time to laugh;
> a time to mourn, and a time to dance;
> a time to cast away stones, and a time to gather stones together;
> a time to embrace, and a time to refrain from embracing;
> a time to seek, and a time to lose;
> a time to keep, and a time to cast away;
> a time to rend, and a time to sew;
> a time to keep silence, and a time to speak;
> a time to love, and a time to hate;
> a time for war, and a time for peace.

This is the human perspective on time, heightened with all the resources of poetry and eloquence. What do we learn about time as we ponder this poem?

We notice first the mixed nature of life in time. Human experience in time is neither uniformly good nor uniformly bad. It is a mingled web, good and bad together. The good and bad, moreover, are arranged in a harmonious rhythm.

The poem also implies human limitation. Many of the events listed portray a world of events that people cannot control. Furthermore, we cannot remove ourselves from time as we can from space. We speak of killing time, but time does not actually die.

Herbert Alleman also observed that "the most apparent application of these verses is the lesson of timeliness."[5] In other words, although we cannot control time, we can plug into its flow. The implication for

5. Herbert C. Alleman, *Old Testament Commentary* (Philadelphia: Muhlenberg, 1948), 630.

work and leisure is that there is a dynamic rhythm to life to which we can conform for our benefit as we are open to what life brings. The God-centered passages of Ecclesiastes offer as the secret to life an "openness to [God]: a readiness to take what comes to us as heaven-sent."[6]

This poem about time gives us contrasting pairs of experiences and treats them as a complementary whole. Although the list does not name work and leisure the application is obvious: there is a time to work and a time to play.

Resignation to Time

Is this famous poem about "a time for everything" positive or negative? To answer that question, and to grasp exactly what the implication of the poem is for work and leisure, let us consider the four responses that the human race has given to the problem of time.

One response has been a hedonistic, "seize the day" philosophy. It is the attitude that we should eat, drink, and be merry, for tomorrow we die. Its opposite is asceticism—attempting to escape from time by withdrawing from life. A third response has been fatalistic despair—a giving up on life.

A fourth response is calm acceptance of time as God's gift. Time is here viewed as the medium of our existence and something that we should make the most of, under God. This note of resignation is the keynote of the poem in Ecclesiastes on there being a time for everything. In different ways, the other three responses to the problem of time refuse to accept it. A more excellent way is encapsulated in the psalmist's sentiment, "This is the day which the Lord has made; let us rejoice and be glad in it" (Psalm 118:24).

To accept the limitation of time in regard to work and leisure has at least two consequences. One is a refusal to think that if we work hard enough and long enough we can get everything done. We can't. To submit to time means letting go at a certain point. Secondly, therefore, the attitude expressed in the poem about "a time for every matter" implies that we should find a time for leisure as an acknowledgment of our creaturely limitations. We cannot master life completely. At a certain point we have to let ourselves be mastered by the nonacquisitive and nonutilitarian.

In this we can see an important truth about the nature of leisure. An overly stimulated lifestyle is as much a foe to leisure as is idleness. The goal of leisure is not to multiply distractions but to make our life abundant. Robert Lee correctly notes that "a Christian understanding of time beckons us to accept all time as God's gift, including our leisure; to live our leisure in terms of the quality of its events."[7]

6. Kidner, *A Time to Mourn*, 58.
7. Lee, *Religion and Leisure*, 260.

Yet another implication of accepting the limitations of time is the wisdom of accepting our lot. This is a major theme of Ecclesiastes. The speaker got himself into trouble by assuming that he had to look far and wide to find enjoyment and satisfaction in life. His final lesson was that he didn't have to look far at all—in fact, not beyond the daily routine of work and leisure. "The gift of God," he discovers, is "to accept [one's] lot, and find enjoyment in his toil" (5:19).

The Momentousness of Life

A final stance that the Bible encourages in regard to time is an awareness of the momentousness of time. Time matters to God and should matter to us.

Time is momentous first of all because it is part of a much larger picture than just the present moment. Time in this life opens out into a spiritual world above and beyond time. We noted earlier the conspicuous emphasis in the God-centered passages of Ecclesiastes on time as the sphere in which God accomplishes his sovereign purposes. Since this is so, time is the medium in which people establish their eternal identity. Kingdom time is daily time. Daily time is kingdom time.

The work and play that we do in time therefore deserve our best effort. Using the most evocative images of zest and festivity that he knows, the writer of Ecclesiastes offers this picture of the good life:

> Go, eat your bread with enjoyment, and drink your wine with a merry heart. . . . Let your garments be always white; let not oil be lacking on your head. Enjoy life with the wife whom you love. . . . Whatever your hand finds to do, do it with your might (9:7–10).

Here is an endorsement of both work and play.

Earlier centuries had a great phrase by which to denote earthly life lived as an extension of eternal life. They called it *sub specie aeternitatis*, meaning "under the aspect of eternity." While this has sometimes led to an ascetic disparagement of life, it need not do so. The writer of Ecclesiastes follows up one of his vintage commendations of enjoying eating, drinking, and work with a truly astounding paradox. The person who enjoys life most, he writes, "will not much remember the days of his life because God keeps him occupied with joy in his heart" (5:20). Success in life is being distracted from life by God.

The perspective of life *sub specie aeternitatis* is the subject of a sonnet that the English Puritan poet John Milton penned when he took stock of the problem of time on his twenty-third birthday. Milton begins with eight lines of self-laceration over his lack of achievement to date, and then moves toward a solution to the problem of time:

> How soon hath Time, the subtle thief of youth,
>> Stolen on his wing my three-and-twentieth year!
>> My hasting days fly on with full career,
>> But my late spring no bud or blossom showeth.
> Perhaps my semblance might deceive the truth,
>> That I to manhood am arrived so near;
>> And inward ripeness doth much less appear,
>> That some more timely-happy spirits endueth.
> Yet, be it less or more, or soon or slow,
>> It shall be still in strictest measure even
>> To that same lot, however mean or high,
> Toward which Time leads me, and the will of heaven:
>> All is, if I have grace to use it so,
>> As ever in my great task-master's eye.

The two parts of the poem highlight a perennial tension in human experience. The octave considers the speaker in terms of *doing* and comes up with a deplorable record of underachievement. Here is the human predicament in miniature: we can never do enough in either work or leisure to allow us to feel that we have accomplished as much as we would like.

In the sestet, Milton shifts the focus from *doing* to *being*. Time, which had been a thief and enemy, is now pictured as a guide and friend. This view is possible only because the perspective widens out to include a spiritual level of reality. Time is viewed as an agent of God's providence, as signaled by the phrase "the will of heaven." Beyond that, the last two lines assert that the speaker is responsible to God and not subject to human standards of achievement. Time is the medium of God's grace, the arena within which the speaker will perform his labors under God's eye—in other words, under the aspect of eternity.

Time as a Quality

The general drift of my analysis is to assert that time is not so much a quantity as a quality. Our use of it needs to be measured not only in terms of *doing* but also *being*. The question to ask is, "In this moment, in this activity, in this relationship, in this task, in this recreation, am I all that I can be?" The goal is not to cram as many experiences into our time as we can, but to insure their quality.

G. K. Chesterton claimed that in Christianity "the instant is really awful," that is, awe-inspiring.[8] Writing without a Christian commit-

---

8. G. K. Chesterton, *Orthodoxy* (Garden City, N.Y.: Image Books, 1959), 136.

ment, the Victorian prose writer Walter Pater painted a similar picture of the momentousness of human life. He spoke of "the splendour of our experience and its awful brevity," quoting with approval Victor Hugo's sentiment that "we are all under sentence of death but with a sort of indefinite reprieve."[9] Pater's proposed solution was the wrong one—to fill life with as many sensory experiences as possible and not even take time to contemplate the meaning of those experiences. In place of such an overstimulated lifestyle the Bible proposes living in an awareness of what Jesus called the abundant life. This is not a life of idleness, nor is it opposed to people's accomplishing a lot. But the abundant life consists more in what a person *is* than what a person accomplishes. The crucial question at any moment is not how much one can do but what the quality of one's work or leisure is.

Two famous biblical verses about time imply this view. One is Psalm 90:12, where the Psalmist prays, "So teach us to number our days, that we may get a heart of wisdom." Implicit in that prayer is an awareness that there are various ways to number our days, including the one that numbers them in terms of units of clock time and quantity of tasks accomplished. A heart of wisdom, by contrast, is qualitative, not quantitative.

The other verse is the one from which I have taken the title for this book—Ephesians 5:16. It is variously translated as "redeeming the time" (KJV), "making the most of the time" (RSV), and "making the most of every opportunity" (NIV). Although this verse is used by some to promote extravagant time management (viewing time as a quantity), the context (especially verses 15 and 17) makes it clear that we are being commanded to view time as a quality—to be wise in our understanding of God's will for our use of time, not to cram as much as possible into our allotted time.

Summary

Time is not primarily a quantity but a quality. So are work and leisure. In a sense, the moment is simultaneously everything and decidedly secondary. It is everything in that it offers the possibility of our being all that we can be at that moment. It is secondary in that its true meaning lies beyond itself in its relation to an eternal world and a personal God.

We can never have *enough* time for work and leisure. What we can work toward is insuring the quality of the work and leisure that we undertake within the arena of God's gift of time. At the end of a day, we

9. Walter Pater, conclusion to *The Renaissance*, reprinted in *English Prose of the Victorian Era*, ed. Charles Harrold and William Templeman (New York: Oxford University Press, 1938), 1410.

can feel good about ourselves if our work and leisure have been *the best* of which we are capable, even if we did not accomplish *as much* as we might have wished.

Further Reading

John Marsh, *The Fullness of Time* (1952).
Robert Lee, *Religion and Leisure in America* (1964), Part 4.
Niels-Erik A. Andreasen, *The Christian Use of Time* (1978).
Robert Banks, *The Tyranny of Time: When 24 Hours Is Not Enough* (1983).

Conclusion
The Divine Harmony
Work, Leisure, and Christian Living

Contrary to the prevailing practice of discussing work and leisure separately, the key to living Christianly in regard to work and leisure is to put them into relationship with each other. God intended them to be a divine harmony.

As I put things together in this conclusion I will relate three things: work and leisure in relation to each other, work and leisure in relation to the Christian doctrines they share, and work and leisure in relation to the contemporary problems noted in the first unit of this book.

Work and Leisure in Relation to Each Other

We usually think of work and leisure as being separate from each other. After all, we experience them separately. They serve such different purposes in our lives that it is easy to think of them as opposites.

But work and leisure belong together. Together they make up our daily lives. They are complementary parts of the single whole of our existence. Because this is so, our well-being depends on our satisfaction in both. Stanley Parker, a leading sociologist of leisure, has said that "research in the various social sciences shows that both work and leisure are necessary to a healthy life and healthy society."[1] In his analysis

---

1. Parker, *Leisure and Work*, xii.

of the same situation from a biblical perspective Robert K. Johnston notes that "play and work go together. . . . Christians are created and called to consecrate both their work and their play."[2]

Work and leisure take their meaning from each other. Without leisure, work narrows life and damages the worker. Leisure by itself also robs a person of fullness. Without work, people feel useless and lack adequate purpose in life, as the unemployed, injured, and retired can attest.

Models for the Work-Leisure Relationship

How then should we view the relationship between these two necessary ingredients of life? Authorities on the subject have come up with a widely accepted framework of three possible models to describe how work and leisure mingle in people's lives.[3]

One possibility is variously known as the *spillover* or *identity* or *extension* model of leisure. This means that people find their work so satisfying that they carry over their work experiences and attitudes into their leisure. In fact, they may do many of the same things in leisure that they do in work because this is what gives them enjoyment. People in this position do not make a sharp distinction between work and leisure, usually because they enjoy their work and experience a quality of leisure in work.

The second model of how work and leisure combine in daily living is the *compensatory* or *opposition* model. Here people perceive their work and leisure to form a distinct contrast. Leisure serves the function of compensating for deprivations in work, which in this model is ordinarily unfulfilling in one way or another. People in this category deliberately seek out activities that are different from the daily grind because they need a break.

The third way of relating work and leisure is *separation,* or *neutrality.* Here people keep their work and leisure in separate compartments. Stanley Parker notes that "the neutrality pattern consists of having leisure activities which are generally different from work but not deliberately so, and of appreciating the difference between work and leisure without always defining the one as the absence of the other."[4]

Is one of these models more Christian than the others? Robert Johnston thinks so.[5] He rejects the identity model that extends work into leisure and the "split" model that values leisure as a compensation for what is lacking in work. Johnston prefers the model that assigns sep-

2. Johnston, *Christian at Play*, 128, 134.
3. A convenient summary of leading models of the work-leisure relationship can be found in James F. Murphy, *Concepts of Leisure*, 2d ed. (Englewood Cliffs, N.J.: Prentice-Hall, 1981), 44–52. The best extended discussion is by Parker, *Leisure and Work*.
4. Parker, *Leisure and Work*, 88.
5. Johnston, *The Christian at Play*, 128–34.

arate value to work and leisure. But work and leisure are more interrelated than this view allows.

We should be slow to baptize any one of the three models as being more Christian than the others. Before we weigh the merits of the individual models, we need to note the broad principles that underlie any Christian view of the relationship between work and leisure. Once we have done so we will find that these principles might be practiced within all three of the models. Also, some writers use the term "integrated" in misleading ways when discussing the relationship between work and leisure. To the extent that the three models regard work and leisure as complementary parts of a whole, all three are equally integrated. The question is how to integrate these complementary activities.

Integration as the Goal

The foundational principle is that both work and leisure are good. God created both of them for the benefit of the human race. This means that we must reject one of the most common tendencies of the human race through the centuries—the tendency to regard either work or leisure as good and the other as bad. Most people in our culture seem to subconsciously regard leisure as good and work as bad. The opposite viewpoint occurs whenever an overly strong utilitarian ethic makes people feel guilty about leisure.

The wisdom of social science research tells us that people function best when their attitudes toward work and leisure are integrated—when both are valued as complementary parts of a whole. Parker writes, "Maximum human development in both work and leisure spheres requires that they be complementary and integrated rather than that one be regarded as 'good' and the other as 'bad.'"[6]

Christianity says the same thing. According to Genesis 2, the account of life in Paradise, people in a state of perfection performed the work of cultivating the garden, but they also enjoyed the beauty of the garden, human companionship, and the worship of God.

The complementary nature of work and leisure is reinforced by the fourth commandment which states:

> Six days you shall labor, and do all your work; but the seventh day is a sabbath to the Lord your God; in it you shall not do any work . . . for in six days the Lord made heaven and earth, the sea, and all that is in them, and rested the seventh day (Exodus 20:9–11).

Here we find the divine harmony—the God-ordained pattern of work and rest in complementary rhythm.

6. Parker, *Leisure and Work*, xii.

Assessing the Models for the Work-Leisure Relationship

With this as a framework, all three of the models for relating work and leisure can be Christian. Everything depends on the specific situation of a given person. There are pluses and minuses in each model, and we need to be aware of these.

For example, people whose work tends to be inherently fulfilling enjoy a very great blessing. People whose work possesses the leisure qualities of freedom, self-fulfillment, and enjoyment already have leisure in their lives before they leave their work at the end of the day. It is natural that such people would experience a lot of continuity between work and leisure. Nor is the autonomy of play necessarily threatened in such continuity. Leisure in work is still leisure.

But there is a price tag attached when people's avocation (what they most enjoy doing) is also their vocation (what they do for a living). One of the functions of leisure stressed throughout this book is its status as a break from routine and obligation. This is what gets lost when people work in their free time. The Christian view that we need times of rest from work and have a moral obligation to spend time with family and friends sets a limit to the practice of merging work and leisure. The biblical Sabbath leaves no doubt about the need to include breaks between work and rest in our lives.

When we consider the second model, which stresses the contrast between work and leisure, we again need to be balanced in our assessment. It is a law of human nature that we need retreats from burdensome reality. When work is tiring or unfulfilling, there is nothing wrong with seeking compensation in leisure. I suspect that people who fall into this category often value leisure more than the person whose work is of the type that encourages work "after hours." Paradoxical as it may seem, I sometimes find the prospect of an evening at home more inviting when I know I am too tired to do more work after dinner.

Of course there are problems here, too. People whose work has qualities of leisure in it probably have more overall leisure in their lives. Furthermore, several studies have found that leisure does not, in fact, compensate for lack of satisfaction in the workplace.[7]

A similar ambivalence occurs when we weigh the pattern in which work and leisure are largely independent of each other in a person's life. On the positive side, this model is capable of protecting the separate integrity of both work and leisure. Both can be valued for what they are in themselves, without having to answer to the other. In this they respect the boundaries God has established between the spheres of work and leisure.

7. These studies are summarized by Godbey, *Leisure in Your Life*, 111–12.

Here, too, there can be problems, because we function best when we are whole people. Our work is impoverished if our play never extends to our fellow workers, for example. We become split personalities when we live in two different worlds having no significant carryovers. In the fourth commandment the worker does not cease to be the same person when he or she rests from work. Later in this chapter I will note the Christian doctrines that apply equally to work and leisure, and we will see that we cannot be totally separate people when we work and play.

In sum, we should avoid trying to find *the* Christian model for the relationship between work and leisure. There are too many variables to allow for a single right relationship. That relationship varies according to the person, type of work, and even day of the week.

Some Practical Considerations

In general, the main influence on our leisure patterns is the nature of our work. The less leisure quality we can import into our work, the more separation between work and leisure will be desirable. If our work wears us down physically or emotionally, our leisure will involve a high degree of contrast to our work. But if our work contains a balance between solitude and social interaction, between physical exertion and repose, our leisure is likely to resemble our work in these same ways.

The important principle underlying everything is that work and leisure are complementary parts of a divine harmony and God-ordained whole. To maintain the importance of both will help keep either from becoming an idol or tyrant that usurps all of a person's devotion.

Another aspect of the relationship between work and leisure is that even though the content of the two may be very different we can strive to import the ideal qualities of one into the other. The usual assumption is that our work will be enriched if we can incorporate the qualities of leisure into it, including a sense of choice in what we are doing, enjoyment, creativity, and self-fulfillment. But the influence can flow in the other direction as well. Our leisure will be richer if it produces some of the same satisfactions that work can provide, including a sense of accomplishment, purposefulness, action (as opposed to idleness), and good use of time.

In chapter 3 we noted the diagram on time usage. Between the poles of work and leisure is a category of semileisure. It consists of activities that are obligatory but can assume some of the positive qualities of leisure. Cooking can be routine work that is drudgery but it can also be semileisure if, for example, it involves the creativity of trying a new recipe. One way to redeem work from the curse is to move as much of it as possible into a realm that makes it share the refreshment we associate with leisure.

If I am right in saying that we must avoid christening any one model as the "Christian" view of relating work and leisure, then we are free to see partial truth in some common formulas that by themselves are deficient. There has been a long debate, for example, over whether we work in order to live or live in order to work. Christian writers on the subject (including Dorothy Sayers) imply that the second is the Christian position. I question this conclusion; it is as incomplete in itself as the other formulation. There is a measure of truth in both statements. Similarly, people argue about whether we play in order to work or work in order to play. I do not see why we should try to choose between these. Our sense of balance tells us that there is truth in both ideas.

The Shared Theology of Work and Leisure

Further unity between work and leisure emerges when we consider the Christian doctrines that apply to both of them. For example, both work and leisure are rooted in the biblical doctrine of creation. God created both of them. In fact, God himself alternately worked and rested when he created the world. Moreover, in the Garden of Eden God prescribed that people would combine work and leisurely enjoyment. The fourth commandment roots both work and rest in God's creation of the world. We can therefore speak of both work and leisure as creation ordinances.

A second principle that work and leisure share is time. Both occur in time. Together they make up our daily allotment of time. The more time we spend on one, the less time we have for the other. When we realize that they are this interrelated, we are in a better position to exercise the balance between them that a Christian outlook encourages.

Work and leisure also share the Christian endorsement of pleasure or enjoyment. Contemporary attitudes would have us believe that we can expect to find enjoyment in leisure, while work is incurably unpleasant. The Bible suggests something different. God intends both work and leisure to be pleasurable. One of the things that makes the Book of Ecclesiastes so refreshing is its fusion of work and leisure in a zestful enjoyment of life: "Behold, what I have seen to be good and to be fitting is to eat and drink and find enjoyment in all the toil with which one toils" (Ecclesiastes 5:18).

Another Christian doctrine that applies equally to work and leisure is the doctrine of sin. Human sinfulness makes possible the abuse of work and leisure. Some of the abuses are identical. In both work and leisure we can be guilty of idolatry, of ingratitude, of poor stewardship, of sloth. Both work and leisure can be corrupted by immoral practices and attitudes. We can also make the mistake of undervaluing either work or leisure.

Work and leisure also share a quality of worship in the broad sense of that which makes us conscious of God and relates us to God. In this definition, our work can be an act of worship, something we undertake in obedience to God's call, in dependence on him, and in a spirit of service to him and to humanity. Leisure, too, can be worshipful. It makes us grateful to God by making us aware of his gifts. It affords moments of reflection when we think about God.

Both work and leisure call for moderation. To pursue one or the other single-mindedly makes us unbalanced. Excessive attention to either leads to a dereliction of the duty we owe to ourselves, our families, and our society. The rule of "neither too much nor too little" applies to both work and leisure.

Finally, the doctrine of stewardship joins work and leisure. God is the giver of both. He holds us responsible for our actions in both spheres. Both work and leisure require from us a commitment to excellence, a desire to make the most of what God has given, in a spirit of gratitude for what we have received.

To sum up, work and leisure are obviously much closer to each other than we might naturally think. Despite the difference in content between the two in most people's lives, the same Christian doctrines tend to be applicable to them. They are, truly, part of a divine harmony.

Christianity and Contemporary Problems in Work and Leisure

This book has been based on a premise that work and leisure need rehabilitation in the modern world and that the Christian faith can contribute to that process. We should, therefore, take another look at the contemporary problems noted early in this book.

Christianity and Contemporary Problems in Work

One problem is an excess of work in what is, after all, a work-oriented society. For some people at some income levels and at some stages of their life cycle there are no easy answers. There is simply too much to be done at certain points in life.

Some of the excess of work in the modern world, however, is avoidable. Much of it is engendered by an acquisitive lifestyle that could be simplified if people chose to do so. Some people work excessively because they worship the success that attends such work, and others because they have not learned to value anything besides work.

The Christian response is to insist that people have been made to rest, play, and worship as well as work. One day in seven is exempt from work. One of its purposes is to protect workers from themselves.

The Christian faith sets limits to the impulse to work. It declares a rhythm of work and rest, obligation and freedom.

A second malady that afflicts the worker today is dissatisfaction with work. We should not direct all the blame for alienation on the job to a technological age. There were as many unfulfilling jobs before the technological revolution as there have been since. Furthermore, no job is satisfying all of the time. Some tasks, whether around the house or in the workplace, are inherently unpleasant or unfulfilling. What does Christianity say to this problem?

For one thing, it does not deny the problem. It does not share the naive optimism about work that nineteenth-century Romanticists expressed, nor the false posters of beaming workers displayed in socialist countries. Christianity acknowledges the effect of the curse on work. It therefore saves us from false guilt about burdensome work.

But Christianity also offers solutions to the problem by supplying attitudes that transform how we regard our work. It assures us that God intends us to work. Added to this is the assurance that God calls us to tasks and that to perform them honorably is to obey God. Further, by elevating the concept of serving humanity, Christianity offers a way to transform work that in itself may be distasteful.

The revolutionary aspect of the Christian doctrine of work is that it focuses on the inner attitude of the worker. This contrasts with the Marxist answer to the problems of alienation in work. The Marxist solution pins its hope on institutional change. A changed social structure will somehow make all work satisfying.

Christianity is not opposed to constructive changes in the values by which people live—changes that would have the effect of eliminating some of the demeaning jobs in our society. But Christianity does not share the confidence of Marxism that structural changes can answer the problems posed by work that does not carry inherent satisfaction. Instead it locates the possibility of finding satisfaction in work in the attitude of the worker.

Christianity speaks to two additional aberrations on the current scene. One is the problem of undervaluing work. The results of such undervaluing are poor work and laziness. The Christian doctrines of vocation, stewardship, and commitment to excellence stand as an alternative to the decline of the modern work ethic. In a Christian view, all legitimate work is honorable and worthy of one's best effort.

In our society, work is overvalued as well as undervalued. Christianity offers an alternative here as well. Work is not the highest value in life. It should not occupy all our waking time, nor is it meant to be destructive of our relationships to God and others. The workaholic usually worships success and prosperity. In place of these goals for work Christianity substitutes the glory of God and service to humanity.

Many in our society take their identity from their work, but in a Christian view our identity comes from being God's people and new creatures in Christ.

Christianity and Contemporary Problems in Leisure

A Christian response to the problems of leisure in our culture begins with a commitment to protect the quality of leisure life. Such an outlook rests on the twin pillars of knowing that God commands leisure for people and wanting to be a good steward of the gift of leisure. In addition to providing this impetus for guarding and fostering the quality of our leisure, Christianity offers practical solutions to modern problems in leisure.

For one thing, those who acknowledge the Christian view of the necessity of leisure will find time for leisure. The prohibition of work on one day in seven is the starting point. It shows that a boundary must be drawn around human acquisitiveness. If we take this principle seriously, we avoid the syndrome of the harried leisure class who are so busy acquiring goods and doing the things society expects that they experience a time famine. The words of Jesus stand as an effective antidote: "consider the lilies of the field" (Matthew 6:28); "a person's life does not consist in the abundance of his possessions" (Luke 12:15).

Another problem in our society is low quality in leisure. This is not surprising, since leisure always reflects the values of an individual society. Christianity calls people to excellence. Its central truth is that it is not enough to leave fallen humanity where it is. Applied to leisure, this means not being content with the level of leisure most people in our culture seek. The Christian life calls us to something better than the triviality, mindlessness, and immorality that characterize much of the leisure scene today.

As is true of work, leisure in our culture is both undervalued and overvalued. To those who cannot value leisure apart from work or who feel guilty about time not spent working, Christianity affirms the necessity and legitimacy of leisure. The Bible endorses rest, festivity, and enjoyment, and it encourages us to protect the value of the nonutiliarian.

Christianity is equally opposed to making an idol of leisure. For one thing, Christianity asserts the necessity and honor of work. This at once disarms those who overvalue leisure at the expense of work. Christianity declares that many things in life are worthwhile in addition to leisure. They include work, worship of God, service to people, and commitment to one's family and friends. When these are given their proper place, one does not have time to overemphasize leisure.

Work, Leisure, and the Balanced Christian Life

We can be deeply appreciative for the provision that God has made for human life in the rhythm of work and leisure. That rhythm sounds so simple and self-evident when we encounter it in the creation account of Genesis and in the fourth commandment that it is easy to miss its significance. Yet all the analysis of the problems of work and leisure in society comes back to the keystone of the goodness of both work and leisure in human life.

Not only are work and leisure good in themselves; they also balance each other and help to prevent the problems that either one alone tends to produce. If we value work and leisure properly, we will avoid overvaluing or undervaluing either one.

Every one of us faces choices in work and leisure. It is a rare person who can be said to "have it all together" in these areas. Work and leisure are neither more nor less important than such Christian concerns as personal holiness, evangelism, family, and the church. But work and leisure, unlike the other topics, have not received the attention they deserve and require. When I came to write the chapters of this book that place work and leisure into a Christian context, I was struck by the scarcity of helpful published material. The church in our century has not given its best attention to work and leisure.

My goal in writing this book has been not only to encourage correct thinking about work and leisure. The right ideas are a starting point. The goal is a thoroughly Christian lifestyle.

At the heart of Christianity is a conviction that we can change our patterns of life in a Godward direction. We are not doomed to perpetuate wrong attitudes toward work and leisure. Constructive change is always possible. It may be necessary as well. The choice is ours.

Scripture Index

Genesis
1 159, 165
1–3 110–11
1:26 174
1:26, 28 222, 231
1:26–27 162
1:31 161, 167, 254
2 159, 285
2:1–3 166
2:2 160
2:15 176
2:21–22 160
2:3 168, 204
2:7 160
2:8 160, 205
2:9 180, 205, 221, 263
3 159
3:16 184
3:17 184
3:17, 19 16
3:17–19 184
12:1 191
18:1–8 242

Exodus
3–4 194
3:1–10 215
16 166
20:3 255
20:9 245–46
20:9, 11 162
20:9–10 205
20:9–11 285
28:2 181

29:8–11 178
31:1–5 215
31:1–6 194
31:16–17 169
31:17 167, 204

Leviticus
23 206
25 179

Numbers
18:1–7 193
28:18, 25, 26 179

Deuteronomy
8:17–18 186
16:16 206
28 177
30:19 141

1 Samuel
11:5 215
15:17 194

1 Chronicles
9 215

Nehemiah
4:6 164, 246
6:16 164
6:3 164
6:9 164
8 206
8:14–15 206

8:17–18 206
9:6 206

Esther
9:17 241
9:19 241

Job
40:20 170

Psalms
8:3 160
16 263
16:6 263
16:11 263
19 181
19:1 160, 181
23 236
24:1 162, 213
27:4 181
29:2 181
36:8 263
37:4 262
37:7 169
72:19 213
78:70–71 194
78:70–72 215
81:2 263
90:12 281
90:16–17 163
96:6 181
104 170, 175, 180, 246
104:2 180
104:10–11 180

293

Subject Index